Also by
Earl Llewellyn Goldmann

Bounce Back, a memoir

Intestinal Fortitude

Intestinal Fortitude

A Memoir

Earl Llewellyn Goldmann

www.brooksgoldmannpublishing.com

Intestinal Fortitude
A Memoir

Copyright ©2022 by Earl Llewellyn Goldmann

This book is a memoir, a work of nonfiction. The author Earl Llewellyn Goldmann faithfully renders events and experiences detailed herein as all true as he remembered them to the best of his ability. Various names, identities, and circumstances changed to protect the privacy of all the individuals involved.

No outside entity of Brooks Goldmann Publishing, LLC, may use any part of this book or reproduce it in any manner whatsoever, graphic, electronic, mechanical or digital, including photocopying, recording, taping, or by any information retrieval system without the express written permission of the author, Earl Llewellyn Goldmann, except in the case of brief quotations in critical articles and reviews.

Editing/interior design by Book Shepherd Ann Videan, ANVidean.com
Cover design, Kristi Wayland, www.electronicink.com

1. Memoir. 2. Alcoholism. 3. Spirituality 4. Sports

ISBN: 978-1-0880-3829-1 (paperback)
Also available in eBook

Library of Congress Control Number: 2022900884

First printing, Brooks Goldmann Publishing Company, LLC trade paperback edition June 2022
Manufactured in the United States of America.

For more information:
Brooks Goldmann Publishing, LLC
www.brooksgoldmannpublishing.com
intestinalfortitudebook.com

DEDICATION

I dedicate this book to my wife Patricia L. Brooks,
an award-winning author, who tirelessly typed my manuscript
while conducting a proofread and critique for me.
Her expertise as an author of three memoirs, president and founder of
the Scottsdale Society of Women Writers and our publishing company
Brooks Goldmann Publishing LLC, adds to the quality of her efforts to
help in launching my second memoir.

Patricia and me in Scottsdale.

INTESTINAL FORTITUDE

A man's word and his intestinal fortitude
are two of the most honorable virtues
known to mankind.

Jim Nantz,
American sportscaster

TABLE OF CONTENTS

DEDICATION
ACKNOWLEDGMENTS
INTRODUCTION

SPORTS   1
The Dixie Classic Basketball Tournament, 1955   3
Penitentiary   14
The Substitution   18
The Life of a High School Punter   23
Annie's Basketball Game   28
Dick Lundy and Jack Streeter   30
Garibaldi's Infamous Football Field   34
Taft Football Game   37
Vernonia   39
Tillamook/Astoria Rivalry   44

FAMILY   47
Immigration and Migration   49
Goldmann with Two Ns   54
Family   59
Psychology Class   65
Charles   69
Almon   77
Creel   84
Burned Balls   89
Karen and Tony   92

FRIENDS   97
Glory Days   101
Date   103
College   108
Hathaway Meade Gang   116
Leroy Vanover   125
Jim Schroeder   129

Howie	133
Rod Carrier	138
Roger	145
Lou Zarosinski	148
Lou and the Dump	151
Lou, Mike, and Joe	156
Deer Hunting	161
San Francisco and Pebble Beach	164

ALCOHOL AND DEPRESSION — 173

Introduction to Alcohol	175
Alcohol	176
More on Alcohol	191
Driving Drunk	196
Mystical Wheels of Justice	200
Making Amends	206
Anxiety	210

RELIGION — 217

Church as a Kid	219
God: A Skewed Look	226

PERCEPTION — 235

Perception	237
Spokane Landing	248
Portland Landing	250
Ups and Downs	253
Mary's Peak	256
Heart Attack	260
Closure	263

REQUEST FOR REVIEW
ABOUT THE AUTHOR

ACKNOWLEDGMENTS

I hereby acknowledge my wife, Patricia L. Brooks, and the members of her critique group, Darlene Ziebell, Dr. Rose Garlasco, and Courtney Schrauben, who have spent countless hours helping me own my truth and tell my story. If not for them, this story might never have happened. I might still be silent to the world.

I appreciate the therapists I encountered over the years while dealing with my post-traumatic stress and healing from trauma. It is with their guidance I came to a place of peace and understanding about who I am.

And I honor too my editor and Book Shepherd Ann Videan, for all her effort on my behalf. Also, Kristi Wayland, who designed this cover with her creativity.

Finally, I recognize my friends and family who supported me with my writing adventures when I desperately needed their friendship and love.

To all of them, I say, "Thank you."

INTRODUCTION

Intestinal Fortitude, my second memoir, is a composition of stories about my life recorded in individual vignettes. Using short stories and essays, I reveal to the reader events and circumstances that impacted me throughout my life. A significant percentage of the stories, some humorous, some serious, changed my life in ways exemplary for my growth and some questionable for my depression. But triumph prevailed.

My writing was guided along with the expression, "Is it true and is it useful?" Readers may judge my viewpoint of past events but, with that knowledge, I wrote wholeheartedly the way I remember events to identify a moral for each story.

Writing a memoir is like looking through a window and recording what you see. Hopefully, you will enjoy reading the narrative of my life stories as much as I enjoyed writing them. They are humorous because they reflect life's funny side. They are also inspirational since it took my intestinal fortitude to survive. You may find them insightful, too, as my in-depth stories reveal my personality, philosophy, and certitudes.

With the stories in this book, I intend to spark memories, emotions, and even admiration as you reflect on their own past adventures and achievements. I authored this book to delve in further than my memoir *Bounce Back,* to tell my truth about my alcoholism, the horrendous car accident that changed me during my college days, and the closure and happiness I found later in life. With this, I hope to help you will move forward too. I would like nothing better than for you to perceive your past as exceptional and your future bright.

SPORTS

When the going gets tough, the tough get going.

K. Rockne,
former Notre Dame football coach

Tillamook High School baseball team playing at the Oregon State Penitentiary, Salem, Oregon, in 1953. I am in the front row on the right.

That's me, number 23, making a layup shot against Taft High School in 1953. Number 20 is my close friend Bud Gienger.

Me again, making a layup shot for Tillamook High School in 1951.

THE DIXIE CLASSIC BASKETBALL TOURNAMENT, 1955

I made a trip home to Tillamook, Oregon, for Christmas in 1955 from Oregon State College. I practically walked on air during that time in my life. I felt elated to play on the OSC basketball team, which was about to make a cross-country trip to Raleigh, North Carolina. On December 27th, we played in a tournament called the Dixie Classic. Coach Gill put me on the team just before Christmas, one of the best presents I ever received, and I was on cloud nine.

My Christmas gifts that year included money from parents and relatives, an unusual experience since I usually found clothes of some kind under the tree. Because I was in college, everyone must have thought I needed a little financial help. The Christmas money was a gift sent from heaven.

An overcoat was needed to make the cold winter trip to North Carolina, so I immediately went to downtown Tillamook to the Man Shop, a men's clothier. I had been in the store often during high school, so the owners knew me. I practically drooled over the nice sweaters, shirts, and pants but never had enough money to buy anything. All through high school, I went into the shop just to look at the clothes and dream about wearing them. This time was different as I had some money in my pocket. Now I could go in and purchase a smart-looking overcoat to make the trip east in comfort.

I picked out a medium-blue tweed coat to wear over my navy-blue team blazer. It made me feel like I had finally reached adulthood—or at least look like it. What a great feeling to take with me as I left the store sporting my new coat. Carl, the owner, wished me well on my upcoming trip with the OSC team. I could tell he was proud of me and really meant it.

Local basketball celebrity, Harvey Watt, had gone to the "Final Four" with the OSC Beavers basketball team in the late 1940s. The people of Tillamook backed their youth and their basketball achievements, and they had backed Harvey. I was now the first one from Tillamook to make the varsity basketball team at OSC since him.

The Trip

I returned to Corvallis in time to catch the bus ferrying the team to the Portland Airport for the first leg of our trip east via Chicago and Washington, DC. The Portland Airport terminal in 1955 resembled a large house. The terminal, such as it was, sat more to the west of the present-day structure near the Columbia Edgewater Country Club. The new terminal would not be built until the 1960s.

Few passenger planes flew in and out of Portland in 1955. It wasn't at all like today, seventy years later, with all its heavy traffic.

We flew on a prop plane, a DC-9 Stretch B. The large plane, one of the biggest prop planes still in use in the United States at the time, shot fire continuously out of the back end of the engines. My teammates and I were concerned, but the stewardess said not to worry because they spewed fire on every flight. This wasn't very comforting for young college boys on their first flight, especially during the night when the flames lit up the sky. After about seven hours, we landed safely at Midway Airport in Chicago. Midway was a busy, cramped, and dingy airport.

Airline passenger service was just starting to build in 1955 in the United States. The use of jet aircraft passenger planes was evolving from propeller planes. O'Hare Airport in Chicago would later open to passenger service to take the pressure off Midway Airport in 1955, a pivotal year in air travel.

While there, we were easily recognized as basketball players because of our team members. Wayne Moss stood six feet, nine inches tall, along with Dave Gambee, who was six-seven. Not too tall by today's standards of seven or more feet, but the team towered over most people, except for me. I was the only player on our team under six feet. People gawked and stared at us as we moved through the terminal, some asking what team we represented. Dave Gambee was our best player and, in a couple of years, would be picked as an All-American. He later spent many years playing as a professional in the National Basketball Association.

We left on our next leg of the trip, heading toward Raleigh, North Carolina. This included a second stop in Washington, DC. The Dulles National Airport in the nation's capital had a cramped terminal much like Midway in Chicago. After traveling through the night and the next day, we were growing tired of flying. When we landed at our destination, though worn out from the trip, we were excited, especially since the flying had been a first for the team.

The South

We were eager as well to see some of the American South's culture. It proved quickly to be much different from our life in Oregon, starting with the Carolina accent's interesting rhythm and cadence. Thankfully, I had my new overcoat. In Raleigh's cold climate, everything looked brown in color, with its foliage in dormancy for the winter. Coming from the green of the Northwest, it looked strange. I'd never seen so many brown lawns before. It depressed me. I soon realized the Pacific Northwest, with all its greenery, was a lot more cheerful. Of course, some people don't think the green quite offsets the winter's gloomy skies and constant rain.

We checked into the Raleigh Hotel, a lovely old-world venue, well-kept and historic. The Holiday Inns and Best Westerns wouldn't come on the American travel scene until the Eisenhower years. Something I noticed first off was the Negro—in the common nomenclature of the time—bellman's worn-out clothes. They hung on his slender body like a scarecrow's. The soles of his shoes were separating from the uppers, and I could see his toes. My thought was,

How could the hotel let him dress like he did and still work there? The sad realization came over me that this represented the condition of many Negro men in the South.

The White North Carolina population was familiar with such haggard folk, as we would observe as we spent the week in Raleigh learning about the culture. The White population wanted the Negro people to stay in an extremely limited and dependent condition. During my time in North Carolina, my perspective of the people in the South took a jolt I wouldn't forget. Life there was extremely different from what I knew growing up on the Oregon Coast. The trip gave us so much more than basketball.

During the tournament, we had a free day without a game, so a few of my teammates and I decided to explore the city of Raleigh. Exploring to us meant meeting some Southern ladies. It seemed easy, as the locals acted and looked more mature than the young women back in Oregon, and they liked guys from the West.

We met a few Southern gals in a restaurant, and they soon invited us out to one of their homes. The first people at her home who caught my attention were the Negro gardener and the maids the family had working for them. Hers was a middle-class family with Negro people working for them. They obviously could afford to hire them because they paid them little in wages. The South maintained a class system as late as 1955 and even later, placing the Negro at the bottom and the White population at the top.

Civil Rights

Brown v. Board of Education was passed in 1954 and would give the Negro population a big victory and, more importantly, hope on a path to equal rights. Victories would come slowly, but there would be a renewed dream.

The Civil Rights Act of 1964, passed under Lyndon B. Johnson's presidency, came ten long years later. Not until Martin Luther King Jr.'s leadership did equal rights receive a big boost in the movement toward a more just and equal condition for the Negro in the South. Today, it is still a work in progress in America, and always will be.

It was enlightening to be in the South the year following Brown v. Board of Education and witness the plight of the Negro. I left North Carolina with an expanded wisdom of the culture of the people.

Basketball

The tournament involved eight teams, so a lot of college basketball players descended on the town from such places as the University of Minnesota and the University of Wyoming. We played North Carolina State in our first game in the tournament. At the time we played them, they were ranked number three in the NCAA basketball polls. We took them down to the wire and had the shots to win at the end of the game, but it didn't happen. Bob Allard, our forward on the team, couldn't convert his jump shots. I liked Bob. We had enrolled at OSC in the same class and played on the first-year team together. He had a beautiful jump shot, with good balance. It was fundamentally correct, with a nice release. His problem was he couldn't put the ball in the basket, a major issue when you shoot.

Of the eight teams in the tournament, not one had a Negro player. The four teams who were invited from outside the South didn't, either. The Dixie Classic was all White, by design. The first Negro player that integrated the Southeastern Conference didn't play until 1967 at Vanderbilt in Tennessee. Perry Wallace garnered scholarship offers from eighty colleges before choosing Vanderbilt. The thought was the first Negro player must be an excellent player who couldn't fail.

The Big Ten Conference had integrated sports by 1945, but Minnesota didn't until 1964 and recruited three. The Beavers of, then, Oregon State College didn't have a Negro basketball player until 1960 even though the Pac-12 Conference had integrated in 1925 some thirty-plus years earlier. Oregon State's first Negro basketball player was Norm Monroe, a walk-on in the 1960–61 season. He quit the team halfway through the season, though the circumstances of his departure are not recorded. Not until 1966 did Charley White become OSC's first Black basketball scholarship player, integrating the team and playing for coach Paul Valenti.

Even though a conference might integrate, individual coaches and schools could decide not to play certain players if it fit the situation—or not even have them on the team. It was obvious that only teams without Negro players would be invited to the Dixie Classic in 1955 in Raleigh, North Carolina.

The Proposition

A middle-aged, well-dressed man hung around our team in the lobby of the hotel. He seemed nice and wanted to know all about Oregon. Finally, one night, he followed us upstairs and, somehow, we all ended up in my room. Eventually, he and I were the only ones remaining. My teammates had gone down the hall to another player's room. I still didn't understand what was happening, but it didn't take long before I did.

He propositioned me, wanting to know if I was interested in a gay relationship. Unbeknownst to me, he had been grooming me for two days and finally made it into my room with only the two of us present. I had come all the way across the country to be asked for sex by a man. I wasn't alarmed or irritated with him, but I insisted he leave, and he did without the slightest hint of a scene or even another word.

I went next door to the room filled with my teammates to tell them what had just happened. Once I arrived in the room, I was apprehensive about saying anything. It was the 1950s and I knew, even though nothing went on between the gay man and me, I would be forever suspect by association if I said anything. A lot of things weren't talked about in the 1950s and homosexual behavior was one of them.

Looking back at it later, I thought the man was pretty patient, waiting for his chance to proposition me. It gave me a chill. This was a new experience for me. I didn't know anything about homosexual behavior. It surprised me, too, because we were in the South. I thought there weren't any gay people in the southern part of the country. I must have imagined that it wouldn't be a good place for homosexuals since the place was overpopulated with "rednecks." I pictured a bunch of White males riding around in pickup trucks, carrying rifles in their back windows, with an antagonistic demeanor toward homosexual people.

Almon

During this trip, my brother Almon returned from the Korean War and was stationed at Fort Lee, Virginia. He surprised me by coming down to Raleigh with one of his friends from his base. They "hitchhiked" their way through Virginia and North Carolina and arrived the day before our first game with North Carolina State. They figured they would sleep on the floor of my hotel room to save some money. I told Almon it wasn't a clever idea, fearing I might get in trouble with Coach Gill. It's a decision I have regretted every day since because of the disappointment on Almon's face.

Looking back on it today, I think, *Who would have known?* Coach Gill always respected our privacy in our rooms, so the odds of him finding out would have been minimal. It just wasn't a very brotherly thing to do. Almon and his friend had just returned from the Korean War Zone and South Korea, yet I couldn't bring myself to honor their commitment to America, or my own brother, with some hospitality. It would have been the least I could have done for Almon. I was young and stupid. Though it still bothers me, I never discussed it again with my brother.

Selling My Ticket

On the final day of the tournament, we played Minnesota in the afternoon for seventh place and lost. We lost all the games of the tournament and were upset.

Someone on our team said, "Let's skip the championship game between Wake Forest and North Carolina State and sell our tickets."

We had all been given a pass for the whole tournament so we could see all the games. North Carolina is easily one of the most basketball-crazy regions of the country, so there was a lot of interest in the tournament, especially the championship game.

It was a sellout. A lot of people wanted to buy a ticket and get inside the R. J. Reynolds Coliseum, named after the cigarette baron. Four of us went to the arena just before the game, figuring we could scalp our tickets for a tidy sum.

With a lot of people milling around out in front of the arena looking for a ticket to buy, it was a seller's market. I caught the eye of a guy about forty years old in a leather bomber jacket who wanted to buy a ticket. I walked up to him and told him I had a good ticket. He asked the price, and I gave him a number way over the face value of the ticket. I was hoping he would say yes to the sale and I would make some easy money.

He opened his jacket. Instead of pulling out his wallet, he opened a large Federal Bureau of Investigation badge.

"I wouldn't do that if I were you," he said.

I stared at the FBI badge, which looked about twelve inches high and six inches wide. It was so big I can still remember it. Stunned, I swallowed deep and choked out an "okay" as I put the ticket back in my pocket. The FBI agent must have been satisfied my scalping escapade was terminated, because he let me go.

There I was pursuing my first scalping transaction and picked an FBI agent as my prey. I haven't ever tried to scalp a ticket since. I told my teammates the details and that he let me go. They were as surprised by the FBI story as I was. We decided to go to the championship game, and my teammates followed me into the coliseum to watch it.

Washington, DC

After getting sidetracked by the FBI and not making that little extra money, I flew out of Raleigh for Washington, DC, with the team the next morning. Our athletic director, Jim Barrett, and Coach Gill had plans for the team to spend some time seeing the sights of the nation's capital.

The team again landed at a small, crowded airport, but this time it was the Dulles Airport in Washington, DC, the forerunner of Reagan International. We went downtown into the city center to the famous Mayflower Hotel and made it our base. The Mayflower was where dignitaries of foreign countries and legislators from our government had stayed at various times in the past. It was the place to meet people and stay in 1950s Washington, DC.

Coach Gill arranged for the team to board a private sightseeing bus to tour the Capitol area. The bus took us around the National Mall to see the Jefferson, Washington, and Lincoln memorials. The driver stopped at the different historical places so we could get off the bus and read the inscriptions on each monument. We drove around the Capitol buildings, the Supreme Court, Library of Congress, and the White House.

At the end of our excursion, we went to the National Cemetery and the tomb of the Unknown Soldier and witnessed the "changing of the guard." It impressed me. The soldiers on guard at the tomb were very rigid when they moved, with their eyes straight ahead. I'd never seen anything like it. They had complete concentration to detail. They made me wonder if I could give such a performance.

I turned twenty-one just days before the trip, but I could still be a little bizarre at times. I thought of myself as the opposite of those soldiers guarding the tomb. But that's a good thing. Who would want to act that uptight?

The tour took up the afternoon and was a wonderful experience. I was amazed to see the monuments and other sites previously seen only in my school government books. It might have helped me make the decision later to teach government, social studies, and history to high school students for twenty-eight years.

Mayflower Hotel

We returned to the Mayflower Hotel, split up into smaller groups, and made plans for dinner. Before we ate, I sat in the hotel café drinking a cola and waiting for my dinner partners to show up. Coach Gill came in and sat down with me. During our conversation, "Slats" got down to the reason he was there.

"Would you have enjoyed taking the shot at the end of the North Carolina State game?"

He clearly wanted to see and hear my reaction.

I said "yes" with as much conviction as I could muster up without showing abundant surprise at his question. I knew this meant he was thinking about putting me in a game later in the season to take an important shot, and he wanted to know if I could do it. Now he knew.

That night, I ate dinner with Dave Gambee, Kenny Nanson, and Dick Wilson. We decided to dine at the Mayflower Hotel. We figured, why try to find some famous restaurant when the Mayflower itself was so well known. We sat down to great filet mignons all the way around. It was an impressive day in Washington, DC. One to remember.

We were to fly out of DC on a "red-eye" flight at eleven that night, so we had time to take in a movie. I remember I had a tough time staying awake. I told my teammates to remember to wake me at the end of the movie. I didn't want t to miss the flight home to Oregon.

When we flew out of Washington, DC, in the middle of the night, all the monuments were lighted, which left a lasting memory. It was a wonderful windup to a trip of a lifetime for a young guy from Tillamook, Oregon. When we arrived back in Corvallis, it was like returning from a pursuit of knowledge. I'd learned so much about myself and the culture in Raleigh, North Carolina.

Flying on a passenger plane was a new adventure for us—and for a lot of the country's residents. The 1950s and 60s are called the "Golden Age of Airplane Travel." That industry in the United States and the world "took off" during that period. At first, air travel was expensive, but it provided many amenities for the passengers: food, drinks, leg room, and pretty stewardesses giving the flying passengers a feeling of being special. Airplanes offered only one class in the beginning, giving the distinction that all flyers were in first class.

People wore their finest clothes when they flew. It's a whole different scene on airplanes today with passengers dressed in flip-flops, shorts, hoodies, and t-shirts, as well as bringing their pets on board. On the downside, the "Golden Age" was a dangerous time to fly, resulting in many disasters around the world. Also, the passengers' cabin often filled with smoke from cigars, cigarettes, and pipes. It might have been the "Golden Age," but it was hard for passengers to enjoy it when looking through and breathing the blue haze of tobacco smoke. Besides the air travel, the trip enabled me to see Washington, DC, up close and the culture of North Carolina in 1955, before Martin Luther King, Jr. came on the scene.

We remained home in Corvallis for three days before flying to Los Angles to play UCLA and USC. We missed a lot of classes during the season, so I took only the minimum number of hours to stay eligible. In my speech class, I gave a talk about my trip to Raleigh and received an A grade. I remember the class because the teacher was an attractive young woman not too much older than the students, and I didn't get a lot of A grades my first year at Oregon State.

The trip to Raleigh was a tremendous experience and left an indelible impression on me and on my teacher.

Penitentiary

In 1953, when I was a senior at Tillamook High, we had a good team and ended up qualifying for the Oregon State High School baseball playoffs later that spring. We lost to Milwaukee High School in the first round. Jerry was a left hander, and I pitched from the right side. We won other doubleheaders too. In one against Astoria High School, we pitched back-to-back no-hitters but didn't win either game.

In the game I pitched, batter Mickey Utti walked. He made it around to third on a stolen base and a groundout. Then Mickey scored from third with the winning run for Astoria. Corky Riggert, our catcher, couldn't handle my wild pitching, so our two no-hitters produced a win and a loss.

Earlier in the season, our baseball coach, Herb Johnsrud, scheduled a doubleheader for us with the Oregon State Penitentiary in Salem. Our team was made up of high school students ages fifteen to seventeen. The penitentiary team consisted of grown men of various ages who had broken the law in some way and had been sentenced by a judge or jury to serve time.

Like several of my teammates, I was intimidated when we learned about our opponents for our next away game, but there was no discussion about it. Coach had the last word. We played the inmates on their field at the prison since they weren't allowed to travel. Their schedule consisted of only home games.

Intestinal Fortitude

When we entered the prison, we were anxious about what was going to take place. Crossing the threshold of the prison understandably produced anxiety. We were about to compete in this sports contest up close and a little personal.

Nervous, I walked past the intimidating divider along the perimeter and into the large chain-link-fence holding pen. The prison guard counted us to confirm the number of team members. We encouraged the officer to be sure the count was accurate since he was going to check us again when we left.

For safety reasons, they ushered us into the prison barber shop to dress into our uniforms. Then we were shown through another bolted door and out into the prison yard where the baseball field was located. Three separate security checks were required to enter the yard, as the facility leaders didn't want the inmates to escape unexpectedly.

With time on their hands, the inmates meticulously maintained the field. The diamond was well laid out with only dirt on the infield and grass covering the outfield.

The wooden bleachers were filled with inmates. The prisoners wore gray shirts and pants that made them look spiritless and tired. Some had tattoos on their necks, faces, and arms. The tattoos looked odd since we had seen them only on ex-sailors home from World War II (WWII) and a stint in the Navy.

We intermingled with the actual criminals. Our third baseman, Howie Fritcher, was closest to the prisoner's dugout and bleachers and heard their banter. They yelled about how the prison would have a better team once we were incarcerated.

We played a doubleheader with Jerry Johnson pitching the second game after I'd pitched the first one. Feeling edgy, I inadvertently allowed the first two inmate batters to single off my pitching during the first inning. As I turned and looked out toward center field that beautiful day, I said to myself, "This is going to be a long day if this keeps up." Finally settling down, I pitched well and never gave up a hit the rest of the game.

Interestingly, two young prisoners from Tillamook sat on our team bench for a brief time during the game. Windy Conner and Ross Defoe were a few years ahead of me in school but had been incarcerated for robbery. Windy had been a neighbor of mine in

Tillamook when I was about to graduate high school with Ross's sister Mary. Living in a small town like Tillamook, people knew one another and everybody's business. These two young men had been in our house more than once.

Windy was a little hyperactive, always on the move, going from one adventure to another. He dropped out of school early. Windy talked fast as if perpetually excited. That's how he'd earned his nickname.

Ross was younger than Windy, immature, and a poor decision maker. Windy easily influenced Ross on several occasions, including the day that led to their incarceration. They became prime prospects for the state prison when they had gone on a robbery spree in Central Oregon a couple of years earlier. Word had it they drove up Highway 395 and robbed nine gas stations along the way. Who knows what they were thinking, or not thinking, but it did not serve them well. They were paying for their criminal romp.

As Windy and Ross sat with us, they inquired about their old friends and relatives back home in Tillamook. They were so close to my age it seemed inconceivable they were in prison and couldn't go home with us on the team bus. How depressing to see them in captivity in the setting of the state penitentiary and not as neighbors, classmates, or acquaintances. The reality of knowing them well created a strong impact on me.

They felt a bit downhearted and it showed on their faces. They enjoyed the game and welcomed us. I tried to be encouraging to them by talking about their siblings, but I really didn't know what to say. Seeing me and our team, and talking with us, hopefully brought them a reprieve from the confining position of prison life. We reminded them of life on the other side of the big gray wall and offered some hope to return to a life they'd once known.

"Do you see my brother Bud?" Windy asked.

We had nothing to give him.

"How about my sister Mary? Any of you see her in class? She's in your class, isn't she, Earl?" Ross questioned.

Again, I shrugged but had no news for him.

I'll always remember how excited they were to see us the day of the game but how disappointed we had nothing newsworthy about their siblings.

Intestinal Fortitude

They were a lot like many young guys I knew, interested in sports. Knowing their brothers and sister formed a connection between us, whether we had news of them to share. Windy's family still lived in the house where I was born over in Hathaway Meade, a neighborhood in Tillamook. Thinking of the two of them gave me a sinking feeling in my stomach and made me sad and depressed when I considered what it must be like—always trapped and in fear.

A portion of the twenty-foot-high gray prison wall served as the left field fence. Hitting a home run over that roadblock was a colossal achievement. Amazingly, our second baseman, Harvey Fritcher, smacked a ball off their incredible barrier for a triple that scored two runs and won us the first game. We also won game two. Both Jerry Johnson and I threw two-hit shutouts against the inmates and won with identical scores of two to nothing.

I never saw Windy or Ross again after our brief encounter at the state pen. I was never told when they were released or whatever became of them. They were good guys, except for their penchant for robbing gas stations. It's hard to picture them as criminals when I remember them as kids in school. Windy and Ross were paying the price for an unwise decision made at an early age.

It would have been much easier to play a ballgame at the prison if all the inmates had been strangers and we'd remained unemotional about it all, or at least detached, but we could not. This hit close to home for all of us.

On the bus ride home, talking to my teammates about how it would feel to be incarcerated made me shudder. It provided a sensible lesson for us, which showed how obeying the law can significantly impact your life. That had to be why none of our parents opposed the idea. The trip to the state penitentiary made an impression on me and my teammates. We shared how grateful we were for our freedom. Our coach, Herb Johnsrud, did us a great service that day by exposing us to incarceration and the loss of freedom.

THE SUBSTITUTION

While playing basketball my sophomore year at Oregon State College in Corvallis, I was severely injured in an auto accident. Due to my detriment, I was unable to continue playing for the Beavers following my recovery. My injuries didn't allow me to compete for the remainder of the season or to return at the level of my previous performance.

With some scholarship eligibility remaining, I transferred the next year to a smaller school, able to play after my two-year healing hiatus. Oregon College of Education (OCE) in Monmouth recruited me to play basketball. The competition wasn't as intense, but the rigorous education requirements were still demanding.

OCE competed against three other schools in the league: Southern Oregon College (SOC) in Ashland, Eastern Oregon College of Education (EOCE) in La Grande, and Portland State College (PSC) in Portland.

PSC dominated the league in all sports. Each year, they produced a formidable team. The metropolitan area of Portland gave them the advantage of recruiting outstanding athletes from all the Portland high schools in addition to the surrounding area.

Because Portland State was a larger school than the other three, their outstanding enrollment allowed them more students to draw from for sports and other activities. The three remaining schools in the league were frustrated by PSC's dominance, which created feelings of animosity. However, of all the sports, basketball was the game the other schools in the league could best compete in against them.

The year I participated in basketball for OCE, Eastern was leading the league standings by one game over Portland State with two games left to play in the season. Eastern had the last two games of the season scheduled with OCE. We stood in their way to the championship. They needed to win just one game against us to mathematically clinch first place and go to the National Association of Intercollegiate Athletics playoff. The games were to be played on Eastern's home court in La Grande.

Our team enthusiastically loaded into four cars for the trip, sharing an abundance of positive chatter about the game. We headed up the highway alongside the Columbia River and over the Blue Mountains to the picture-perfect college town of La Grande. We admired the town's streets lined with green trees, and the rushing water of the Grande Ronde River running through it. The town was a stop on the old Oregon Trail in the 1840s and had a comfortable feel.

We arrived on Thursday ready to play Friday and Saturday nights. The team was surprisingly relaxed, casually discussing the game and looking forward to playing the league leaders. We were the underdogs and not expected to win. But, for some unknown reason, our team felt confident we would give Eastern a good game on Friday night. It showed in our swagger.

Before the game, the EOC players smiled a lot during warmups and looked confident to play. When the game began, we bounced off to a fantastic start, taking the lead and holding it. Our fast entrance frustrated Eastern and seemed to tighten them up, as noted by their stressful looks. As the game progressed and Eastern did not manage to take the lead, their fans in the student section became testy. They started to yell a few choice words at us, such as, "Losers!" Hostility crackled through the gym. We felt the crowd's demeanor permeate the game, but our team fed off their contentious attitude and played even more intently.

With four minutes left, we still led by ten points, controlling the game on cruise control. While moving toward a sure victory, we played like the team leading the league.

Without any explanation, our coach pulled all five of the starters out of the game, even though we were playing well. He substituted five replacement players for us. These inexperienced players were barely our second-best on the team. They had sat on the bench the entire game before coach called their names. Even worse, they were not warmed up.

As my fellow teammates and I came off the court and sat on our bench, we looked at our coach in confusion, questioning his motivation amongst ourselves.

"Why do you think Coach took five of us out of the game at once?" I asked our center sitting next to me. "If he took one or two of us, I wouldn't be too surprised, but all five makes a statement."

Our center just shook his head in disgust.

As we sat on the bench and watched our team fall behind, we realized our coach either was a horrible leader or wanted Eastern to win the game. The momentum of the game shifted immediately. Eastern did win the game, easily making up the ten-point deficit and then some. Our fans were somber and left quietly.

Initially, we were unwilling to accuse the coach of such a traitorous act as giving the game away. But, as we thought more about it and discussed it further, we felt double-crossed. Confusion turned into anger and agitation. It was difficult for any of us to accept the coach's decision since there was no reasonable explanation.

After the game, the team headed to the dressing room, not knowing what to do and hardly thinking about showering or going back to the hotel.

I questioned the coach, "What was your intent for substituting our five best players at such a critical time in the game?"

We received no answer. The murmuring of our players exploded, detonated by my inquiry, and some began questioning the coach in an accusatory tone.

"What happened, Coach?" two of them asked in unison.

Still no answer. Even the most timid players took part in the questioning. The dressing room went from skepticism to outright incrimination with no hesitation.

Finally, our coach became defensive and held his ground. "The substitutions weren't a big deal. I just wanted to change the lineup."

Intestinal Fortitude

Though it was a weak answer, he didn't say any more. With his reply, we forced ourselves to settle down and head to the showers, convinced there was an ulterior motive. We all went quiet, realizing the game was over and we had no choice but to accept his explanation. But "why" consumed all our minds that night.

Eastern also won the league championship over Portland State, which might have been the coach's motivation for removing his five best players.

PSC should have won the Oregon Collegiate Conference Championship one more time but was denied it by a questionable substitution. Our players found it difficult to truly accept what they'd witnessed that night. It seemed unbelievable our coach would intentionally "throw" a game, especially at the college level. Even knowledgeable fans were stunned at our coach's ability to do such a thing. Many a head shook as they watched OCE's victory disappear.

Initially, it did cross my mind that our coach so badly didn't want PSC to win the league that he changed the outcome of our game that night to influence the later outcome. His players weren't children. We were not too young to understand the controversial substitution which led to a deliberate loss. I was twenty-one, and a couple of the other players were too. We had played enough basketball by the time we entered college to understand how the game was played—and not played. We knew there were things you didn't do during a game and substituting all five of your best players with a slim lead late in the game was one of them. We knew the decision killed our team's momentum and jeopardized our chance to win.

"The game is over. Let's move on," I said before leaving the locker room. "Hashing it out isn't going to change anything. We need to get ready for another game tomorrow night."

Before Saturday's game, the team walked to the Eastern Oregon gym, which was a few blocks from our hotel in downtown La Grande. As we dressed in our uniforms for the game, the team room was subdued and mostly silent. Everyone was uneasy, including the coach. The players kept their heads down and did not talk.

When it came time to play, the coach broke his silence. "You guys think you know so much about coaching, let's see how you do tonight."

His challenge sounded more like a threat, and it obviously referred to our questionable loss the night before and the lineup of the players, including me, who'd challenged him the most about Friday's game. Those of us on the starting team held a short meeting on the court before tip-off. We pledged to give it our best effort, just as we had the night before.

We played well and won by eight points. I scored twenty-seven of our points while the opposing guard scored fifteen. Our center took over and ruled the boards, coming down with fourteen rebounds. The game was close, as Eastern lost all its edge in the wake of our free-wheeling onslaught.

After returning to school on Sunday, no one voiced any more implications about the coach. His throwing the game was something impossible to prove. A coach can substitute any way he wants to in a game. No one thought about bringing it up to the athletic department. It was better to just let the whole thing slide, and we did. We had won the second game.

When Portland State didn't win the league championship that year, some of the players for OCE and I were sure we knew why. If our coach hadn't substituted and caused us to lose the Friday night game, we would have taken both games and knocked Eastern out of first place.

Basketball is also about life decisions, not just winning or losing. It's "just a sport" but it's still about good sportsmanship and trustworthy coaching. Sometimes you don't get answers and must live with the consequences and decide not to question authority. Sometimes, for a ballplayer to be a good leader, he must be a good follower, too, even with no inspiration and bad communication skills.

THE LIFE OF A HIGH SCHOOL PUNTER

While I was the worst football punter in the history of high school sports. The only way a kicker might have been worse would involve missing the ball with his foot. Our coach, Larry McKeel, wanted me to do the punting for our team because I could catch the ball when the center snapped it to me.

Sometimes the center would send the ball skipping along the ground. I would then have to field the ball like a shortstop in baseball before trying to punt. Sometimes the ball would be high and I would have to jump to catch the ball.

Our team's punter had to have capable hands first, and if he could kick, all the better. Coach knew I was agile and had skillful hands to handle the punting for our Tillamook High School football team. Fourth down was a real event, trying to get a kickoff to the other team without them blocking the punt. I didn't dread fourth downs, but I admit I didn't look forward to them, either.

Sometimes when kicked on fourth down, the ball might be a nice spiral searing into the Friday night lights. But more times than not—or than I would like to remember—they were what we call a bad fly ball in baseball: "a dying quail to the right field." My kicks were, unfortunately, inferior.

Delay of Game

One Friday night, we played Central Catholic in Portland on Liberty Field behind the junior high school. It was 1953, and Central would win the State Championship of Oregon that year.

We found ourselves in trouble against such a formidable team, and they often forced us into fourth-down situations a lot. That of course gave me plenty of chances to try to punt the ball.

During the game, our team received one of the strangest penalties in a high school football game during a fourth-down punt. The penalty was for delay of the game. What caused the delay penalty was our nearsighted, almost blind tight end, Loren Leach. When he caught my kick and ran for what he thought was a touchdown, it turned out quite comical.

When the ball was snapped to me, I had to hurry to manage the kickoff before some big Central lineman bent on blocking the kick trampled me. My kick spun in a low spiral and just cleared the line of scrimmage. It looked, to our nearsighted end, like a pass. As he ran downfield to cover the punt, he looked back and saw the ball coming at him. He caught the ball and ran seventy yards.

The Central players just stepped aside and let him run for the end zone. It took Loren a while to reach the other end of the field, then return to hand the ball to the referee. They penalized our team for delaying the game. It was the perfect storm. Loren's poor vision and my kicking the ball so it looked like a pass right to him caused the "hard to believe" penalty.

What was also funny was that Loren, with his poor vision, normally couldn't catch a pass when I, the quarterback, threw it to him. To my surprise, he hauled in that punt like he was Jerry Rice of the San Francisco 49ers.

Because of Loren's poor eyesight and glasses with lenses like those of a Coke bottle, his nickname amongst his teammates was "Peepers." Through much name calling by his teammates, "Peepers" eventually became "Peaches," by which he was then forever known.

Bud Geinger, our team's running back and captain, dreamed up both of those nicknames. He thought the names sounded the same, but the latter was easier to say. Our team captain liked nicknames and had them for many of his friends and classmates.

Bud had his own nickname, attached to him by his friends at Tillamook High School. All his friends knew he liked to complain with regularity, so we nicknamed him "Always Bitching." You couldn't say those types of words around other people or at school because, in the early 1950s, bitching was considered a cuss word. We shortened Bud's nickname to "AB." After much use, it became "Abby," which his buddies at Tillamook High School used frequently.

Another story of my punting prowess happened against the North Bend Bulldogs, a team that would also win the State Championship in the year we played them. We played a lot of tough opponents when I was at Tillamook High. We again played at Liberty Field behind the junior high school. We were being beaten badly as we couldn't do anything against their defense. We trailed by four touchdowns late in the game, and the outcome appeared evident even to the most diehard Tillamook fan. For obvious reasons, I had also been doing a lot of punting in the game. I'm not sure we even made one first down all night.

We had the ball on our own five-yard line, it was fourth down, and I had to kick the ball. As I pointed out before, I never knew what kind of a punt would transpire when I set out to kick the ball. What took place mystified the Tillamook fans, the opponents, and me. It was almost mystical, having a spiritual reality that is apparent neither to the senses nor to the intelligence. In other words, no one knew what happened...

Chet Patton

With the ball on our own five-yard line, I would have needed to stand in the endzone when I attempted the kick. In fact, I backed up to the end of the endzone, off the end of the field. Ready to receive the ball, I moved right next to a parent and friend, Chet Patton, who stood just off the field. Remember, this is a high school football game in a small town in America on a Friday night. Lots of fans and parents watch games, standing on the sidelines.

As I watched for the snap, Chet said, "Earl, why don't you try a pass?"

He had obviously seen me punt the ball.

It was late in the game, we were behind in the score, and it was too much of a spread to catch up. I thought Chet had a clever idea, so I called time out. As we huddled, I told our end, Loren "Peaches" Leach, the one with the questionable vision, to look for a pass. About that time, our coach, Larry McKeel, figured out what was going on and yelled at Chet not to interfere with the game.

We lined up again. I went through with the first plan to kick the ball. I was ready to kick it when the snap of the ball came toward me, but it didn't make any difference if we passed, ran, or punted. The ball sailed high over my head, out of the endzone, and into the crisp night air. As the center sent the ball flying out of my reach, I looked at Chet and, in unison, we shrugged our shoulders. It was that kind of Friday night.

Nehalem and Erv Garrison

Our junior varsity football team played a game against Nehalem High School one fall afternoon in 1952. Tillamook High played them with their junior varsity. I was on the JV team that afternoon and, as usual, played the punter position for Tillamook. It was odd that no other player could kick better than I could. But, as I mentioned, it was more important for the punter to be able to catch the ball from the center than be able to kick it.

We played the game at Nehalem, a small town in northern Tillamook County in the northwest part of Oregon, within a couple of miles of the Pacific Ocean. Quite naturally, the Nehalem team nickname was the Seagulls.

Nehalem High and the town were built on a hill with a view of the Nehalem River Valley below. The school was built near the top. Since it wasn't all that extensive a space, it offered minimal room for a football field. In fact, there was so little land, when they laid out their field, they had only enough room for an eighty-yard gridiron instead of the usual one hundred yards.

Also, at one end of the field ran the Pacific Coast Highway 101. On the highway end of the field, they didn't have a goal post because if you kicked a field goal or extra point the ball would sail onto the highway and cause a car wreck. After a team scored a touchdown at that end of the field, the teams would go to the other end of the field to try for the extra point.

Nehalem had a good team made up of loggers' and farmers' sons from around their hometown. Their best player was a big, fast, talented player named Erv Garrison. On that afternoon, he was running the football and piling up the yards against the Tillamook High School JV.

Erv was also Nehalem's punter, and a good one. What Erv did that day surprised even him. He had punted a couple of times in the first half and each time caused our kick returner, me, to backpedal to catch his punts. In the second half, Nehalem drove down the field, headed for the Highway 101 end, and we finally stopped them at our forty-yard line. It was again time for Erv to punt on fourth down.

I hung back, waiting for the kick on my own goal line. Nehalem snapped the ball to Erv from the forty-yard line to where he stood at least ten yards behind his line of scrimmage. He got off a great punt that soared over my head, traveled beyond the endzone, and continued onto Highway 101, a total distance of about seventy yards.

The ball missed all the cars traveling on the highway, avoiding a wreck. Some of Tillamook's players thought the ball got caught in Pacific Ocean winds. I had a good look at the punt in the air going over my head. No wind caused that ball to cover seventy yards. It was *some* kick.

Canby High School

Thirty years later, Erv would coach my son Eric in football at Canby High School, south of Portland. One of Oregon's better high school football coaches. He produced strong football teams year after year. I coached the Canby High School boys' basketball team at the same time. We won our league championship and competed in the Oregon High School Basketball tournament. Erv and I remained good friends until his death.

ANNIE'S BASKETBALL GAME

My daughter Annie attended Barclay Grade School in Oregon City, Oregon, in 1972, where she played on her fourth-grade basketball team. Barclay played against other elementary schools in Oregon City and West Linn, across the Willamette River. She was fortunate to be able to play organized basketball at such an early age due to Title IV coming into effect a few years earlier. This basketball program's goal was aimed at involving the female students in learning the game early on.

Annie was a skillful player. Her mother and I watched the games each week of the season as proud parents. One game day, I was out of town, missed her contest, and didn't see her play. When I returned home after my trip, Annie was excited and wanted to tell me how the game had finished.

She said it was a close game and went into overtime four times.

"Wow!" I said. "That must have been some game, going into overtime repeatedly. Tell me about the game."

She explained to me that her team scored right at the end of the game, on a last-second shot, to tie the game and send it to overtime. Then she told me her team scored right at the end of the first overtime to send the game to the second overtime. Then they scored at the end of the second overtime to move the game to the third overtime. They did it again to go to a fourth overtime. At the end of the fourth overtime, they scored that last-second shot and were victorious.

I asked her, "What was the score of the game?"

She said, "Thirty-two to thirty."

"And how many points did you score?"

She answered, "Thirty-two."

Annie went on to Oregon City High School and played on the girls' basketball team. The team went to the Oregon State Basketball Tournament every year she was in school. She was one of their better players, and I continued to watch her as a pleased dad.

Today, Annie is an executive with Intel Corporation and lives in both Lake Oswego, and Bend, Oregon, with her partner, Suzanne, and her dog, Lucy. They are avid runners and hikers.

Celebrating my 85th birthday in Scottsdale with my son, Eric, and daughter, Annie.

DICK LUNDY AND JACK STREETER

When I played football on the Tillamook High School team in the fall of 1952, I had two teammates we called small in physical stature. They were not only short but slight in build compared to their high school teammates and opponents. Neither weighed very much soaking wet, like jockeys or featherweights.

Their slight sizes for football never seemed to bother them much. Dick Lundy and Jack Streeter were notable examples for me and our teammates. Because they were as undersized as they were and played the game well, it gave none of us the excuse we weren't big enough.

They were also brave to play against bigger opponents, leading by example. I always thought if Dick and Jack could do it, there was no reason I couldn't.

Both Dick and Jack were intelligent, which isn't saying much about the two, given that they chose to play football. Besides being smart, both were armed with, or afflicted with, unmitigated gall. They didn't think it was strange to be on the football team in their miniature condition. To top it off, they showed no timidity toward any opposing team scheduled by the Tillamook High School Cheesemakers.

Intestinal Fortitude

Dick

Tillamook had the custom of playing some big schools each year, such as Catholic Central and Astoria. When Dick and Jack were juniors, Tillamook also played the powerful Medford Tornadoes on their field. Dick played in the backfield as a running back. We wondered how he could be tackled by some big lineman and not be crushed. Dick's height of five foot six and weight of 123 pounds helped him in many instances. He could more easily slip through a small hole in the other team's line, and his modest stature made him hard to tackle. There simply wasn't all that much for a tackler to grab.

Also, Dick was fast and shifty when running with the football. Being slight created another advantage for him. The opposing team couldn't see him in Tillamook's backfield until he burst through the line and ran off for a touchdown. Another important aspect about Dick's prowess as a running back was his positive thinking. He always believed he would run the football for a big gain or a touchdown every time he carried the ball.

Jack

Jack Streeter would cause anyone to be curious as to how he could play in a high school game and live to tell about it. The question isn't how, but why? As high school football lineman go, he was small for such a pastime. At a height of five foot five and only 140 pounds, and being of sound mind... "Why?" is an honest question. The thing about Jack was he never looked big playing against opposing lineman about twice his height and weight. Often, he held his own against them.

Jack had some attributes to even the playing field against some goliath across from him on the other team's line. He was strong and quick. He would have been a good wrestler if Tillamook High School had had a team at the time. On the football field, he often beat some big giant with his speed to a spot they couldn't default.

Jack played on the Cheesemakers' defensive line. His mind had one goal: get to the other team's ball carrier and make the tackle. He would go around some big, slow adversary or go over him.

Occasionally, he would go under him, applying something he called his "submarine" move.

Entertainment

Since both Jack and Dick were smart guys in the classroom as well as on the football field, they used that attribute in other areas too. During the season, our team traveled long distances in our yellow school bus to away games. It was easy for our players to grow bored and weary trekking to these events. Tillamook is located out on the Pacific Shore of Oregon, west of the Willamette Valley, where most of the Oregon population lives.

Jack memorized the lengthy poem "The Rime of the Ancient Mariner" and recited it for the team on away games. He didn't just deliver the words verbatim. He put his unique presentation to the prose as our bus rolled down the highway toward our next game. Jack also trusted to memory the equally lengthy story of "The Signifying Monkey," a humorous rhyme he introduced with a flare only Jack could portray. We all leaned forward with anticipation to Jack's telling of the poems on the long bus rides.

I remember a line in "The Signifying Monkey" when the monkey said to the lion, "Some things about your grandmother made me mad," as the monkey tormented the lion from the safety of the tree.

Our coaches, Larry McKeel and Herb Johnsrud, taught the team some of their old college drinking songs. This activity also helped keep our minds off the lengthy rides and hard seats of the buses. They knew quite a few songs, which may or may not have meant they had drained a few beers during their college days. It was fun to sing the tunes since they made the trip go faster and gave us the feeling we were doing something college boys did. It gave us the notion that pursuing a higher education must be a lot of fun. College had to be a good stint if we had time to sing all the songs we learned from our coaches. A lot of us were excited about going to college when we finished high school. Between the college drinking songs and Jack's poems, the bus trips were a lot more enjoyable.

Intestinal Fortitude

Side Note

I played on the Tillamook High School football team with Dick and Jack during the 1951 and 1952 seasons, their junior and senior years. We still enjoy following Tillamook and Pac-12 college football and stay in touch. We remain lifelong friends.

Jack is a former pharmacist now retired and living in Banks, Oregon, with his wife, Elaine. Dick's career was in architecture. He is retired, too, and lives in Sherwood, Oregon, with his wife, Mary. Jack and Dick were both eighty-eight years old at the time of this writing.

Garibaldi's Infamous Football Field

Tillamook High School's junior varsity football team was once again to play Garibaldi High School's varsity football team. The game was played on Garibaldi's infamous field on the edge of Tillamook Bay. I say infamous, but only to the other high school football teams in Tillamook County because the field was usually flooded with water on one end.

They should have named the field "Tide Flats" because it was laid out on the tide flats of Tillamook Bay, and the incoming tide submerged the south end closest to the bay. The part of the field lying above the water line of the bay was only about six inches in elevation. The games played on the field should have been scheduled for a low tide, but that must not have been a concern to those who oversaw scheduling.

All the schools in Tillamook County in the early 1950s—Nehalem, Wheeler, Bay City, Nestucca, and Sacred Heart Academy—were familiar with the flooding. Many a story originated from Garibaldi's notorious field by Tillamook Bay. These typically covered how, after being tackled and landing facedown with an opponent on top, the ball carrier had almost drowned. Or how the center trying to snap the ball needed to gather a clump of grass to set the ball on, keeping the ball out of the water so it wouldn't float away or be wet when the quarterback handled it.

During our game between Tillamook's JV team and Garibaldi's varsity team, it rained pitchforks, a real downpour. With the field under water on one end and the rain coming down sideways off the Pacific Ocean less than a half mile away, the sheer amount of water made us think the Biblical ark would show up any minute. The field was saturated with water.

A most unusual play took place during this competition between Tillamook and Garibaldi. It only added to the attitude that the game would be played even in often-fluid conditions that increased its mythical history.

Harvey Madding was the quarterback in Tillamook's T-formation offense, trying hard to keep a hold on a slippery, wet ball. Passing the ball was futile since he found it almost impossible to get a good grip on the wet ball. Plus, the receiver had a tough time running out for a catch on the soggy field, especially when he had to look back at Harvey through the downpour. It made it almost impossible to complete a forward pass against Garibaldi's defense and the rain. Harvey didn't call any passes. Instead, he went with running plays, where the ball carrier drove straight ahead at Garibaldi's line.

A run around the end was also an impossible achievement as the runner needed to change direction as he made a cut up the field. Cutting on the waterlogged gridiron was beyond all comprehension. That left Harvey with only one choice: to have the runner move straight ahead with the ball. Even when he handed the ball off to a running back moving straight ahead into the line, it was hard to make a clean exchange of the ball. The water would also slow the running back as he headed toward Garibaldi's line. This detail helped generate one of football's oddest performances.

Harvey took the ball from Len Bishop, Tillamook's center, turned, and attempted to hand it off to Tillamook's running back, Frank Kenyon, who wasn't extremely fast in the first place. Frank ran straight ahead into Garibaldi's line and, because of the wet conditions, was extra slow getting to Harvey's handoff.

In what seemed like a split second, Stan Hushbeck, a Garibaldi lineman, burst through a hole in Tillamook's line. He took the handoff from Harvey, sidestepped Frank, and sloshed down the field. Or should I say waded down the field?

Harvey was dumbfounded for a second, then gave chase after Hushbeck. But Stan had enough of a head start that Harvey couldn't catch him on the soggy field.

I was playing in the backfield with Frank and made a lunge for Hushbeck as he went by me. My dive for Hushbeck became more of a plunge, as I missed the tackle and went facedown in the water, only to come up sputtering from a mouth full of muddy water.

Harvey hadn't fumbled the ball; he was just holding it out so Frank could take the handoff. Instead, Hushbeck had gotten to the ball first and took the handoff in the opposite direction. Then he splashed his way down the field for an improbable Garibaldi touchdown. What an astonishing play.

The field, being inundated by the rain, played into this amazing touchdown. Also, some credit should go to Hushbeck for his heads-up. His timing was perfect as he pushed through the line and sidestepped Frank for the touchdown.

So, the Garibaldi football field produced another story unique to the legendary gridiron next to Tillamook Bay.

TAFT FOOTBALL GAME

The Tillamook High School Cheesemakers had a football game scheduled with the Taft Tigers one Friday night in September of 1952. The game was to be played in Taft, a town south of Tillamook on the Oregon Coast. Taft is built on the edge of the Pacific Ocean with its Main Street running along the beachfront. The distance from the beach could be measured in yards, not miles.

The climate along the Oregon Coast in the fall and winter can be cold, rainy, and foggy. Many of the schools along the coast of Oregon play football games in these conditions every year. The weather that Friday night was, thankfully, warm and mild, like an extended summer day.

Taft's field lay less than a mile from the ocean on a hillside. The field fell to the same problem all schools along the Oregon Coast face, finding enough flat land to lay out a football or baseball field. The mountains of the range along the Oregon Coast stretch west to the very shoreline of the Pacific Ocean, with the mountains plunging down to the edge of the ocean.

Taft's field was new, having just been bulldozed from the top of the hill overlooking the ocean. It was so new it didn't have any grass growing on it. The flat surface was prepped for Taft to plant grass and complete it. Unfortunately, the dirt was clay. Grass doesn't grow well in clay. The game couldn't be played on the dirt surface as it was too hard. Also, if it rained, the field would be a mud bath. The question arose: How do you play a game on a dirt field that might turn muddy from the clay and be very slick and gummy?

Taft High School produced a plan. Their answer was to apply wood shavings all over the field. They would spread the shavings out evenly, approximately four inches deep. This would render the field softer to land on and keep the players from getting dirty. Also, if it rained, the shavings would retain the water and keep the field from becoming a muddy mess. This idea had to rank as one of the most ridiculous decisions in the history of athletic fields.

There was also one other problem with the shavings. How do the yard lines on the field stay in place? Visualize a field of shavings with white yard lines all laid out ready for a game of football. The lines eventually became obliterated, causing the referees to only guess as to the initial line locations.

Another problem arose for the players. As the game proceeded, the shavings were kicked into piles with each play. It was difficult to run on the uneven field and gain consistent footing. I remember spitting shavings from my mouth each time a Taft player tackled me. The dust from the shavings, which broiled up off the gridiron like heat waves, hung over the field. All the players, coaches, and crowd members tried to fan them away.

Eventually, the game was called early, cutting short the usual full period of four quarters. Also contributing to the shortened game was the score. Tillamook was ahead 60–0 in the third quarter. In those days, nobody stopped the game or had a running clock. The Cheesemakers had a fullback named Bobby Riggert who ran straight ahead and couldn't be stopped by the smaller Taft players. He didn't need to run and cut on the questionable surface or go around the end. He ran straight ahead and had a field day!

When Bobby graduated in 1952, he went on to Oregon State College and lettered for three years in football, playing for the OSC Beavers. He continued to be a good friend and avid Oregon State fan until he passed away several years ago at the age of eighty-three. I miss meeting him at Oregon State games later in life and sharing Cheesemaker football stories.

Vernonia

Vernonia is a small town nestled in the Coast Range of northwestern Oregon. It is close to the Oregon Coast with the Pacific Ocean to the west and the small town of Banks to the southeast. Its location is out of the way from any population center, fifteen miles off a main road called the Sunset Highway. The highway connects the large city of Portland to the east and the Oregon Beaches to the west and runs straight west to the Pacific Ocean. Driving west at sundown, you have the sun in your eyes all the way to the ocean.

The word "remote" best defines Vernonia's location. It once had a large lumber mill as the basis for the area's economy. It was a town of blue-collar workers who labored in the woods or in the mill, which is why the high school team's nickname became the Loggers. Quite a few taverns lined Main Street and were frequented by the industrious citizens. Vernonia was known to some people as a rough town, with quarreling easily found in any of its taverns. Sports teams at the high school were considered challenging because they played very physical ball. You had to be ready for a tough game when you played Vernonia High School.

Tillamook High School played them in basketball in their gym on a frosty night in December 1952. The weather may have been freezing outside but our team, the Cheesemakers, burned red-hot inside. We made every shot we threw at the basket. This, of course, didn't make their team happy, and it further frustrated the hometown fans.

Earl Llewellyn Goldmann

Players

Vernonia had a talented player named Kenny Nanson who stood six foot one and could practically jump over the gym. I later played with Kenny at Oregon State College, where he made the All-Conference Team. He was that good. They also had a player named Gordon Crowston who was a heck of a scorer. When he was in eighth grade, he set the Oregon State Grade School Tournament scoring record with forty-four points.

Our team had to overcome these two special players for the Tillamook Cheesemakers to have any chance of winning the game. Because our players had the hot hand that night, we managed to come away with the victory over Vernonia, 66–60.

Vernonia also had a Negro player on their team, which seemed strange because Vernonia was so far from the inner city. Most Negro players in Oregon in 1952 lived in the central part of Portland, and many attended Jefferson High School. Along with this player, they had a feisty little guard on their team who was a bit of a wise guy. I was assigned to guard him, and he guarded me as well. It wasn't long before we were locked in a competition that night as to who was the better player on the court. We became a little physical as the game wore on, fouling each other with barely any extra force. By the end of the game, I had scored quite a few points on him, and he wasn't a happy guy.

As both teams exited the gym floor after the game, retreating to their respective dressing rooms, the feisty Vernonia guard launched one more smart remark to me over his shoulder. By then, I'd had enough of this wise guy and his nonsense.

I made a move for him, pointed my finger in his direction, and yelled, "Wait right there!"

Everyone in the gym heard me and turned their heads in my direction. He didn't wait. Instead, he made a hasty exit for the safety of his team's dressing room. Standing behind the feisty guard was their Negro player. It looked as though I was threatening him instead. The whole situation reversed on me in seconds, as I was the bad guy, like I'd challenged the Negro player. In response, the students and fans began filing off the bleachers. It was obvious the townsfolk planned to defend him.

The Vernonia students and parents weren't happy in the first place. Tillamook had won the game and I was one of our team's leading scorers. Among sullied fans and students, truly little was worse than a put-down. The scene was set, with the maligned Negro player and me, the antagonist who had cast aspersions upon the whole town. As I turned away to our dressing room to shower, I knew this confrontation was just getting started. I worried that their indignation was building into anger for challenging their player. To some of the crowd, the fact that he was Negro and singular in the community made a difference. They thought I had accused him—of what, they weren't quite sure—and they were going to defend him.

In addition to the player issue, I had scored most of our team's points in beating the home team. The Vernonia fans now had a real prospect to turn their frustrations on... me.

The Crowd

A crowd of parents, cheerleaders, townsfolk, and ball players assembled on the front porch just outside the gym door. They also crowded the steps leading up to the gym outside the porch and spilled out into the parking lot in front of the gym. The Vernonia contingent of followers stood waiting for me to come out of the gym.

As soon as I reached the front door, I saw all the people through the door's glass windows. It was quite a scene. I contemplated my next move. I knew one thing for sure: Anything could happen and there was no way to tell what it would be before I walked out of the door. I was in a tricky spot and on my own as everyone else was already on the bus. It was quite a misunderstanding I'd gotten myself into, but that was not something to think about at this point.

I knew trying to tell the crowd it was all a misreading on their part wasn't going to fly now. As I stood waiting to go through the doors, I thought this was no time to show fear in the face of the crowd. How far the Vernonia people were going to go with their resentment of me was the big question. One thing was for sure: I had to be strong.

With a knot in my stomach, I remembered reading somewhere that a mob has an IQ of zero.

I pushed the gym door open, held my head up, put the bravest look on my face I could muster, and walked straight into the crowd. Their cheerleaders and players made it hard for me to squeeze through. The scene was tense. You could feel the electricity in the chilly night air. I pulled up my jacket collar, looked straight away, and made no eye contact or odd movements.

After a few comments, the crowd went deathly silent in the freezing darkness of the night. Everyone was waiting for something to happen. No one jostled me, but they breathed down my neck as I pushed my way through. I made it across the porch through the cheerleaders and players to the steps of the porch. I would next need to confront the parents and townspeople. My apprehension as I tried to keep under control reminded me of the movie *High Noon,* starring Gary Cooper as the sheriff.

My coaches and teammates did not anticipate the situation and sat motionless on the bus, watching the uneasy drama. I thought this might be a suitable time for them to step up, but no one moved from the bus's interior. The crowd again started to make it hard to walk through them across the parking lot.

As I reached our bus, the last fan I passed stared intently at me. "You're one lucky son-of-a-bitch," he said.

I didn't reply, only looked in his direction, made eye contact, and nodded. That fan captured the scene. I was one lucky guy. With a sigh of relief, I entered the team bus. I had just gone through one of the tensest situations of my life. All over a misunderstanding.

Our coaches and players didn't realize the volatility of the confrontation. Or they knew waiting for me on the bus would make for a more favorable outcome. If they would have gotten off the bus to back me, it would have inflamed the situation. It would have been them against us.

The setting was ripe for trouble. Fortunately, we also had a few fans from Tillamook who understood the situation and the conflict that could arise in a split second. These fans stayed after the game and their presence served as a deterrent to trouble breaking out.

Intestinal Fortitude

We were a long way from adequate police protection. We were also badly outnumbered. I was glad that cooler heads had prevailed. This could have turned into an ugly confrontation if someone had thrown something or hit me. I felt fortunate to get out of Vernonia intact that frosty night, escaping a simple misunderstanding that could have escalated into an ugly affair.

On the bus ride back to Tillamook, I marveled at the passion of the Vernonia townsfolk as they revealed their indignation and defended their Negro player. I wasn't sure it was about me. I had just become a symbol. The reality that the town was all White, with blue-collar jobs, made me think that player had become a unique representation of the town's acceptance of all Negroes. They wanted to defend their tolerance of all people. I've always been curious as to what the reaction of the crowd would have been if things had been reversed and he had been White.

I brought the scary situation upon myself. I couldn't pass on the feisty guard's smart mouth. Sometimes a person doesn't think things through in an emotional moment. Certainly not as a young high schooler. I learned from it, happy to leave Vernonia unscathed.

Tillamook/Astoria Rivalry

The Tillamook High School Cheesemakers and the Astoria High School Fighting Fisherman were rivals on the basketball court and on the gridiron. Because they were adversaries for many years, struggles between them grew more intense with each passing year. The two schools had nicknames that represented the economy of both towns. Tillamook had many dairy farms, and cheese was an important export. Astoria had a fleet of fishing boats with canneries along its waterfront and was known for exportation of canned salmon and tuna.

    Each town's citizens perpetuated the competition with stories that became bigger with each accounting. The antagonists would battle with each other, trying to counteract the other's adverse behavior. It continued over generations.

    The final straw that diminished the rivalry's adverse behavior, and brought the authorities into play, took place in Astoria. One of their enthusiastic fans finally went too far with his devotion to the Fighting Fisherman. He loosened the lug nuts on the tires of the Tillamook team's bus. When the yellow school bus collapsed as the Tillamook Cheesemakers left Astoria, the rivalry might have diminished with it. But that was not the case. No one was injured when the bus came to an unexpected and surprising stop. But the real possibility of gravely harming the bus's occupants could not be overlooked.

Rivalry

In 1951, I was a sophomore on the Tillamook High School basketball team, and the rivalry was still going strong. I remember our team bus receiving a barrage of eggs and tomatoes as we entered Astoria with a police escort. The police greeted our bus in Warrenton, a suburb on the outskirts of Astoria, and accompanied us to the Astoria Armory downtown, the game location.

As we exited the bus, we walked about twenty yards to the back door of the basement dressing room in the Armory. Walking the twenty yards, we passed through a line of Astoria police officers and school administrators to reach the door. They protected us from young and wild Astoria fans who yelled insults and threats at us. It would have been impossible for our team to enter the arena if not for the police. Their intimidation tactics made me a little leery about leaving the safety of our bus. At only sixteen years old, I'd never seen an angry mob held back by police to protect me and my teammates.

The atmosphere was thrilling at the same time, with a mixed bag of emotions. The young Astoria fans reminded me of the wild hooligans who follow European soccer. Even older fans of both schools were confronted by incidents of rude behavior. Fights after the game outside the arena were commonplace, usually among recent young graduates of both schools. The name of Astoria's team, the "Fighting Fisherman," was a nickname taken to heart by some of the town's faithful.

It wasn't a promising idea to cruise around Tillamook or Astoria in your car before a game, as groups of young local fans would stop you, looking for trouble with a makeshift roadblock. The atmosphere was a little edgy and not fun for fans of either school.

These schools took sports rivalry to a whole other level, losing sight that this was high school sports. It created an environment that could easily lead to injuries if the contention continued to escalate.

The Oregon School Activity Association (OSAA) threatened to penalize both schools if the hostility continued. When Tillamook and Astoria realized the OSAA was earnest, they organized a goodwill exchange assembly at their respective schools. Each school reached out to their individual communities as well, as much of the problem rested with unruly ex-students. The goodwill exchange appeared to work. Future athletic events became incident-free even though no love was lost between the two schools when they competed against each other.

FAMILY

**Other things may change us,
but we start and end with family.**

**Anthony Brandt,
author and editor**

My mother, Dorothy. Goldendale, Washington, where she attended high school in 1929 and played basketball for the girls' team.

My father, August. Confirmation, age sixteen.

My mother, Dorothy, second from the right, playing golf with her Aunt Bertha who is swinging her driver.

IMMIGRATION AND MIGRATION

Though he was German, my grandfather, August Beno Goldmann, was born in Silesia, a part of Poland, on February 2nd, 1873. Germany, at that time, occupied the area. He served in the German Army from age seventeen until the age of twenty-one, when he left the military. My grandfather, by choice, directly boarded a ship to America, dressed in his army uniform, for an opportunity he believed was waiting for him in the United States. He arrived at Ellis Island on September 29th, 1896, and shortly thereafter homesteaded in North Dakota.

He was trained in Germany as a leatherworker. While living in North Dakota, he herded sheep, farmed, mined for gold in the Badlands, worked as a grain elevator manager, served as a justice of the peace, and was president of the Golden Valley School Board.

My grandfather played both the piano and the organ in his Lutheran church and won prizes working crossword puzzles. Since English was his third language—German and Polish being his first two—he worked hard to never lose the ability to complete the puzzles in English, which exhibited a firm grasp on his new language in America. He died in 1939, at the age of forty-six, and was buried in Golden Valley, North Dakota.

My grandmother, Carolina (Lena) Schroeder, was born January 29th, 1879, in Westphalia, Germany. She immigrated to America with her parents at the age of two. They first lived in Illinois, then homesteaded in Hebron, North Dakota. A Schroeder family member still farms the original land. She was one of ten children. Upon marrying August Goldmann in 1899, she gave birth to fourteen children, including two sets of twins. She died on October 27, 1963, at the age of eighty-four, and was buried in the Schroeder family plot in Hebron.

My father, August—the first son of August and Lena's union—was a twin and named after his father. He was born in Golden Valley, North Dakota, and left North Dakota at sixteen years old, working his way west. He washed dishes in a restaurant in Dickenson, North Dakota, where he survived the influenza epidemic that swept the United States and Europe from 1918 through 1922. The woman who cooked at the eating establishment nursed him back to health as he lay in his bedroom apartment in the attic of the restaurant.

Young, restless, and determined to keep moving west, he made his way to northern Nevada and the Buena Vista Cattle Ranch, near Elko, where he became a cowboy. The rugged individuality of the cowboy's life fit his character. He didn't waste words and was usually stoic and enjoyed the rugged outdoors. My father broke horses and, in his words, "peed blood" after riding the bucking broncs and experiencing the sudden violent contact with the horses that caused pain and injury.

My father later left the ranch for American Falls, Idaho, where he farmed with a younger brother named Carl. They applied for the land from the government as part of a homesteading concept at the time.

In 1929, at the age of twenty-eight, he beckoned my mother, Dorothy, to come to American Falls and marry. They had met a couple of years earlier in North Dakota and stayed connected. My mother suggested they meet halfway between American Falls and Goldendale, Washington, where she lived, to get reacquainted. They connected in Boise, Idaho, and later married in American Falls.

At the time my mother made this proposal, she lived with her aunt Bertha and uncle John—from 1921–1930. She attended the high school as a good student and an outstanding athlete, playing on the girls' basketball team. She also played golf with her aunt for recreation. She left high school after her junior year and married my father in American Falls in January of 1930.

My oldest brother, Charles or "Chuck," was born in American Falls in 1930. In 1931, my parents moved even farther west to Tillamook, Oregon, on the Pacific Ocean, to seek work. My father was hired on at the Archie Pye dairy farm north of town to milk cows. A year later, he moved over to the A. G. Beals dairy farm on Bayocean Road, west of Tillamook, for an increase in pay.

The dairy farm employment was a secure industry, especially during the 1930s Depression era when jobs were scarce. As the main hired help, my father was afforded a place to lodge along with dairy products for food. My brother Almon was born there on the Beals's farm in 1932 in the hut where they lived. The place still stands today. He was delivered by two of my mother's sisters, Corrine and Lillian, who had come over from Salem to help.

Two years passed, and my father went to work in the woods north of Tillamook for the Charley Stone Logging Company. Our family rented a small house on Evergreen Drive in Tillamook. In December 1934, I was born in our home, delivered by my aunt Lillian.

Decades later, on her death bed, in her eighties and extremely ill, Aunt Lil told me, "I helped you get you into this world and now it is your turn to help get me out."

She died shortly after making that statement as I stood beside her bed. I was too emotional and unable to respond. I had forty aunts and uncles—my mom came from a family of eight, and my dad a family of sixteen—but Aunt Lil was special. She had always been good to me.

Working in the woods as a logger was one of the most dangerous jobs in the United States. The felling of trees, bucking of logs, choker setting, tree topping, and log truck loading and unloading set the stage for many tragic accidents. My father often told the story of when he jumped into a hole as a big log broke loose above the hillside and rolled over him. If the hole hadn't been there or if he hadn't used his quick wits, the log would have crushed him. There was a constant chance of injury or death in the timberland in Oregon.

My father left the tall trees behind, due to the danger, to become the caretaker of the local Tillamook County Fairgrounds in

1936. We lived for two years in one large twenty-four-by-twenty-four-foot room—a concession stand. It included an outhouse but no other amenities. He thought this position would be a good fit for him since he could start a herd of milk cows on the grassy infield of the racetrack. My father planned to bring them to maturity, then use the herd as collateral to secure a bank loan to purchase land to farm.

His plan was well founded, but tragedy befell his strategy. He bought a railroad carload of alfalfa hay for the cows. The boxcar, just previously before the alfalfa load, had carried a material poisonous to cows. The newly purchased hay killed most of the new herd.

This was a sad time for him. Also, at that time, he lost the caretaker job because politics among the County Fair Board caused changes he could not control. He lost his support there but put his heartache aside in 1938 and returned to the logging industry. Though it was a challenge to care for a family during the 1930s Depression in America, my parents exhibited a powerful ability to survive. My mother's determination to keep our family together also guided our household onward. Her cheerful outlook, which she possessed throughout her lifetime, carried us forward.

While living on Evergreen Drive in the Hathaway Meade neighborhood in Tillamook, Oregon, in 1939, my father bought a 1938 Ford Country Sedan. He also purchased four acres of land across the street from their rental and built a house. We moved into our new home by 1940, just before WWII. It was quite different from the concession stand we'd lived in during the days on the Tillamook County Fairgrounds.

Just prior to the move, my father became an employee in the timber industry again, returning to work for Charley Stone. Charley was a jovial, heavy-set man who always wore a navy-blue suit. He looked like he was from a distant planet when he stood next to his workers dressed in their red flannel shirts and corked boots. He drove the biggest navy-blue Cadillac sedan money could buy. I've owned a few Cadillacs over the years and always thought it was because of Charley's influence. I always wanted to be like Charley when it came to cars because he looked impressive in his cars and suits.

In the 1950s, my father moved upward and became a lumber grader for Diamond Lumber Company in Tillamook until his retirement in 1962. He passed away at the age of sixty-six in 1971 in Salem, Oregon. The cause of death was an aortic aneurysm that burst.

My father and my mother were capable people with many life skills that would have benefitted them in any era. They were efficient and effective, and they expected to be so by their own standards. We always had a roof over our heads and food on the table.

My mother died on May 7, 1988, at eighty-five, sitting in her chair one morning while reading the Bible. She passed on in style, making it difficult for the Almighty to turn her away from the Gates of the Kingdom. My grandmother Barnes, on my mother's side, passed away in her nineties. Many others in the Barnes family—aunts, uncles and grandparents—also lived long lives, making longevity a possibility for me to have my mother's family in my life for a long time.

My mother left me with two sayings to live by. One is, "Too much of anything is not good for you." I've tried to stay away from excess because of those words, and most of the time I've succeeded. The other is, "Save a little, spend a little." I am a person who can save money. Putting away part of my earnings for safe keeping seems natural to me. These words of wisdom have stayed with me for a lifetime.

GOLDMANN WITH TWO NS

The name Goldman spelled with one N usually depicts a person of Jewish descent. My family name, spelled with two Ns, is considered a German name and not Jewish. The question to ask is: Did a family member previously add the second N to escape being considered a Jew? I haven't met a Goldman with one N who wasn't Jewish.

Because of the persecution of the Jewish people as recorded in world history, some Jewish families might have added the extra N to avoid being thought of as a Jew to avoid persecution.

My grandfather Goldmann was born in German-occupied Southern Poland in 1873, before the turn of the 20th century. Goldmann was spelled with two Ns on his birth certificate. When he immigrated to America through Ellis Island in 1896, he was dressed in his German Army uniform and spelled our family name with two Ns. Did someone in our family add the second N before 1873 or on his birth certificate before he came to the United States? During World War I (WWI), he considered going back to Germany and fighting in the German Army in that uniform.

My brothers and I were lax in signing our names with the second N, usually leaving it off. Our parents were also guilty of not adding the extra N when they signed their names on letters, certificates, and documents. On my birth certificate, Goldman is spelled with only one N, and it stands that way today, never corrected.

So, my parents weren't very diligent in maintaining the second N even though it was never changed legally.

I have been mistaken and referred to as Jewish by many people and organizations over my lifetime. At first, I was bothered by those references even as an attempt at humor; they were racist, nonetheless. Now, after having been called a Jew so many times and knowing more about Jewish history and culture, I am not offended. I've been told by Jewish people and others that someone in my past family history added the second N so others wouldn't think our family was Jewish.

Honorary Jew

I entered Wilson Elementary School in Tillamook, Oregon, in 1941. On December 7th of that year, the Japanese attacked the United States at Pearl Harbor in Oahu, Hawaii. The assault forced the United States into WWII, declaring war on Japan and the other Axis Powers, including Germany.

Reports came out of Europe about Hitler and the Nazi Party of Germany persecuting the Jewish people of Europe. From 1933 to 1939, most of their civil rights were terminated. There were incidents such as the "Night of Glass" when the Nazi Party broke out the front windows of Jewish storefronts across Germany. Also, they burned books, discontinued labor unions and library cards, and ended land inheritance. Many Jews fled to the United States and other countries to escape the oppression and brought their stories of the enormity of the onslaught faced with the Nazis.

At that time, my father decided we should make sure our last name was spelled correctly with two Ns. My brothers and I were told by our parents we should tell our teachers to spell our name the correct way, with two Ns.

My first-grade teacher, Mrs. Maxwell, who could have been a German storm trooper, listened with a good deal of indignation when I told her to change my name to Goldmann. I don't remember if she was more upset that a first grader was telling her what to do or if she really thought our family was Jewish. Either way, I had to tiptoe around Mrs. Maxwell for the rest of the year, as she ran a tight ship in her first-grade classroom. She balked at first, but when I produced a note from my father, she complied with the second N. So, from 1941 on, the name Goldmann in Tillamook schools was spelled correctly by our family—and hopefully by everyone else.

Years later—when retired and living in Scottsdale, Arizona, with my wife, Patricia—we bought a condominium in a high-rise development. After living there a brief time,, we realized we'd bought a unit in a primarily Jewish community. Many of the residents were Jews from Chicago and New York. It was only a slight surprise that two other families in our building were Jewish with the name Goldman, spelled with one N. With three families named Goldman or Goldmann in our building, we received a lot of the other Goldmans' mail by mistake.

One of the older Jewish ladies who had survived the Holocaust often reminded me I was really a Jew. She told me in her heavy accent, "You're part of the tribe."

One day, while having a conversation with the little Jewish lady—she was only four feet, eight inches tall—I told her my name was German. She told me I couldn't fool her, that someone in our family had added the second N to elude the unvarnished truth. She was a delightful soul whom I enjoyed seeing and still miss today. To her, I was a Jew. Being thought of as Jewish did work for me on occasion.

Oregon State College

During my first year at Oregon State College, I was living in such a protected environment in the fraternity house I wasn't growing. I was a student on a college campus with an athletic scholarship and a lot of people looking out for me. Life was a bit artificial, like living in a large bubble of protection.

As an example, OSC had a Dean of Men whose primary responsibility was to look after the young men on campus. He was good at his job description as he seemed to find out about any problems that arose amongst the male students. Being on scholarship, I played on the first-year basketball and baseball teams. My coaches always knew what I was doing. Astute at behavioral awareness, they knew where I might be day or night. My living on campus was controlled by the rules of the fraternity, Sigma Chi, and its upperclassmen. With so many people looking out for my welfare, it was a little unrealistic. I wanted to be on my own and look out for myself.

I moved back to Portland the next year to take a break from school. I rented an apartment on Broadway across the street from Portland State College and paid thirty dollars a month for a one-room walkup that included a community privy, or bathroom.

I applied for work at the largest department store named Meier & Frank. The store, also on Broadway, usually warranted a visit on any excursion to the city's downtown. Two old Jewish families owned the store. I interviewed with Clifford Dowd, the manager of the high-fashion shoe department. After he hired me for forty-two dollars and fifty cents a week, we shook hands.

He said, "You will go a long way in this company with a name like yours."

He was obviously referring to my often-misunderstood name. Selling expensive shoes and purses to nice ladies, as it turned out, was not going to be my life's work. They wished me Godspeed as I headed back to college after only a few months.

During the summer of 1970, I sat at the bar at the Ritz Carlton Hotel in Chicago with some other young men. They had bet me I couldn't gain entrance to the Jewish wedding reception going on across the hall just by using my name. I was in Chicago to attend a textbook conference and looking for something to do. Also, everyone at the reception appeared to be dancing and having a fun time, so I accepted the challenge.

I went to my room, put on a suit, and headed for the soiree. I knew there would be a few attendees with the name Goldman. If not, the name Goldman would have to be hard for the door attendant to turn down. I won the bet as I sat in for a drink with the maid of honor, the sister of the bride, and the mother and father of the bride, toasting their good health. I was able to "crash" the wedding by just using my name.

From the skeptical Mrs. Maxwell, my first-grade teacher, to the wrongly assuming Clifford Dowds in my life, I was well acquainted with people thinking I was Jewish. I went from not really knowing the history of the oppression heaped on the head of this population to today being more aware of the painful legacy that has followed the Jews through the ages. Knowledge of the Jewish people has been compelled on me throughout my life. Today, I comprehend more of their plight since many people believed me one of them. I have taken it upon myself to know more about their culture through books, film, and conversation.

It took Hitler's treatment of the Jews in Europe during the 1930s and 1940s to convince my father to make sure the second N was always on our name. At the beginning of WWII, no one knew for sure who would be the victor. My father decided to not take a chance on the outcome.

It wouldn't have bothered me to be Jewish, if in fact I had been born so. I wasn't offended when considered Jewish by other people. Even when a person tried to upset me by calling me a Jew, which happened when I was young—enough times to give me an indication of what racism was all about.

FAMILY

Mother

Shortly before her death, my mother requested I take her to Tillamook. She wanted one last look at the place where she had lived for thirty-some years before her move to Salem.

Our family laid down roots there in 1932, so we considered ourselves natives of this beautiful coastal county. If I took her there, she would go to the house my father built in 1940 on Evergreen Drive, east of town. She'd raised three boys in that house and seeing it might bring back a lot of memories.

Surely, she'd want to drive out to Netarts and Oceanside to see the Pacific Ocean one more time. Maybe even walk the beach for an hour in her bare feet and let the surf remind her of the many fun times the family had experienced in the place together.

Each summer, we packed food for a dinner on the beach. When we arrived, we immediately built a big fire with driftwood, some pieces drifting into Oregon from as far away as Japan. Wood always washed up on the shore. After dinner, in the darkness, with the fire as our illumination, we roasted marshmallows on a stick. It was great fun. The sparks from the fire rose into the night air, leaving us with the magical feeling of a special experience.

Oceanside became a popular retreat for our family over the years. I grew up running in the surf on its sandy shoreline. A couple of large mountainous rocks offshore function as sentinels. My mother would surely recall the time she and my brother Almon walked out to the rocks during a record low tide in 1946.

She'd enjoy driving around the city of Tillamook to see the streets and buildings familiar to her, especially a drive by the Redeemer Lutheran Church on Third Street where our family worshipped. We were close to the Lutheran church for many years. My father taught Sunday school and counted the money from the collection plate after the minister's sermon. My brothers helped on Saturday. They washed the stained-glass windows and brightened the pews and the wood floor while my mother dusted the alter and pulpit. My job: to mow the lawn.

I knew she'd want to visit the Tillamook County Fairgrounds east of town and visualize the small refreshment stand, now gone. Our family had lived there for two years from 1936 to 1938. The twenty-four-by-twenty-four-foot building had only one room, a wood stove, and chilly running water. I remember heating water on the stove, once a week, for a bath in a tin tub in the middle of the room. My mother would remember the carnival music during Fair Week, along with the shrieks of the fairgoers as they rode the wild rides on the midway, just steps from our one-room home.

She would want to visit the Beals's Dairy Farm west of town on Baycean Road, including the hired man's farmhouse where she gave birth to my brother Almon in December of 1932. I'd buy her a five-pound loaf of their famous cheddar cheese at the new Tillamook County Cheese Factory north of town. Every area in the county had their own cheese factory in the old days, when our family had first come to Tillamook County. Today, all the cheese factories have consolidated into one association.

We'd drive out to the blimp hangars south of town, a reminder of Tillamook during the World War II years. The base, built there during the war to house the impressive blimps, would provide early detection of an attack by the Japanese. People in Tillamook worried about an assault after what had happened at Pearl Harbor on the island of Oahu in Hawaii. My mother would remind me of the air raid sirens and blackout practice Tillamook held at that time in preparation for a real strike. We'd also remember hearing the blimps overhead, sounding like large lawn mowers on their way to the Pacific Ocean. We'd then loop around the Trask River and pass the Wyss farm, remembering her oldest son, Charles, and his marriage to a Wyss girl named Dorothy.

After a bite to eat at the Fern Café and saying hello to the owners, Katie and Smitty, we'd head back over the coast range to the Willamette Valley. My mother would be satisfied with her day back on the Oregon Coast and reminded of the people and places a part of her history in Tillamook. She'd be appreciative of my taking her for her last trip to the land of cheese, trees, and ocean breezes.

All of this would have been wonderful for my mother, but it never took place. I didn't take the time. I've always regretted not doing it and wished from the time of her death I had taken her back to Tillamook for one last drive down memory lane.

Father

I was raised in a German household with precise discipline dispensed by my parents. When I was a young child, it felt like rules formed the cornerstone of the family. As a hyper youth, I always bumped up against an expected form of rational behavior. We were German Lutherans with a big toe still back in the old country when it came to family.

My parents taught me to accept their authority and the basics for becoming an upstanding citizen. If I knew anything, it was right from wrong, and I patterned my life after family, country, and God.

Because of my father's emphatic discipline, I built up a considerable amount of animosity toward him. Sometimes his punishment passed beyond the limitation of modest boundaries. He did not hesitate to lay a hand on me when he deemed it necessary.

When I enrolled at Oregon State College (OSC) to play basketball, my coach was "Slats" Gill. His style of play involved a controlled, regimented game plan. He was a no-nonsense type of coach. As it turned out, I was prepared to play basketball at OSC more than I'd imagined because of my childhood upbringing. I knew how to follow orders.

Earl Llewellyn Goldmann

I looked forward to playing for "Slats" and the positive direction he coached. I felt I could accept his demands. Needing a promising avenue to follow, someone who would act in my best interest, I trusted Coach Gill. When I met him during my senior year at Tillamook High School (THS), he struck me as honest, so I went to OSC and walked on in basketball. He promised to award me with a scholarship and, in time, kept his word.

I liked "Slats" too because of his loyalty to his players. I used to say, "As long as I have a dime, Coach Gill has a nickel." He influenced me like Mr. Shepherd at Wilson Elementary School and Barney Swanson at Liberty Junior High School. These two important coaches, for many of the same reasons, set me on my way to basketball at OSC. Though I was beginning a new journey at OSC, my harsh past with my father was still visible in my rearview mirror.

As I looked across the coliseum basketball court at my parents, who had come to OSC to see me play, it reminded me of the stern discipline I'd withstood from my father when I was younger. Without thinking, I compared him to Coach Gill. An unfair parallel, but my reflection revealed the scene. I watched my mother, sitting beside my father, not saying too much, intent on the setting in front of her. She was thinking back to when she had played basketball for Goldendale High School in Washington in 1928.

As I advanced toward maturity, my relationship with my father started to feel different to me. I was expanding outward from under my father's grip on my life. I wanted to crawl out from under a dark cloud as I could make decisions without his approval. I was a little anxious to realize, along with my newly found freedom, there came responsibility for my behavior. Although not sure what the future fostered in that respect, I grew confident and felt it.

Breaking away while being young made for an unsettling period. Making personal decisions while trying to continually appease another person charts a blueprint for disaster. It would take many years for me to fully understand our relationship.

I sat on the team bench, thinking how to tell my father his discipline, though harsh, had helped prepare me for the standards of Coach Gill. I didn't understand praise because it didn't exist in my life. I had never thought of saying thanks to my father for his tutelage.

How could I express my gratitude for his punishment throughout my childhood? I wasn't going to bring it up.

My father sat in the front row of the gymnasium, immersed in the game. Coach Gill was to my left, intent on competing against the Bruins of UCLA in the arena named in his honor. The uproar of the crowd, the pretty cheerleaders, and the raucous band made the atmosphere exhilarating. I wondered if my father perceived the same emotion I was experiencing.

I hoped for a favorable connection with him until the day he died. We were never close. It seemed like we had nothing in common, such as fishing or golf. He spent that type of activity with my brother Charles. Though my father's approval was an aspiration I sought, invariably it was missing.

From an early age, I sought an answer to what my father thought of me. He never said. It was discouraging to go through life missing any responses to my activities. Was he proud I was a member of OSC basketball team? I'll never know.

As he continued to sit across from me, I contemplated his opinion. I wanted the word "proud" to ring in my ears for the rest of my life. Or he could utter the words "nice going" or "I like what you're doing." But I knew it would never transpire, just as it never happened at any other time in the past. My stomach took on a familiar empty, hollow feeling once again.

"Slats" called my name, "Goldmann," which roused me from my thoughts about my father. I returned to the confines of the coliseum and the game at hand as I bounced off the bench to enter the game. I was excited. My parents saw me play for the Beavers of OSC.

After the game, I said goodbye to my parents before they returned home to Tillamook. It was an awkward moment between my father and me. I knew he wanted to get started for home, but I kept waiting for his favorable reaction to the time he just spent in Corvallis. We, again, were like two ships quietly passing in the night, silent and uncertain. There wasn't any hugging or even a handshake, as a show of affection wasn't something we did in our family. He said nothing about whether they'd enjoyed seeing the beautiful OSC campus, the small college town of Corvallis, or the impressive Gill Coliseum, including the brief time I'd played in the game.

Earl Llewellyn Goldmann

Everyone has a story about how they were raised by their parents. Most parents try to do the best they can. I overlooked my past until ten years ago when I authored my book *Bounce Back*, contemplated my life with an eye of objectivity, and let bygones be bygones. I'd pushed them back in my mind, disappointed and hiding the truth of my father's rejection and stern correction. I moved these stories away through a life of alcohol abuse, love addiction, and depression. Writing my memoir helped me understand myself as well as my family.

My father was a strong, diligent worker, but he was also quiet and stoic. With his abuse of me, I saw a difficult person, different from the one the world saw.

I took down my father's picture from the top of my dresser last year. So it would no longer sit amongst other family photos, I placed it in a dresser drawer under my socks. "Out of sight, out of mind" was my reasoning. But that didn't last long. I returned his picture to its rightful place amongst the family pictorial collection, with an understanding that it was best for me to forgive my father and move on.

PSYCHOLOGY CLASS

In September of 1962, I married Karen Smith, whom I had met at the beach in Seaside, Oregon, and courted briefly. Afterward, I decided to return to college for the fall term at Portland State College in Portland, Oregon. I was determined to complete undergraduate school. Graduating was a big step for me after having spent many years as a college student. I believed marriage, a bachelor's degree, and getting a real job belonged together. By earning a secondary teaching certificate, I could land a position as a high school teacher and coach.

I'm not sure why, but while taking classes at PSC, I registered for a course in psychology. The class was one of the most interesting educational experiences during my many years in college. Two women working on their doctoral degrees in psychology offered the course, not part of the curriculum. However, before I enrolled in the discussion, I had to go through an interview procedure to qualify. To be accepted, students needed to have a problem the two women could help you work through. They wanted to analyze and assist in resolving a psychological issue each member of the seminar was experiencing. Also, members of the lecture actively participated in solving each other's issues.

During my interview with the two women, they asked me what problem I thought I had or what worry for which I'd like to find an answer or solution. As my first comment, I expressed an interest in working on my relationship with my father. As soon as I said, "My father," I burst into tears and became overwhelmed as years of frustration and emotion came gushing out.

I said to them, "I guess I have a problem."

There were three boys in the August Goldmann family of Tillamook, Oregon. Charles was the oldest, Almon was in the middle, and I brought up the rear. We were all two years apart, and my father clearly favored Charles.

All the physical abuse I'd experienced as a child, the absence of love and affection, the disregard for me while my father showed favor to Charles, came pouring out. Before taking this group of lessons, I had never confronted these issues or spent time working things out with anyone, let alone a psychologist.

The class turned out to be a gift. It seemed like the perfect time to have someone to help me with this lifelong stifling condition hindering me from living a healthy, mentally wholesome life.

With my new marriage, I adopted my wife's son, Tony, from her previous marriage. I needed a clear head to parent. Being the father of a six-year-old happened overnight. One day, I was childless; the next day, I had a young son. The situation took some getting used to when it happened that quickly, I learned parental skills on the fly.

The discussions helped me see, first, that I had a problem with my father. Though I knew to a point I had issues with him, I never knew the depth of my emotions until I spoke to a professional.

The prognosis of my troubles became apparent as the course came to the end of the semester. My classmates, through discourse, proposed my course of resolve. I was to confront my father to get everything on the table and out in the open. I gave this solution a hard look but, sadly, couldn't do it. He had too much control over me, and I had too much anxiety about approaching him. As a result, he continued to hold me under his power. His personality and the history of our relationship were still too strong in his favor for me to challenge his domination of so many years.

His rule over me was too dominant, and it didn't diminish when he died in 1971 at the age of sixty-six. Even then, he held a place in my mind, symbolizing my lifelong anxiety. I experienced conflicting feelings at the time of his death. I grieved for having been cheated out of a more fulfilling relationship with him. I was sorry he'd died, but not because of love for him. Love was an affection I couldn't fathom when I thought of him. I felt bad more out of respect for him and the fact that he died young.

I was supposed to be sad with his passing, but it felt more like an inkling that a piece of my life's puzzle had gone missing and I would never get it back. He had such a hold on me that it was a sense of relief when he died.

On his deathbed in the Salem Memorial Hospital in Salem, Oregon, he told me he didn't want to die. What was I supposed to do about that? It was like he was asking me to intercede for him or pray for him. He might have been trying to reach out to me finally, but I'll never know for sure. I had no idea how to react to that comment. I didn't discern what to say to him. We had never had a satisfactory relationship from which I could draw on words or a recollection of an enjoyable experience together. We hadn't shared anything of value I could remember. We weren't close and it showed. I mumbled something about him having a good life with many accomplishments, and the short conversation ended. The brief encounter represented our usual concise conversations.

A few minutes later, he was dead. He died the way he'd lived: without tears. I would have given anything to have loved him. He didn't give me the chance.

When children are abused, they sometimes emulate their abuser. It's a learned behavior used to cope with a hurtful situation. I put my father on a pedestal when I was incredibly young. That foundation crumbled under the harshness of beatings. When I turned eleven years old in the fourth grade, my mimicry was overwhelmed by anger.

Forces worked in my mind. I was angry and sought his approval. It baffled me, and the uncertainty lasted for many years, stretching into adulthood. I didn't want to make a decision that confronted my bewilderment because I feared it would be negative toward my father. It was perplexing that I was afraid of losing what relationship I had with him, my abuser. I sensed it would be better to hold on to whatever relationship we had. Fearing everything might be lost if I challenged my father, I worried about how a clash would turn out, especially since he won every disagreement I ever had with him. Honestly, coming to grips with how I really felt, and trying to act on it, was not as easy as a bystander might think.

The psychology class benefitted me in that I came to understand more fully my struggles with my father. It offered a solution which I couldn't follow. I was unable to challenge my father before he died, and I was left where I'd started, not standing up to him.

My father lurks in the shadows of my mind, waiting for an opportunity to reappear and say a word of praise or bring about memories of a lost relationship.

CHARLES

My oldest brother, Charles, always appeared to thrive at the top of his game. Though successful in so many ways, he hadn't attained two accomplishments that might have bothered him. Charles never went to college or played intercollegiate athletics like he had always dreamed. At times, he appeared jealous when I told my stories of college life and sports.

Charles could have attended college and played sports, especially football. At six foot one and 185 pounds, he made a good defensive back his senior year in high school. It was easy for him to excel in class there, too, as he was certainly intelligent enough. He was the only one in our family to consistently make the honor roll.

I watched Charles play for the Tillamook High School football team against Astoria High School, where I am sure he made every defensive tackle. He ran at the speed of a jackal and embodied the physical attributes to shine on the gridiron. My brother was quick enough to cover a pass receiver from the National Football League (NFL), like Jerry Rice of the San Francisco 49ers. He was also blessed with one other important and special characteristic—he played the game without fear of physical contact or injury.

I could have played football at Stanford. The university offered me an athletic scholarship upon my graduation from THS in 1953. Charles was a much better football player than I when coming out of high school but was offered no scholarships. He would have done well to continue with football and graduate with a degree, but he chose a different path to success. I don't know how many times he asked me about college through the years, but he brought it up enough to make me think he missed attending. I suppose he thought many times in life about not attending college and how his life could have been different if he had been on campus somewhere.

Circumstances were different for Charles when he left high school. For him, going to college was a consideration, but not as significant as when I graduated. By my era, just four years later, there was a strong positive change in attitude and interest in higher education. The GI Bill of 1944 had an influence immediately after the war and was making an even greater impact on education in the early 1950s. Just a few years later, an increased number of high school students wanted a college education.

Some of my teachers included those who had returned from WWII and taken advantage of this benefit, part of the Serviceman's Readjustment Act. The bill gave every veteran a free college education. I was taught by instructors who appreciated their college degrees. Many felt an urgency to make up for lost time during the war years and to start a professional career. By the act's last year in 1956, almost eight million veterans had used it.

My teachers Larry McKeel, Herb Johnsrud, and Barney Swanson preached of the importance of earning a college diploma. They knew if we earned a degree, we could be successful. They encouraged me and my classmates to pursue higher education.

"Go to college even if you don't know what you want to do in life. You'll figure it out when you get there," they said.

These men encouraged me to earn a teaching degree and helped me to attain athletic scholarships to Willamette University, Stanford University, and Oregon State College. These were for all three sports I played in high school: football, baseball, and basketball. My coaches encouraged me to teach school for four or five years because they believed teaching would prepare me for other lines of work, especially sales. Not surprisingly, I taught school for four and a half years and then moved into textbook sales.

Charles was coached and taught by many teachers who had stayed home during the war. The veteran teachers who taught me felt a self-confidence and a sort of "cockiness" from winning the war. The reception they received when they returned was like no other, and they relished in it. Charles's teachers were of a different mindset than those who educated me.

They'd fought for a country that emerged from WWII as the strongest nation in the world and felt good about themselves and their country. Following the war years, the 1950s were a unique economic period in our history, particularly for the middle class.

New career fields were opening with the development of inventions used in the war effort, such as plastics and jet propulsion. It seemed, when I was leaving high school, an engineering degree was every schoolboy's dream. Charles graduated just ahead of this craze. He attended a trade school in Portland and took a course in refrigeration. He later returned to Tillamook and accepted a position with Roby's Furniture as a repairman. Charles graduated high school at the youthful age of seventeen since he did not attend kindergarten. This might have held him back initially career-wise, but he was young and smart while working at Roby's. I saw his confidence soar as the store made him a salesman, and he grew mentally and physically.

After working for Roby's for a year, he took off in another direction, which became his life's work. He was employed in a new position as a collection representative for a small credit bureau in Salem, Oregon. As the business grew, he grew with it. He later became the president of the company. Their head office was in San Francisco, California. Eventually, he went on to purchase his own credit bureau in nearby Fairfield, California. He owned it for many years before selling to his daughter Kathy, who has since sold it to her daughter Kelly.

Charles was not encouraged by our parents to attend a four-year institution of higher education. I thought it unfortunate because he was a confident and smart guy in school. They were stuck in the rationale of the 1930s, Depression Era thinking. If you attained a skill and were employable, hang on to your job. I graduated from high school four years behind Charles with a not-quite-so-impressive grade point average but was encouraged by coaches and mentors to attend college despite this thinking.

Earl Llewellyn Goldmann

Today, my father and mother would be considered public school dropouts. My father stopped attending school in the eighth grade. My mother left high school in the eleventh grade to marry my father in 1930. At that time, most states only required a child to complete the eighth grade. Times were exceedingly difficult in the 1920s and early 1930s due to the pandemic in the beginning of the decade and ending with the financial collapse in America. Attending only that far was an accepted practice, especially in an agricultural state, which most were at the time. Manual labor was highly regarded.

I remember the day the topic of college produced comments from my mother.

"Why don't you stay in Tillamook and work in the lumber mill?" she asked me as I opened a letter from the Oregon State College Athletic Department awarding me a scholarship.

OSC wanted me to come to Corvallis, Oregon, and play baseball and basketball. I loved my mother, but I had been striving toward college sports for five years, and now I had an opportunity many would relish. I had to pursue my athletic ability.

My answer to her was an unequivocal "no."

Since I was the youngest, she was a little intimidated by such a large school and my leaving home for the first time. Fortunately, my mother became a solid supporter once I'd officially enrolled. I didn't realize at the time the importance of that acceptance letter to my future. It enabled me to leave home and begin a life for myself. College opened a path to more education and a professional life. I primarily attended by my own choice and self-determination. That's the way it was supposed to work out.

"I am going to Oregon State," I told my father with some excitement in my voice.

He listened to me and appeared happy by his attentiveness, but he did not respond and never let on what a crucial step I was taking. Times like this in my life helped me surmise my father suffered from mental depression, represented in his lack of emotion, moodiness, and fear of change for us. I was undertaking a milestone in my life, yet he couldn't get excited for me. Like my mother, though, once I was in school, he became an unyielding champion of my experience.

My father and I didn't interact much in all the time I knew him, especially after the childhood abuse years he'd put me through. Being beaten by your father repeatedly at an early age wasn't a safe way to start a casual conversation or build a close relationship later in life. I lived my childhood epoch on the edge of fear.

He assisted me with money at various times for emergencies at school, though he didn't consider them handouts. He kept a ledger of every dollar loaned to me. I didn't want to owe him the money and paid him back every nickel after I graduated, just as we'd agreed to at the time of the money transfer.

He came once to watch me play basketball that one time at Gill Coliseum on the OSU campus. I was one of the younger players on the team—and a good one at that. Even though he didn't say much about me being on the team, I took it as a gesture of earning his approval. His silence left a hole in my heart though. I felt empty inside and tried not to show my disappointment when I wanted to slump my shoulders and tighten my lips. Instead, I swallowed hard and held back my tears.

My father once told me to learn how to use a shovel. "You will never be out of work if you can use a shovel." His idea of security was manual labor skills. He could not relate to anything learned in the classroom or in sports with his level of education. He always thought he still lived in the 1930s and continued to remember the tough times of the Depression Era even though the country was leaping to the opportunities of the 1950s.

When I received my bachelor's degree from Portland State College—now a university—Charles asked me, "How did you do that?"

He was curious how I'd continued with school for so many years to obtain a diploma, even with time lost due to a horrendous car accident and inadequate funds.

I playfully punched him on the shoulder and told him, "I knew for many years I would complete my higher education. Graduation was always my objective."

His question didn't surprise me. Marrying his high school sweetheart so soon after graduation and having the responsibility of children early in life made his opportunities far different from mine. He wanted to go to college. Marriage closed a few doors, including earning a degree, and made others more difficult to open in the business world. Nonetheless, he persevered. All the time I was in school, I never saw myself in his position. From various conversations, I surmised Charles's decision to marry so young was something he reflected on later in life.

I never thought of Charles as a genuinely happy man. My father's demeanor had a strong impact on determining his life, even more than mine, because they were so close and spent so much time together.

Our father often appeared to suffer from mental depression, a condition many alcoholics experience. From my own drinking, it is easy for me to recognize the clues. When I was five years old, my father stopped drinking and didn't take another drink the rest of his life. The beatings ended for me, but he became moodier and more unpredictable in his behavior. He knew by then, with his probable depression, it was risky for him because it could lead to violence.

Charles's controlling treatment of his wife and children, his intolerance and impatience with other people, and his stern manner were all indicative of our father. The influence of the Lutheran church in our growing up years, with its dampening doctrine of "you're full of sin," matched his personality.

The Lutheran church was a detriment to a happy life for me with all its rules and regimen, so no wonder I saw him as anxious. Constantly filled with the Lutheran's "original sin," who wouldn't be?

For the two years before Charles died, he came to Arizona in the winter to attend spring training baseball games with my wife and me and play golf with friends. Throughout my life, I found it difficult to be comfortable around him. It never really happened, and he never thought of us on equal footing. Our time together always felt awkward. It put me on edge as we golfed, ate dinner, or watched spring training baseball games. He must have felt the same uneasiness toward me since we hardly knew each other. It always seemed like he wanted to tell me something but couldn't express himself.

His cautionary demeanor between us always marred any bona fide relaxed occasion. You could sense it in the air. Charles represented my father to me. I thought of them as alike in so many ways, with their serious demeanor. They also resembled each other in their taller heights. My resentment from childhood about how my father and he stood apart from me—exemplified by their attitude of greater importance—never changed as we all grew older.

Charles and my father fished together and spent hours on a riverbank talking about many topics. They communicated differently to each other around the dinner table, around the barn, or in the car than they did with me. They sounded unlike me all their lives.

As their elusiveness with one another grew, I further realized my difference from them. Charles wanted to be like my father and wanted him to be his best friend. They were a matching pair. I don't imagine my brother could escape acting as our father's noble son even if he had wanted to change.

Charles came to Arizona to see me and say goodbye shortly before he died. We knew he was terminal at that time but did not discuss it directly. His apparent tentativeness showed he had something on his mind, but he returned to California without expressing his feelings.

He was hesitant toward me when he said, "Well, I guess this is goodbye." We knew it was surely the last time as we stood in a business district outside of Phoenix after lunch with a lot of people milling around.

We didn't embrace with a hug. We said a formal goodbye and shook hands. It was a small gesture from each of us, a singular handshake at the end of a couple of hours spent together. We both knew we wouldn't see each other again but could not express ourselves anymore. There was no "see you later."

Charles slowly walked away, frailer than I had ever seen him in my life. He was with the woman he traveled with at the time, which might have altered any exchange of feelings between us. My wife gave him a slight embrace, but I extended nothing further since he did not seem receptive to the idea. After moving a short distance down the sidewalk, he stopped without looking back. He clearly was mulling something over in his mind but continued walking around a corner. Once out of sight, he was gone forever.

It was the last time I saw him. His final trip to Arizona didn't work out the way I'd anticipated it would or the way he'd planned it in his mind. He appeared so hollow to me. I regret he came for a simple hug of affection and a final goodbye that wasn't meant to be. Our last encounter was indicative of our past associations of keeping each other at arm's length and with little-to-no emotion. Neither of us showed any feelings.

After he left Arizona, I wrote him a letter regarding my feelings toward him, knowing he would die soon. I strove to make him feel good in his final days.

Today, I wondered if I was truthful when I wrote, "You were a mentor and someone I looked up to growing up."

I felt better but, on the other hand, I questioned if I was a hypocrite. That sentiment in the letter was a fallacy. He wasn't a mentor of mine or someone I was in awe of, though I admired his accomplishments in the business world. As a young boy, I looked up to him as a younger brother might, since he was a good athlete and had done well in school. All that ended with my father cementing his relationship with Charles on the bank of some river in Tillamook County and leaving me behind.

I looked back on my relationship with my older brother and, in retrospect, wished he and I would have been closer. The breakdown in our relationship started when I was young and impressionable, and it continued into our senior years. It was never resolved. I wish I had known him better. We are both to blame.

ALMON

Our father was a hired hand at the A. G. Beals farm in 1932. The farm was located west of Tillamook, Oregon, on the road to Bayocean. As a family, we lived in the hired man's house, where my brother Almon was born. The 1930s Depression Era was beginning to heat up.

    This period in the United States lasted a decade and ended with the start of WWII in 1941. America was forced into the war when Japan attacked our Navy base in Hawaii on a beautiful Sunday, December 7th.

    Born in the 1930s, Almon and I were "Depression Era babies." I came along two years after my brother in December 1934, in the same Hathaway neighborhood east of Tillamook. Since we were so close in age, we grew up sharing many activities. We spent a lot of time together as young children and continued our relationship into high school.

    When we were young boys, swimming at the YMCA and in the rivers around Tillamook was a delight. The blackberries and blueberries we picked, our mother made into jams and jellies. We collected the foxglove plant as our first way to earn our own money. It was used to make digitalis, a necessary ingredient in some heart medicines. We peeled bark off the Chittum trees to sell for use in the medical field as well. Almon and I spent hours in the fields and forests around Tillamook collecting these two plants to sell to a medical dispensary for needed cash.

It was a typical childhood for two brothers growing up together in rural America during the 1940s and 1950s. Even though our father favored our older brother, Charles, we stuck together. My father and Charles excluded Almon and me most of the time, shamelessly leaving us behind, notably when they went fishing. Discouraged, we realized a meaningful relationship with our father or Charles would never happen. We were simply not a part of their lives and chose to rise above it with a good attitude, looking at the glass as half full, not half empty.

While in school together, Almon and I attended movies on Saturday with our friends and participated in school dances after ballgames. We looked for girls from Portland vacationing during the summer down at the beaches on the Pacific Coast. They were at dances in towns such as Seaside, Rockaway, and Ocean Lake.

Almon stood five feet, ten inches tall with a stocky build and wavy black hair. He was friendly to everyone. I should say "almost" because he could spot a phony a mile away. My brother was dark complected and didn't look like me. I was light skinned and blond. We were the same height, but he was heavier than me. Almon was relaxed and I was usually hyper, which made us look like complete opposites to most people.

Both of us sang in the school choir, but Almon had the superior singing voice and was often picked to perform the melody in our musical renditions. He crooned in talent contests held during the Saturday matinee at the Coliseum movie theatre in downtown Tillamook. The competitions included all types of talent, such as singing and dancing. I doubt Almon ever lost the first prize for singing to anyone during those contests. Other girls and boys competed on stage between the playing of the newsreel and the Popeye cartoon, but to no avail.

When he stepped up on stage, although smartly dressed, I felt uneasy, hoping he would remember all his lyrics. Most of the other kids in the theatre knew we were brothers. So many of them glanced at me and then back to him. He usually shouted out well-known tunes from our era. I shouldn't have worried. He always did an admirable job by belting out the songs to win the prize every time. He made me proud.

Almon was always outgoing, friendly, and knew most everyone at Tillamook High School. When a new student enrolled at THS in the middle of the year, they told me later how grateful they were that Almon immediately reached out to welcome them before anyone else at school did. School was our social focus, and my brother was in the middle of it all the time with his unassuming and unabashed friendliness.

When the latest fad in clothing started in Tillamook, or anywhere in the United States, Almon wore it first in Tillamook. From Stradivari shirts and argyle socks to Arminshaw's saddle shoes, he had to wear them before the rest of us. My brother was also the first one in Tillamook to have a pair of blue suede shoes. When Elvis came out with the song "Blue Suede Shoes," Almon went to Portland, a two-hour drive from the coast, and bought himself a pair. I went to Portland to buy a pair, too, but he returned home before me to be sure to be number one. He always held an odd job to earn enough money to be first.

In the 1940s and 1950s, many of the fads centered around military surplus left over from WWII. Navy peacoats, Army field coats, and Air Force leather bomber jackets were the rage. Almon wore an authentic brown leather jacket throughout high school, to the chagrin of his friends. He was a first-class dresser showing us the latest craze, often ahead of his classmates.

Almon played football at THS. As a three-year starter, he was determined to play right guard and make All League his senior year. When my brother was a junior in high school, he was also a cheerleader at basketball games. The school hadn't had a male perform this role that anyone could remember. He used his letterman's sweater as his uniform and took the floor at timeouts to lead the students in cheers.

He devised his own set of unique hails and shouts. His most notable was one where he got down on all fours and pounded on the gym floor with his fists to set the tone. The students were stunned as he thumped the hardwood. At first, they appeared a little embarrassed for him, as if they might be irritated. I also felt self-conscious as I watched my brother expose his passion to the crowd. But Almon was undeterred, into the cheer, and didn't for a minute feel any humiliation.

The students were soon overtaken by his commitment and joined in to support him enthusiastically. This beating on the floor became his trademark, with the students expecting his performance at each game. He loved to keep the crowd in abeyance as the game progressed, knowing everyone wanted him to do the cheer. His sense of fun helped him keep them in suspense by performing it only once a game. This was pure joy for him, even if it was a bit bold.

The gym rocked like a volcano when he finally gave the fans what they wanted, this pulsating cheer. He was a big hit during basketball season and a little famous. I became proud of my brother and eventually a bit envious of his notoriety.

Frank Kenyon, Jack Streeter, and Kenny Hahn, three of his friends from the football team, joined him the next year after seeing how much fun he was having leading the fans. Of course, he was able to meet the girl cheerleaders from the visiting teams. He was a unique figure, and the females found him interesting and exciting. My brother wasn't any dummy!

Almon had a job during high school working for a wealthy lady in town doing yardwork. When he found a new and better paying job, he convinced me to take his place as her gardener at her lovely home overlooking Netart's Bay. He said it was an effortless way to earn some money, with little difficulty. Well, I don't know what he considered easygoing. It was hard labor for me. Mrs. Coats gave the orders and I hopped to it.

I pulled out stickery blackberry bush vines by hand, with gloves, then took her garbage to the dump. Her garden needed to be spaded. I did that, too, and raked a lot of leaves, mowed the large lawn weekly, and pulled weeds constantly. All the time, Mrs. Coats gave orders from her porch as my back was about ready to break.

The job was no day at the beach! Almon was always stronger than me, and this proved it. I attempted to discuss the "effortless" job he set me up with that summer when I arrived home after the first day.

"I have blisters on my hands, and my back aches," I told my brother.

Intestinal Fortitude

He chuckled a little about it, but that was the end of the conversation. Needing the summer job, I couldn't quit. My mother wouldn't let me quit anyway as she expected us to pay for school and sports supplies.

One beautiful sunny day, Almon sat at the wheel to take us to high school football practice at Liberty Field. We approached Tillamook from the east on a cool fall morning. The road was a little elevated just before crossing the Southern Pacific railroad tracks. I easily saw three blocks ahead as Almon drove the car into town. My brother was driving a "loaner" car from the local Dodge dealer since our family's car was at their shop for repairs.

Several blocks away, I noticed a car parked in our lane as we drove toward Tillamook on Third Street. Almon on the other hand, with his poor eyesight, didn't see the car until we were too close for him to stop. Although surprised—or more probably dumbfounded—I didn't yell for him to stop. He crashed us into the parked car's rear end, minimally damaging both cars at the speed he was traveling. The city's speed limit in that area was thirty miles per hour, but with Almon's diminished eyesight, he might not have seen the sign. That proved for sure how weak his eyes were. He had just hit a standing car in plain sight, one I'd anticipated from three blocks away.

My brother was in a lot of trouble as we approached the driver of the parked car. He was a middle-aged gentleman, not looking at us, but inspecting the damage of his car. The damage to the loaner car was amazingly small, with most of the damage done to this man's parked car. We knew something would need to be done about the damage to the other car when two police officers showed up.

Almon and I both felt depressed about what had just happened as my brother showed the officer his driver's license, which he hadn't even had for a year.

My brother was often a lucky guy, and this time was no different. His good fortune soared back into sight as the police officer also checked the driver's license of the other driver. It was a moment in life when the unexplainable happened. To our utter surprise, the police officer handcuffed the other driver and put him in the back seat of the patrol car. We were stunned and shared glances with raised eyebrows.

"I don't know what's going on," I said as the tow truck driver arrived on the scene to tow the man's car.

"Me neither. They aren't asking me too many questions," Almon remarked as they took the car away.

The police officer came over to us on the sidewalk. We looked at each other, hoping we weren't in big trouble.

"You hit a stolen vehicle and there is a warrant out for the driver," he said. "We are taking him to jail, and he will be prosecuted. We have been looking for him for a while."

In our shock, we realized we had just assisted the police department with an arrest.

Almon's stroke of luck was in full force now as the officer said, "Go on your way to football practice. No ticket will be issued for the rear-ending mishap. Thank you for helping bring a fugitive to justice."

Talk all you want about good fortune but, that day, my brother had it in abundance.

Both of us spent a huge amount of time together until Almon left for college at Portland State. He played a year of football for the Vikings before enlisting in the Army. Even poor vision did not keep Uncle Sam from allowing Almon to perform his civic duty of serving in the Korean War in South Korea. When he enrolled in PSC, he was the first one from our family to enter college.

After his Army stint ended and he returned home, Almon sold tires for Montgomery Ward, bringing his outgoing personality to the sales floor. He was remarkably successful and made sales bonuses many months. One day, I needed a single tire and went to see him at the Beaverton store where he worked. Almon was not only genial and affable, but he was also downright persuasive. Before I left the store, he had convinced me I needed a complete set of four new tires, insurance on the tires, a membership in the Montgomery Ward Auto Club, and an alignment on the front end of the car. He went on to explain what a good deal I made that day. As I left the store, he enthusiastically waved goodbye. I should have been a little suspicious of him since he'd passed on the gardening job at Mrs. Coats' house and sold me the idea to work for her.

Quite a few years later, after I divorced and moved to Scottsdale full time, Almon came down and stayed with me in the winter for a few weeks. He usually vacationed in March during baseball's spring training season to see some games and play golf. We had a wonderful time going out to dinner with our friends Don Dental, Lance Oliver, and Howie Fritcher, who were there from Tillamook for part of the winter. Those were fun times with Almon. I miss him and wish I could share them once again. Sadly, we weren't as close later in life as we had been, due to marriage and kids and relocating. He died of cancer at the age of seventy-eight.

I eulogized him at his memorial, reflecting on what a unique and important person he was to me and others. Everyone especially liked his down-to-earth manner when looking at life around him.

A favorite story I shared happened on a particular Sunday when I visited Almon at his house. This was after we were both married and had children. We stood out behind his house with his two young sons. They were one and two years old and eating the food from the cat's dish.

"Reid and Paul are eating the cat's food!" I yelled.

"Hell, it doesn't kill the cats."

His comment said a lot about his patience and tolerance of others and with life. He didn't sweat the small stuff and took most things as they came. I learned a lesson from him that morning about prioritizing my life, making each day matter, and living one day at a time.

By remembering him fondly when he died, and feeling quite emotional at the memorial, I was not able to finish the poem I'd planned to read. My wife helped me with the end verses.

CREEL

From as early as elementary school, my brother Almon and I considered ourselves separate from our brother Charles. We were both treated differently by our father. The males in our family weren't a close-knit team; all for one and one for all or a clan. Not even close.

Our father and Charles were a pair unto themselves, even though they were thirty years different in age. Almon and I were a duo as well. We felt like stepchildren in our father's eyes.

My father talked to Charles with a different tone in his voice than when he talked to Almon and me, more sincere and understanding. It was like when you talk to someone with respect. He also was impatient when he dealt with the two of us, hardly taking time to answer our questions. He taught Charles various skills willingly, enjoying himself in the endeavor. Although my father wasn't verbal about his feelings, his behavior spoke volumes to me.

I lived with a little hole in the bottom of my heart that didn't diminish with time. It felt like something wasn't complete when I thought of my father. Almon had some of the same sensitivities. We discussed it a little, but words weren't necessary to us. We had a glance of awareness between us or the drop of a shoulder as a sign of defeat and the language of loss between us. These became our way of communicating without so many words.

It might have been some type of European tradition to favor the firstborn or the first son. If that were the case, at least it would give some explanation to my father's favorable treatment of Charles. As mentioned, they cemented their relationship through fishing. It seemed every weekend they were going off to a river to fish. If they weren't fishing, they talked about fishing or working on their rod, reel, or the special gaff hook.

Almon and I were considered, by my father, too young to fish with them, yet we were all only two years apart. We were shown ambivalence each time they left for their favorite fishing hole, and we were not invited. We understood the message quickly. We weren't going with them.

Today, seventy-five years later, I have a picture in my mind of them together by the creek. I am not sure how Almon felt later about it, but I developed a distaste for the pastime. Fishing took my father and my older brother away from me when I was young.

When I was a kid, I did not emulate my father and my older brother. For the longest time, I held out hope I would look up to them. It was an incomplete process stopped short by their segregated treatment of me and Almon.

I surveyed my life around our home and concluded it was divided. On one side was my father and Charles, and on the other side my mother, Almon, and me. Because of this division, I was not as influenced by them as I might have been. Their guidance was flawed and deficient. They didn't encourage me to play sports or to go to college. My coaches did that for me. It might have been, on the other hand, a blessing since I often saw how Charles struggled during his life to control his temper and his tongue.

Almon and I were forced to find our own ways because of my father's attitude and behavior toward us. Our lives were devoid of what we expected and needed from a father: attention, advice, and guidance. We were seeking companionship and inclusion in tasks around our small farm. The nurturing we sought went to our brother Charles.

My father and Charles fished together until my father died in 1971, when Charles was forty-one years old. They were known on the banks of the Wilson and Trask Rivers in Tillamook County, Oregon, as two of the prime fishermen to lash those waters.

Almon and I found other outlets, mostly at our school. We played sports and took part in many activities offered there. Almon did his lone male cheerleader stint during basketball season until others realized how much fun he was having and joined him. I played on the basketball team, but we all played on the football team together.

We also found other mentors, our coaches, to replace our father and Charles. It's a sad commentary on my family, but we were encouraged to do so by their treatment of us. We were lucky to have some excellent coaches and teachers as positive examples to follow during our years at Tillamook High School in the early 1950s.

Our coaches—Barney Swanson, Herb Johnsrud, and Larry McKeel—were great mentors They had made it through WWII in the Pacific and were stand-up people. Thank God we liked sports and school and weren't into vandalism and crime.

When I was thirty-five years old, I lived in Oregon City, on Madison Street, a location I would eventually occupy for forty years. In my basement, hidden under some dusty boxes, I discovered my father's fifty-year-old fishing creel. He had used it fly fishing for trout in Tillamook County. He had since died, yet I'd somehow ended up with the wicker fishing basket. I don't remember how, but there it sat on my workbench, looking mythical. A lot of fishing stories swirled like an eddy around that forgotten symbol of my father's enjoyment. Even though it was old, it looked good, like a trophy to a life of fishing.

I held on to the wicker fishing basket for a year before asking myself what I was doing with it. The longer the creel sat on my workbench in my basement, the more it became a symbol of my frustration during my youth. Why was I keeping this miserable reminder of the many days my father and brother went fishing without me? It represented their fun and comradeship since they'd fished together so often. If our family had created a coat of arms, it would have featured a fish and a creel on it.

I thought, since Charles had fished with my father so often, he would be honored to have the creel. He could display it as a tribute to our father by putting it in a prominent place in his home where his friends could see it and ask its significance. He could then tell grand stories about how he had fished the rivers of Tillamook County, with his father by his side.

Intestinal Fortitude

I gave Charles a call in Fairfield, California, where he lived, to offer the creel to him. I anticipated he would be pleased to become the owner. When I asked him if he wanted it, he just said, "No." Just, "No." At first, the sound of his voice confused me. All those years I'd watched my father and Charles march off together to their favorite fishing hole, and all I heard was an emphatic, "No." He understood, but I considered asking him again. I passed on the idea, due to the crescendo in his voice—the emphatic "no" still ringing in my ears. It was so resounding, it stunned me. I had expected a different response.

He knew I was offering him the old wicker fishing basket and wasn't under any misunderstanding. As often happened, we traded a few more strained words about the weather, and we hung up.

Boy, I thought, was I mistaken about trying to do the right thing and give the creel to Charles.

He didn't want it or appreciate my efforts, and that was the end of it. He encouraged no conversation as to why he felt that way and, because of his usual cold attitude, I did not ask for an answer.

I was always curious as to why he didn't want the basket whenever we saw each other, however briefly, during our adult life. I assumed he would welcome the memento from his past, to remind him of the many good times he shared with our father, but I was sorely wrong. He never mentioned the creel or fishing to me again.

All those years my brother and my father had fished together didn't seem like a special time in his life anymore, given his reaction to my offer. All those years, I thought they were establishing a great relationship between them. It might not have happened. My rapport with Charles after that time remained hesitant. Beneath the cordial handshake he offered when we met, often in passing, was the doubt that I would ever know the real story. He was more interested in telling me about his latest accomplishment than showing an interest in my life.

Those infrequent times made me question the hours I put in being disappointed we weren't closer as brothers. It was a blessing for me when I realized they didn't have any more fun than it appeared from the wicker basket phone call. For much of my youth, I'd yearned to go along on a fishing outing with the two of them but, as the years progressed, I questioned Charles and my father's actual relationship with each other. I no longer envied what it was they shared.

The creel took on a new hint of implication. What had their time together really been like? It was as if the fishing basket represented something distasteful when Charles unequivocally said, "No," to me. A dark secret might have been uncovered in the basket and he wanted no part of it anymore.

That short phone call was an experience difficult to forget. I tried to do something nice for him and he turned me down, acting as if I was asking for his inheritance. Makes me think there might be quite a bit more to the story, but I won't speculate. It's more than I want to know about the two of them.

I eventually finished cleaning my basement and had a large garage sale. I sold the creel that day with more questions than answers.

BURNED BALLS

When the weather warmed up in the summer, Charles and Almon and I enjoyed swimming in the Wilson River. George and Betty Widmer's family farm, near Riverdale Elementary School, was our favorite spot.

We walked out north of Tillamook on the Southern Pacific railroad tracks to get to the river. This route connected Tillamook to the Willamette Valley. We had competitions between us to see who ventured the farthest on the narrow footpath of the train's tracks before losing our balance and falling off.

This location in the river where we swam was part of the tide water. When the Wilson was at high tide, the water practically ceased to flow. It ran slowly on its way to Tillamook Bay and then the Pacific Ocean a few miles away.

Eddies helped build the sandy beaches along the river's edge. They formed near the bank like an alluvial fan, then protruded into the waterway's bottom. The sand was pure as silk and gentle on the feet. This made for remarkable swimming holes with almost stationary water when the tide was at full crest. The sandy beach gradually went downhill as we walked farther into the river. Spots like this were unique to the area and developed by the flow of the water.

One warm summer day, while at the river's edge, we lay in the sun catching a few rays on the pristine beach. Charles mentioned the topic of nude bathing. While discussing nudist colonies, a dare emerged. Amongst me and my brothers, daredevil activity was a common event and all of us loved it.

"I bet you're afraid to take off your suit and swim in the nude," Almon dared me.

"If I do it, I won't wash dishes at home for a week," I retorted.

They agreed to the grand prize.

This sounded darn good since I loved competition. I accepted my brother's challenge, quickly removed my swimsuit, and jumped into the cool water. After ten minutes, I came out of the river and stretched out on my back in the sun without getting dressed. My brothers laughed at me and jumped into the coolness for a swim.

"You're a nudist," Almon yelled. Their heckling didn't bother me in the least. I ignored him and enjoyed having won a week's reprieve from doing the dishes.

I laid back down on the sand for more sun and a little nap. Suddenly, just as I was about to doze off, a woman's voice called out from the road across the river.

"How is the swimming down there for you boys?"

What happened next was all reflexes. I plunged into the river in record time and was underwater in the blink of an eye. When I hit the wetness, I figured I was safe from the lady's view. But to my sheer amazement, when I landed in that chilly water, incredible pain shot through me. As I bounced in and out of the water a couple of times, the sting shot through me, hitting my groin more sharply and more excruciatingly each time. I'd never thought my balls could sunburn so quickly.

I jumped back out of the water, but then I remembered the lady watching us and jumped back in again. Even though I wanted out of the river because of the insufferable pain in my private parts, I didn't want her to see me holding them. This predicament put me between two dilemmas: hide my naked self or get my burned balls out of the water. My brothers, who were swimming in the water, were no help. For a while, I hopped around, not knowing what to do about the pain or the embarrassment of being naked in front of the lady. She still stood above the river, watching my antics.

I'm sure it was a comical sight for her, as well as for my brothers. Finally, I sprinted out of the water and put on my swimming trunks as hastily as possible. Almon and Charles were laughing hysterically at my dancing but offered no empathy. With my pain not subsiding, we decided it was time to go anyway. The lady left too as we headed home. To their amusement, I made a slow and careful walk back to town, waddling along the railroad tracks.

    I told myself this would be the last time there would be a stunt like this for me. It was a hard lesson learned. However, the thought of not having to do dishes at home for a week made the agony a little easier to take… but not too much.

KAREN AND TONY

Monthly payments and getting married were two typical responsibilities I stayed away from during most of my twenties. I knew better than to buy something over time. Paying on credit meant I needed permanent employment which, in turn, tied me down. Those concepts also limited my social prospects and forced me to be responsible. I wasn't interested. As a result, I didn't own a car that cost me more than one payment, paid in cash.

Staying away from marriage made sure I didn't intend to foul up my happy-go-lucky college lifestyle. Ironically, I didn't look like much of a catch anyway to most young women wanting to marry. Those available weren't exactly breaking down my door while wearing wedding dresses. None of them seemed to want to marry a guy who owned a beater of a car and lived in the Tillamook Fire Hall like an indigent for little-to-no rent.

By a twist of fate, I married Karen Smith when I was almost twenty-eight years old, only six months after I'd met her. I was with a couple of my friends at the beach in Seaside, Oregon, during spring break 1962, and I noticed her blonde hair in the sun. I gathered the courage to talk to her. I was impressed she was bright and responsible, attributes I needed to brush up on.

The better I got to know her, the more I realized she was not just a pretty face. She was bright, had a good personality, and could type. I requested her help with my papers when I returned to school.

Her honorable characteristics, especially responsibility, qualified her for more than I initially recognized. She was either a gambler or a saint for accepting my proposal for marriage when we'd known each other such a brief time.

What I had to offer her when we met was a college transcript full of hours of study and potential. The transcript was genuine, but the potential was questionable, especially by some of my old running mates who knew me well. Karen leaned more toward the potential side of our arrangement.

Nothing was said during our "engagement" about who was going to cook, where we were going to live, or how we were going to pay the bills. We must have been busy with other things, like getting to know each other, as our dating life was short. She lived in the Portland area, while I lived two hours away on the coast in Tillamook. Eventually the basics of life were resolved, and I moved to her hometown so the marriage could become a long-term event.

We were off to a good start since Karen had a credible job at a law firm in downtown Portland and a reliable car, paid for in full. She had an upstairs apartment for twenty-five dollars a month in rent, located above her father's medical clinic in Oregon City. We didn't need medical insurance. For any health needs, we walked downstairs.

The low cost of rent during those early years enabled us to use the extra money for tuition as I returned to school once again, this time to Portland State College, in downtown Portland.

Early on, Karen posed the interesting question to me. "What do you plan to do in life?"

You might think this question would have come up sooner, say during courtship, but it did not. We took things as they came.

By now, you can imagine how my social standing skyrocketed after marrying the doctor's daughter, making college graduation plans, and hanging out at the golf course on occasion with her father, Dr. Smith. I went from the outhouse to the penthouse as far as my old group of companions saw it. I'll admit, I didn't bring too much to the table, apart from a good set of golf sticks. Karen took a major leap of faith believing I possessed some bona fide potential. Her generosity did not go unnoticed by me.

Karen had a six-year-old son, Tony, from a previous high school marriage. When I married her, he was part of the package. His father was out of the picture with their divorce. Karen and I didn't discuss Tony too much, either. We talked extraordinarily little about my parenting skills or whether I would someday adopt him. The three of us were a group, acceptable to those who knew us.

When we married, Tony was in morning preschool, then at a babysitter in the afternoon. I immediately enrolled in Portland State College's night classes, and Karen worked all day for a successful lawyer, Morton Zalutsky. Our family of three didn't spend a lot of time together during the week. This was a good thing as we adjusted to our roles in our instantaneous family, still avoiding the topics we needed to discuss.

Karen had to adapt to living with me and me with her. In addition, I had to work through being an instant father to Tony. This whole scenario was new to me and happened overnight. One day, I'm single, and the next, I'm a husband and a father to a six-year-old who had a gerbil for a pet. Responsibility came in a hurry with a loud bang.

Tony suddenly had to share his mother with another person—and a stranger on top of that. Karen had to balance her love and attention between the two of us. Tony didn't know where he stood, feeling left out in the cold. He often acted out with tantrums. To someone on the outside looking in, our life appeared easy. But the first year we were together each of us was affected differently by these circumstances.

I found it difficult to accept the routine of marriage and family. For Tony and Karen, it must have been terribly disruptive of their established family unit. With little communication going on, the three of us didn't bond well.

Tony suffered abandonment issues when Karen had divorced his biological father. He never really knew where his father, Otto Mott, was living or when he would have another problem with the law. Otto served time in the Washington State Penitentiary and was out of Tony's life. He didn't contest the adoption of his son, either. Tony was emotionally dependent on Karen, not me. They shared a different relationship, one I never knew. When she transferred a portion of her love to me, his abandonment issues surfaced again. Tony became a casualty of our marriage, never feeling a part of our family.

That special bond that can occur between a father and a son was never attained by us, as Tony had vastly different interests than I did, and they did not include sports. For those forty years, we didn't have an extended conversation on any topic of interest without it ending in controversy. We were both opinionated and headstrong. The best years of our relationship, as we grew older, centered around small talk, but mostly it was nonexistent. I blame myself and Karen. As the parents, we needed to take the lead and support and guide him more. We needed to try harder to make him feel a part of our family.

Karen's parents were always there for backup. Although Mrs. Smith, Karen's mother, usually made it sound like she was giving us the key to the family safe every time she helped us financially, whether we paid them back or not. Her father eventually gave us their 1958 Ford sedan when Karen's old Plymouth died an abrupt death. This vehicle was later wrecked when my friend Bob Wynia drove it and side-swiped the Burnside Bridge in Portland on one of our escapades, something I should have outgrown by then. That was the end of the Ford and put Karen and me into a used 1956 black VW.

Karen's question about what I planned to do in life was answered now, with my going back to college to finish my teaching degree. This accomplishment took me only one year to achieve. I earned good grades by putting more time into my studies than running and gunning with my old friends. However, we won't count the night Bob and I crashed the '58 Ford.

I even surprised myself at PSC with the high marks achieved in my classes. Mrs. Smith, who thought I didn't have enough brains to come in from the cold, passionately believed I must have cheated. She was a piece of work and continued to sabotage us with these types of comments throughout our marriage.

Dr. Holland had been my brother Almon's football coach at PSC the year before I arrived at Portland State College, so we knew each other. I had to take a lot of night classes to accomplish my graduation goal, but he constantly encouraged me and supported me to make that a reality. I had a great mentor in Dr. Holland. He streamlined my transcript, accepting various classes already taken, and guided me through in a year. He helped me take my education goal of graduation to fruition and made my experience enjoyable.

We lived in the post-WWII influence, one of the greatest economic times of American history. Prices were still low from the war years, and inflation hadn't started to rise and leave many people behind. College tuition was inexpensive and affordable. College professors' salaries were nominal by today's standards, but the monetary aspect of education at that time was one of the reasons I could afford college. My schooling and the Boom collided beautifully.

When I married Karen, my life took a miraculous turn for the better. I went from a questionable future for my livelihood to what I perceived as an ideal opportunity for a career. It was an enjoyable time for us to be young in America. It took me many years to deeply appreciate and be grateful for this kickstart to my life and to realize what I had done for myself and my future with that one little question, "Will you marry me?"

We parlayed our short-term romance into forty years of marriage, but the last five years we were on life support, and we divorced in 2001. We raised three children together, and for many years, our life was good. We did well financially with her working for the law firm and me teaching, coaching, and selling textbooks. The rental properties in Oregon we shared, and an investment in Arizona, helped too. We enjoyed our younger children's school activities and sports for many years, but it wasn't enough.

When I left Karen, Tony rebelled. He wrote me a letter that said "get lost" in very harsh words. It was hurtful. He has never contacted me since, or me him. He tried to turn my other children against me with that letter, but it did not work. Today, he lives in Palm Springs, California, and works as a flight attendant for Delta Airlines. He is single and stays in touch with his mother, his brother Eric, and his sister Ann.

This last exploit of record for me was extremely difficult. He tried to involve his siblings, my biological children, into signing the hateful letter as well. They wouldn't get involved in his anger, but they have all seen one another over the years.

I'm not optimistic today, twenty years later, that Tony has shed his bitterness by this time in his life. I ask about him on occasion but know extraordinarily little about how he is doing.

Karen still lives in Oregon near our daughter, Ann. Eric lives in California.

FRIENDS

A faithful friend never gets in your way unless you happen to be going down.

Arnold H. Glasow,
U.S. businessman

Jack Streeter and Earl at the Tillamook County Fair in 1952.

GLORY DAYS

While listening to the radio, on came a song I always enjoyed: "Glory Days" by Bruce Springsteen. It's about Bruce's high school athletic exploits. The lyrics tell the story of meeting up with an old teammate and reminiscing about days gone by on the gridiron back in high school.

I soon felt an alliance with Bruce and his teammate. Like Bruce relates in his song, the emotion of playing a football game years ago with my schoolmates—for me, in the 1950s—came flowing back into my memory. I recalled a game I'd played back then and the teammates alongside me on the field.

Today, when seeing an old teammate from Tillamook High, I sense the passion that carried us to victory years in our past. We recognize a common bond held only by those who played the game, a spirit of friendly goodwill and the noble experience of winning together. We are on the field once again, living our past adventures as a team, scoring a touchdown, and winning the game in memory as if it had taken place yesterday.

The story has enlarged itself after the retelling of the action, in a small part defining our lives. Sometimes the game becomes the moment in local history amongst the townsfolk. You become known to your peers for the triumph of the game, a feather in your cap. It signifies to the players the importance the game takes on in their lives. It makes little difference as to the enormity of the game to the uncaring. The perceived magnitude of the game to the players is what matters most. The game played by the young and revered into the gray years.

One game, versus Central Catholic, is recognized and celebrated in the minds of the Tillamook players of my era. As Bruce Springsteen sang in "Glory Days," it is fitting to remember about your past. When the Tillamook Cheesemakers football team defeated the powerful Catholic Central Rams on the gridiron in Portland, it became reminiscent history in the making.

The sun shone brightly on Stark Street that Saturday afternoon in October 1951. Those who played for Tillamook were bonded forever, as one, for the remainder of their lives. The Cheesemakers were giant killers that day. They had defeated their rivals, the invincible Rams, on their home field in the big city. Oh, the feeling of glory over that game amongst the boys who played for Tillamook.

Over the years, the film of that game has been shown at gatherings and reunions many times by the boys who played. It extends the "Glory Days" of my teammates as we escalated into our later years. The old tape was always kept in the safe hands of our best player, Bobby Riggert, who scored the winning touchdown against the Rams.

Like many of my teammates, sadly, Bobby is gone. Where is the film today? It really doesn't matter much now. The game is seared in the memory of those of us who remain. It's the game that defined our team over the years and propelled us into our "Glory Days" in college and beyond.

DATE

As I entered high school in Tillamook, Oregon, I became interested in dating. In the early 1950s, a boy asked a girl for a date and then the two of them did something as a couple, such as see a movie. In today's world, groups of boys and girls go out together. That didn't happen often in our era, though double-dating was part of the picture for me at age fifteen.

Up to this time, I had never taken a girl out, so dating was a new experience for me. Dating caused nervousness and excitement with the thought having a girl sitting alongside of me. I stewed on the matter so much it made asking a girl out a challenge. It was my mission to prove to myself and my friends I could do this, too, and do it well. If I didn't calm myself down, I expected the experience would cause my collapse into a nervous breakdown.

I don't know if every fifteen-year-old boy thinks of girls but, for me at that age, girls occupied my mind continuously. In 1951, I was going to be a sophomore at Tillamook High School in the fall. At that time, culture viewed teenage boy and girl relationships in a unique way. It was a more restrained and conservative era, with some protocol to dating. This was before the free love breakout of the 1960s, when all rules of dating were challenged for the sake of expediency, and rebellion against society's norms occurred. Parents approached the decade with their children as a crossroads of a new liberal movement. Even though the time had its tranquil flower children, the young people started a revolution toward changing society's norms in a hurry.

I was happy to take things slowly in the 1950s. With all my fretting about the realm of romance, I was obviously a real novice. At age fifteen, it took a lot of courage to ask a girl for a date. I really had to dig down deep into my bravery storehouse and discover some backbone I didn't realize I possessed. The possibility of being turned down always lingered inside me. Failure fell hard on this young man packed with hormones, especially when it involved young ladies.

I coupled all my trepidation with the fact that I wasn't old enough to use our only family car. It loomed as another problem to contend with while making my plans. I relied on an older schoolmate to double-date and give me a ride. Not only was I too young to drive, but I also had two older brothers who were lined up ahead of me for just such an occasion. It would be a while before I earned the privilege of using the family car to woo a young lady. I couldn't wait until I was a senior and my brothers, Almon and Chuck, would be out of the house. I would be the only one using the family car for courting girls.

Dating wasn't a simple activity. It involved a nerve-racking process, not only to obtain a date, but also to secure a car ride for the adventure from one of my friends. Two people, my date and the driver, became a part of my commitment for things to happen. I had my first experience with time management and learned some organizational skills quickly.

I desperately wanted to arrange a date with a girl, but not just any girl. She had to be pretty, not a ravishing beauty, but an eye-catcher. A good figure, not necessarily statuesque, and of course a charming personality. Those criteria gauged whether I asked the right girl to go out with me. They were my early aspirations. A guy, I figured, had to have standards.

With my criteria in mind, and as time passed, I looked and looked at every girl possible. Not surprisingly, no one came close to a qualifier. Searching for my perfect girl, I grew increasingly frustrated, wondering if she really existed. I experienced little luck in my pursuit, even though I put in a lot of thought and effort in finding my unique young lady.

Intestinal Fortitude

She might have a good figure, but not be pretty… and so on it went. Something was always missing with every gal. She might have the wrong smile or hair color, be too short, not shapely enough, too quiet, or a little too loud. My search for my perfect girl was much more difficult than I'd thought at the beginning of my exploration.

In the meantime, I couldn't fulfill my eagerness to spend a night out with a young miss. My pals had girls and I didn't. They tried to fix me up with a girl, but she never matched my essentials for dating. I started to question what attracted the two of them to be a couple. I analyzed my classmates, looking for their secrets but found not one characteristic fit all. With time passing me by, I couldn't find a girl for me in this world—or at least in Tillamook County. I was beginning to believe the one I looked for was a little too inconceivable and may not exist at all.

I adjusted my expectations and became more realistic in my approach by looking at dating from a personality and fun-loving point of view, rather than putting my emphasis on good looks. Sometimes a girl's being pretty wasn't enough of a factor when looking for a companion for the evening. Once I started scouting for the girl with the good personality, I found every one of them had an amiable persona. They were prettier than I'd first thought, so I understood where some of the old adages came from: "Beauty is in the eye of the beholder" and "Beauty is only skin deep."

After I took a more sensible view of courtship, it was incredible how my outlook toward girls and socializing with them changed in just a few months. With my modification in attitude, I met a girl who fulfilled my fantasy within two weeks. She was a lovely gal from Garibaldi, Oregon, just a few miles from Tillamook. Joan Kalinowski was slender, had a nice figure, and stood as tall as me at five feet, nine inches. Joan wore her blonde hair on the top of her head, something I liked about her. We met at a basketball game in Garibaldi and, with her pleasant disposition, I found her easy to talk to and witty.

She became my first dating experience. Asking her out was easier than expected since she was such a nice girl with her good manners and pleasantries. I marveled at how I found the right one so quickly after I took a more reasonable view of things. Not surprisingly, it was her pleasant nature that attracted me to her in the first place.

I arranged a ride with Doug McCool to go on a double date with him and his latest girlfriend, Katie VanDomlin. He was a year older and could use his parents' car to go out on weekends. Doug played on the basketball and football team with me and had been a solid friend since we first met at Liberty Junior High School. We had plans to go on to college together and play sports.

Dressing for my date made me nervous. I polished my shoes three times that day. I couldn't decide on the best shirt to wear and kept changing them repeatedly. After asking my brother Almon which one looked best, I wore the one he'd picked out. I wish he had also offered some advice on how to control stress on a first date.

We drove to Garibaldi that beautiful summer evening on old Highway 101, past Bay City and through the curves parallel to the shoreline of the bay, where the tide was out. In Garibaldi, we found my date's home up the hill near the high school. This part of town had a magnificent view of the bay and fisherman tending their boats.

I went up to the front door of her house and knocked, nervous and fumbling when she answered the door.

"Hello," I mustered.

She appeared eager to have some fun and greeted me with a big smile.

"Hello," Joan said, radiant in an attractive blue dress that made her look cheerful, like the girl next door.

I was smitten by her blonde hair and blue eyes. They matched her light-blue dress.

We walked to the car as the evening light began to fall on the small town. Tillamook Bay glistened in the last beams of light as the sun set over the Pacific Ocean. She jumped into the back seat of the car as I held the door for her. She surprised me by sitting close. Since I was on my first date, I didn't know what to say to her or where to put my hands.

When she turned to speak to me, I was hit with a blast of her ungodly breath. It smelled like she had eaten a seafood dinner yesterday or hadn't brushed her teeth in days. My head suddenly retracted, moving backward so quickly it caused a kink in my neck. I was dumbfounded. I couldn't believe the odorous the scent of her breath.

Befuddled, I kept smelling her rank breath as she continued to talk to me. I immediately lost all enthusiasm for her and the evening ahead, wanting desperately to escape from the back seat of the car.

I couldn't bring myself to relax, take her offensive breath in stride, and have an enjoyable time. She was pretty and fun to be around, with her charming personality, but those aspects didn't combat her breath. Being too young, inexperienced, and socially insecure when it came to girls, I didn't have enough confidence in myself to discreetly tell her about her halitosis. It reminded me of day-old clam sauce. Offering gum or mints was not an option—I had none and didn't want to embarrass her in any way. To sit next to her was quite a predicament. She must have thought I was a weird and lousy date because of my constant squirming.

We took in the movie as planned at the Coliseum Theatre in downtown Tillamook and had a cola afterwards at the Fern Café. It was a good thing for me it was a double date. The conversation would have died if it had been up to me. Doug was a talker and kept things going.

We returned to Garibaldi a short time later. I walked her to the door and quickly said goodnight.

I've always wondered what might have happened if I had been more confident and a big enough person to overlook her defective breath—or, better yet, to talk to her about it. Her halitosis might have only been a one-night fluke... I'll never know. I saw her later that summer at the Tillamook County Fair. She was having fun with her friends and pretty as she had ever been. She wouldn't look my way or say hello. I wasn't surprised.

COLLEGE

As a senior at Tillamook High School in 1953, I felt like a student in name only. I was in a fog and passing aimlessly through the hallowed halls, a misplaced period in my life. As a mediocre student where academics were concerned, I effortlessly attempted to graduate without any signs of exertion in the classroom.

Oregon State College required a high school diploma to attend, so that became my goal for the next year: to become a first-year college student in 1953. I'm not sure I learned much of anything from my trek through all grades up to twelve. Playing sports, gaining an athletic scholarship, and going somewhere to college to play baseball and basketball piqued my interest the most.

After visiting Oregon State College in Corvallis twice my senior year, I grew to admire the school for its friendliness, attention to each student, and coaches, such as "Slats" Gill and Paul Valenti. Even with our brief meetings, they showed me a professionalism I could admire as they laid out all the ground rules and expectations.

Contributing to my lack of interest toward high school was a girl. My longtime girlfriend, Joyce, graduated in the spring of my junior year to attend Willamette University in Salem, Oregon. During her first year at Willamette, she was chosen the Sweetheart of Sigma Chi. Not only did I think Joyce was a good-looking girl, but the Sigma Chi fraternity shared my opinion. She truly was a sweet person and I enjoyed being with her. A slender blonde-haired person with blue eyes, Joyce stood five feet, ten inches in height. In addition to her affectionate and tenderhearted personality, I was drawn to her smile and warmth, and not the least by her fair beauty.

We'd dated for two years in high school, but it felt like we'd divorced when she departed. Joyce decided to sever our relationship, not me. She believed it would be better for both of us to have our freedom when we were miles apart at different schools. Even though it was a practical decision, it wasn't favorable from my perspective. I missed her more than imaginable, and high school wasn't the same without her by my side.

One story about Joyce and me in high school centered around another girl who reported around school that she and I had gone out together. She claimed I had cheated and, of course, Joyce was upset as this lie circulated.

I knew Joyce left school on an early bus and would pass my classroom at three in the afternoon. So, one day, I decided to put an end to the rumor. I jumped up from my desk and told the teacher I would be right back. I stopped Joyce in the hall and told her to stay right where she was. I went into a different classroom and found the girl spreading the rumor. In front of her teacher and classmates, I pulled her from her desk by her arm and took her into the hall where Joyce waited. I demanded she tell Joyce the truth, which she did.

I walked back to my classroom after telling Joyce she now had the truth. The two girls were left standing in the hall looking at each other. I heard Joyce make a comment of forgiveness to the girl before she caught her bus for home.

I acted totally on impulse, but it worked.

Ours was a high school romance I came to understand only as my senior year began. I longed for a relationship with Joyce, even if long distance. When she left, a part of me went with her. We had a two-year history between us. We shared a strong bond, and I was in love with her. Her leaving contributed to my depression which became more frequent than occasional. I often isolated and stayed to myself when I used to be more outgoing. I felt abandoned by her.

During my senior year at THS, most of the girls in my class were dating guys in college or veterans who had just returned from the Korean War. The undergraduate girls seemed too young. My prospects of finding a girlfriend in the absence of Joyce, before college, weren't too favorable in the 1952–53 school year. I dated no one from Tillamook my senior year.

Honestly, I was afraid of a commitment to a girl in my hometown and them getting pregnant. I wanted a clean break when I went off to school. I was terrified of any obligation to keep me from playing college sports. If I dated someone my last year, it certainly would turn into a sexual relationship. The attitude toward teenage sex in our small town during the 1950s was surprisingly loose.

With a lot of my friends off to college and the girl situation during my senior year, I became more depressed. I played sports to keep me motivated, but my last year in high school conflicted with my decision to go solo. I had one foot at THS and the other in college, where my heart yearned to be an OSC athlete. My social life with girls was nonexistent most of the time. I set it up that way while waiting for my opportunity to begin at Oregon State on scholarship to play baseball and basketball, or at Stanford which offered me financial assistance because of football.

I later realized I'd shortchanged myself at THS during my senior year by being melancholy and having a resentful outlook about Joyce leaving. I went through the motions and suppressed my depression, but my negative attitude affected my behavior. I wasn't profoundly serious about learning in the classroom that final year. I missed Joyce.

If I may skip forward a bit to bring closure to my relationship with Joyce, let me say that our paths crossed infrequently for the next thirty-eight years, but only because of some event in Tillamook. Usually we were both married, but one time, she was not. That time, we united at the coast when we were fifty-five years old. A friend made the arrangement for us to meet. We connected during the Elk's Golf Tournament in which I participated. Vivian Stangle, whom Joyce had lived with during high school, invited Joyce to stay with her at that time so we could be together. Vivian had always wanted us to marry years before when we were in college.

Joyce and I met for dinner that weekend and reminisced about high school. The evening was emotional as we dusted off the past after so many years. Joyce was single at the time, but I wouldn't leave my

Intestinal Fortitude

wife to be with her. She contacted me several times after that, trying to get us back together, but I had to say no for my children.

It was too late to think about rebuilding our old relationship. I had to let it go. She accepted my decision with much difficulty. It wasn't easy for me, either, but I walked away believing I made the right decision. Joyce died of a massive heart attack the next year, in Seattle, at the age of fifty-six while tending her flower garden. I believed our emotional entanglement over those many years played a role in her death. She was so enthusiastic about us yet had so much anxiety every time we saw each other. It wore on her, especially when we parted. Many have written about their first loves, and I can say it is true we do fondly remember the first one.

Back in my senior year, I found it hard to concentrate. My grades were barely passing. Some of my teachers were caught up in the "give the 'dumb jock' a break" routine and moved me along. My first-period English teacher, Miss Chapman, gave me a pass to the gym to shoot baskets on game days. She tried to help my attitude improve. That spring, I did show enough interest in my schoolwork to pass her class. I played baseball then and pitched our team into the Oregon State playoffs. Baseball was a positive influence on me and helped my effectiveness in the classroom. I kept my sights on my goal of playing baseball and basketball in college.

I didn't learn to study properly in high school. Without any developed study habits, I chose Oregon State to play sports. Once there, I really had to take my classes seriously to achieve passing grades. The professors at OSC cared less if I played on the basketball or baseball team. I learned how to educate myself and attend classes on a regular basis to become an authentic collegian.

I devised a plan my first year which enabled me to pass my college courses and stay eligible for my scholarships and sports. By investigating different major fields of study, I determined the classes I felt I could pass easily. They were usually courses with the number "100" in front of them. Every major had an introductory lecture for a first-year student. As an example, the field of literature had a 101 course in speed reading. I enrolled and earned a B grade. I'd have attained an A but miscalculated and read too fast the first day of class. Unfortunately, I didn't show enough improvement by the end of the term. My mind was only on one thing when I first attended OSC: becoming an athlete. Thinking about earning a degree wasn't even on my radar.

When I finally picked a major field of study, I chose general studies. Initially, I didn't know what I wanted to do for an occupation. I lived in the moment. General Studies was an excellent choice for students who didn't want to stay home and pump gas—in Oregon, only attendants pump your gas—or work in a lumber mill, like my dad, while they figured out their future.

My taking the 100- level options only worked for the first year. Then I had to declare a major. By the end of my first year, I figured out how to continue my education in an institution of higher learning. I understood how to study and become an authentic student, one with respectable grades and an interest in academics as well as sports. Before I left for school, a logger friend in Tillamook gave me some advice.

He said, "Go to class."

It sounded too simplistic, but I knew if I went to class the professors would work with me and provide support. They wouldn't give much help to someone who didn't show up for their classes. I later gave the same advice to my grandchildren when they started college sixty-five years later.

During my first year at OSC, I received a lucky break. My English teacher, Mrs. Butts—her real name—did me a huge favor. I remember her as a diminutive, homely woman who wore a long black coat in the Oregon winter. She was a stern, demanding, and unyielding character with traits I came to respect as the term progressed.

Mine was a serious experience with her. She had a no-nonsense approach involving little conversation or friendly banter. She knew what I needed and held me accountable for my actions. I wasn't going to get away with my old attitude toward learning. That was over. Mrs. Butts helped me learn to write and take school seriously. She was a real blessing for me because I needed her class to remain eligible to play basketball.

When she returned my first essay, across the top of it read, *"See me."* No grade, just, *"See me."* My paper was written so pathetically she made me an offer on how I could pass the class.

"If you attend the class diligently three days a week and meet with me the other two days to write, I might give you a D grade," she told me.

Mrs. Butts had my attention. I took her up on her proposal. I was enrolled in English five days a week and set upon a path to make up for my apathetic behavior from high school. At the completion of the term, I earned a D grade. More importantly, Mrs. Butts helped me learn to write and become an engaged student. She was truly a Godsend to teach me to develop a keen interest in the written word. Later in life, I became a voracious reader and a writer.

I still remember Mrs. Butts and the help she gave me at just the right time in my academic travels. When I'm writing now, I think of her and where my writing might be without her guidance. She would be astonished I wrote two books. Mrs. Butts helped me grow up a bit. I learned to respect her as a teacher and appreciate the English language. I not only honored her as a teacher, but I liked her as a person.

When I later attended Oregon College of Education, now Western Oregon State University, I came to an interesting conclusion about college attendance. I realized I not only could attend college, but I might also actually graduate with a degree. I was moving toward adulthood. When I first attended OSC, now a university, only a few years earlier, I never visualized graduating, what with my focus on sports.

After spending two years at OCE, I was about to earn a degree in general studies—not a major accomplishment, but a diploma nonetheless. I didn't ponder long about what I would do with this qualification, but I would be a graduate. While almost ready to complete this goal, I had second thoughts. I was taking a math class in the spring term 1962, where the professor assigned homework the first day. Anxiety hit me, and a knot of apprehension filled the pit of my stomach.

The realization for me was school was no longer safe. I now had a lot of the pressures of finding a real job, getting married, buying a house and a car, and eventually having children. It was overwhelming to me. Leaving college after almost five years of attendance was more than I could comprehend. I must live my life January to January rather than in seasons, such as fall, winter, spring terms. I couldn't force myself into taking the class or move beyond the concept of not going to college and being a student.

As I was walking out the classroom door, the professor said, "Earl, this class will graduate you."

I'm not sure what I said to him, but it was like, "I'm not ready to graduate."

I was nervous about the notion that if I graduated someone might get the wrong impression and expect me to seek permanent employment. I didn't matriculate the class or graduate from college that year. It was another reprieve from adulthood, something I practiced for many years. I was stuck in semi-adolescent mode into my late twenties. The scary thing about my long journey through college was being petrified at that moment. I knew I would do it all over again the same way if the opportunity arose: a slow rise to maturity, missing Joyce, and a lingering college life. Graduation finally came more than five years later, taking me ten total years to earn a degree.

Within six months, my single life abruptly ended. I met and married Karen after our short courtship over the summer. After a few months of marriage, I became a quasi-contributing member of society, a husband, and a father. With an innocent "I do," I gained a wife, a young son, and her expectations of me. Within a whirlwind year, I finished my degree and obtained a job as a teacher, beginning with Estacada High School in Estacada, Oregon, outside of Portland.

My miraculous feat of graduation from college was finally accomplished with a lot of help from Karen. She was like Joyce with her outgoing personality, but she was more fun. We had a lot of good times together.

Maturity occurred for me at the age of twenty-seven after an extended adolescence and a fun-filled heyday of waywardness. My pre-adulthood sojourn through college life for almost ten years ended. My marriage to Karen promptly compelled me to enter a new phase of my life: adulthood.

People mature at their own pace, some faster than others, and some never do. I was involved with college life during most of my twenties and enjoyed that environment immensely. The academic setting on campus was like a drug for me. I was addicted to it. The high I received while attending school was bigger than me, and I always looked for the next fix. The interaction with my fellow students and professors, my various teammates and fraternity brothers, all set the stage for me to seek and embrace more involvement.

I made friends like Bob Walker, Bob Erickson, Johnny Fredericks, and Lou Zarozinski from Oregon State College, some who are still in my life today. The Sigma Chi house offered basketball teammates such as Dave Gambee, who was an All-American at OSC and later played in the National Basketball Association (NBA). He stays in touch.

Some people move to adulthood by enlisting in the armed forces, like my brother Almon. Others go commercial fishing in Alaska, like my son, Eric. Yet others marry built-in responsibilities, like my brother Chuck. College was where I fled to mature. All the athletic teams, coaches, colleges, part-time jobs, and newfound friends I met along the way enabled me to have a significant journey toward adulthood. The switch for me came gradually. It was fate, but there were people helping me during my twenties in Oregon. I wouldn't recommend my path and struggles to everyone, but it proved beneficial for me. It might have taken me a few extra years to get started, but eventually I achieved a couple of degrees with the help of athletic scholarships and good mentorship; a couple of careers with the support of friends and family; and, ultimately, adulthood.

HATHAWAY MEADE GANG

Hathaway Meade was the name of the neighborhood where I grew up. In 1934, I was born there east of Tillamook, Oregon, just over the Southern Pacific Railroad tracks. We played on the train engines and box cars. It was a mile from downtown and the Coliseum Movie Theatre, where we walked to on Saturdays for the matinee movie with Roy Rogers and Popeye cartoons.

During my grade school years, we had a neighborhood troupe called the Hathaway Meade Gang, a random group of elementary-aged boys and girls. The gang members were diverse, a haphazard group of sizes: short, tall, fat, and skinny. A haphazard collection of ethnic backgrounds made up the assemblage.

Our clan fished in a creek and looked for crawdads. We found it fun to dam up the creek located at the end of our property. We also had a large forest to play in with tall spruce and hemlock trees for hiding places. We loved to walk among them while making trails through vine maple and elderberry bushes. It was like another world inside the forest, peaceful and calm. Amid the trees, we experienced a serene hideaway where we could disappear into the darkness. We often sat on the soft green moss to, if necessary, escape from friends, siblings, or parents.

The tracks behind our house brought hobos who would ride the rails back and forth across America. Physically, they were dirty men in tattered clothing, carrying everything they owned in a bindle over their shoulders. Mysterious men, whom we were afraid of, lived in the hovels next to the tracks. These hobos, or tramps as they were called, came to our back door begging for food, and my mother accommodated them. It was an era of helping others when you could, no matter how little you had yourself. The men eagerly ate the food out on our rear lawn near the garden, then left for their hovel or the next train as it moved through town.

Growing up in our neighborhood was remarkably interesting. It was a good place because those who lived there were a cross section of America. A variety of nationalities, tribes, and ethnic origins resided in Hathaway Meade. For example, the Buckbee family came from American Indian descent, the Goldmanns were German, and the Kowalskis were Polish. There in the neighborhood, ages ranged from several young people beginning their lives to older folk finishing theirs.

My father worked on a reload operation out behind our house, near the Southern Pacific Railroad tracks. He loaded logs from the surrounding forests. They were brought by logging trucks onto flatbed railroad cars for shipment to the Willamette Valley. My father did physical labor for eight hours a day. Moving quickly because of the danger in the job, he hooked heavy steel tongs around big logs that were lifted skyward and placed on a flat railroad car.

Our neighbor from across the street, Mr. Ellingsworth, was a plumber always covered with dirt and smudge, except on Sunday. That day, he cleaned up and, to our gang, looked as different as night and day. We didn't think he could ever get as clean as he did on the sabbath. He took a bath, put on a pressed suit with a white shirt and a tie, and surprised us all.

The neighborhood had few zoning laws. Sometimes there was a lovely well-manicured lawn and a home with pillars out front, and next to it sat a framed dwelling that looked like work halted on it in the middle of the building process. It appeared as if the builder suffered a mental breakdown. The unfinished houses' homeowners or contractors might have forgotten that unpainted sheets of plywood were not final house siding. After a few years, the neighbors would come to understand "what you saw was what you got" as far as the exterior of the home was concerned. It was an attention-grabbing area of Tillamook with the "nice house/strange house" routine.

Earl Llewellyn Goldmann

Throughout the vicinity, someone from the middle class was living next door to someone near the poverty line. Our house landed on more of the strange end of the scale. Though it did have a completed, easy-on-the-eye, green exterior, it was no beauty. It still stands today.

My brothers and I took our turn in Hathaway Meade delivering the afternoon Portland newspaper, *The Oregon Journal*. Chuck took the first paper route. When he grew old enough to hold a job in town or on a farm, my brother Almon took over the route. As Almon grew older, I stood next in line to replace him as the carrier.

There were two large dairy farms just down the road at the end of our property. One was owned by Press Williams, whose hunting hound dogs bit me when I delivered newspapers and left holes in my pants from their sharp teeth. My father called Press to tell him to tie up the hounds, but they always ran loose. I lived in fear of those hounds until I lobbied my parents to allow me to give up the paper route.

Delivering the paper, soliciting new customers, and collecting money put me in a position to know what was going on with my customers. I had the scoop, and it wasn't all in the newspaper. Some of it was exciting to a thirteen-year-old kid with an overactive mind.

Before the dogs hurried my demise of my paper route business, I could only guess what Mrs. Schrobercher was doing at four o'clock on Friday afternoons. The same gentleman showed up at her house in a blue Ford pickup. He wasn't her husband because I knew Mr. Schrobercher. He had a job driving a delivery truck into Portland on Fridays and didn't arrive home until later at night. Mrs. Schrobercher always looked at me in a funny way when I delivered the paper promptly at four. She knew I knew something wasn't quite on the up and up, but we were going to keep it hush-hush. It was our secret. I wouldn't disclose information on Mrs. Schrobercher's weekly rendezvous. For one reason, she paid me on time for the paper. But I did tell my best friend, Bobby, that something funny was going on at her house at four o'clock on Fridays.

Then there was old Mr. Root, who lived around the corner. He only left his house to get groceries in town at Huesser's Grocery. I always had a tough time getting him to answer the door when it came time to collect for *The Journal*. He liked being mysterious and enjoyed scaring the kids in our gang every chance he could. Bobby and I threw rocks on his roof at night to get his goat. It amused us.

One night, Mr. Root was ready and caught us red-handed. He chased us up a tree and, even though he yelled at us to come down, we stayed in the tree for an hour until he felt tired and went into his house. From then on, we left him alone.

Our neighbors across the street were the Andersons. They had two daughters, LaWanda and LaVerne, who always played in our "kick the can" games in the front yard. Mr. Anderson was a quiet loner. We never saw him doing much except going to work and coming home. When I went over to the Andersons' house, Mr. Anderson would always sit in his big chair and listen to the radio. I swear, that's all he did.

Mrs. Anderson was the interesting one. She was a little peculiar and marched to her own drumbeat. She had a five-foot pet alligator kept in a large tub in the front room of their house. During the day, she brought it outside so it could stretch its legs and get some exercise. He was never confined to a leash.

One day, when the alligator was lounging on the front lawn, Mrs. Anderson left the reptile while she went inside the house to get something. When she returned, the gator had disappeared. Mrs. Anderson compelled the kids in the neighborhood into action to find the missing creature. It wasn't long before someone spotted it in the drainage ditch next to the road. Mrs. Anderson retrieved the gator with some of his favorite food and returned it to the front room of the house. Eventually, it grew to about six feet in length and she had to give it up. Everyone wanted to know what she did with her pet reptile, but none of us wanted to ask. She was just too strange to approach, and the mystery was more fun.

We had quite a group of kids in Hathaway Meade. Not only did we represent all sizes and ethnicities, but some also had traits or quirks that made them stand out as unique personalities.

The three Tucker boys liked to play with matches right up to the time they burned down two homes in the neighborhood. The fire was a couple of houses from ours, just down Alder Lane. They were lighting matches in the garage when the blaze started. As the flames spread from the garage to the main structure, the fire grew bigger. The house became engulfed in flames and ignited the home next door. It was quite a blaze. The fire turned into an inferno and sent ashes and sparks flying high in the air. Some landed on the cedar shingle rooftops of other neighboring homes. My father launched the garden hose and sprayed our roof with water since we had a cedar shake roof, too, that would have easily caught fire.

I'm not sure what kind of punishment the Tucker boys received because, without a place to live, the family moved out of the neighborhood. Some referred to them as the "arson boys."

Next, the Easterly kids: Rosemary and Billy. Rosemary was a heavy girl. To be honest, obese. I don't remember her weight being a problem for us kids. She was part of our gang. We didn't make a big deal about it. Her brother, Billy, was a young member of the gang, so no one took him seriously or paid much attention to him until one day.

"Let's ride the donkey!" he shouted. Although Billy was a little mentally challenged, his proposal surprised us, and we listened because his enthusiasm was infectious. Fun was at hand and Billy had become our leader for the first time.

The Easterlys had a field in front of their house where they kept a small gray donkey. No one thought of riding it until Billy, who never was consulted about any of our escapades, produced the idea. So, off we went, the whole bunch of us, to see if we could ride the jackass.

The donkey appeared tame, as he stood in one place for extended periods of time with his head never moving. Our gang of kids stood around the donkey, daring each other as to who would ride him first. The animal never moved, even though we had him surrounded. Bobby stood in front of him. He was always one of the more eager members of our gang. He reached out to pet the donkey's head with his right hand. The animal had enough of all of us kids bouncing around him. He took hold of Bobby's fingers on his right hand and clamped them between his teeth.

The animal brayed as he tugged Bobby's fingers in a death grip. Bobby jumped up and down, trying to pull his fingers from the donkey's mouth and yelling in pain. All of us leapt around, not knowing what to do about the screaming Bobby. He not only yelled from pain but knew he might lose his fingers. It was quite a sight in the Easterlys' field that afternoon.

Intestinal Fortitude

The jackass let go of Bobby's fingers in an abrupt motion. Miraculously, his hand was intact except for the indentation of the donkey's teeth on his knuckles. For the rest of the day, Bobby looked at his hand in disbelief and tried not to cry. He hid his injury from his parents for the next week and did not go to a doctor. The donkey scared everyone so much we gave him distance from then on.

The Easterly kids' father was a state police officer and a nice man, often warning our gang about how many fish we could catch from the creek down at the end of our property. The fish take was limited by the county. The fact that Mr. Easterly was a state trooper didn't keep Mrs. Easterly from going out at night and stealing plants from the local nursery, owned by Mr. Brooks. She drove to the nursery one too many nights to lift some free foliage. After a few nights of losing plants, Mr. Brooks laid in wait behind the rose bushes with his trusty shotgun.

When Mrs. Easterly loaded up more pots, Mr. Brooks came out from behind the roses. He recognized her immediately. She tried to make a fast getaway, but it wasn't fast enough. As Mrs. Easterly sped away into the darkness, Mr. Brooks took aim with his loaded shotgun and blew a huge round hole in the passenger-side car door. Afterward, she drove the car around Tillamook with the king-sized hole in the door. It didn't seem to bother Mrs. Easterly when word got out about the side of her car. It wasn't surprising Mr. and Mrs. Easterly separated soon afterward. The children went with her, as was customary in the 1950s.

As I reached the age of sixteen, a sophomore at Tillamook High School, I took a job in a grocery store downtown. As you might imagine, Carmichaels was owned by two clever guys named Carl and Mike. During the same time, one of the old gang members from the neighborhood, Steven Jackson, went to work in town at the First National Bank. Steven was a few years older than most of us in the gang, but he spent time with us on occasion anyway.

One day at work, Carl asked me to take 1,000 dollars in bills to the bank and get change for the store. A thousand dollars in the 1950s was a heap of money, so I was jittery. The bank was only a block away, so Carl thought the chance of my getting held up or losing my way was minimal in the short distance. It felt gratifying that Carl trusted me to go to the bank for him.

When I reached the bank, the teller was Steven Jackson from our old gang. He was dressed in a shirt and tie, and he acted in a professional manner, so I went along with it. He was all business but put everything in the bag out of my sight. After getting the change from Steven, I headed back to the grocery store and Carl's office, holding on very tightly to my cargo. I dropped off the money bag as I was asked to do and returned to work stocking shelves with groceries. It wasn't long before the store manager told me to go immediately to Carl's office again as he wanted to see me. I didn't question this, although it seemed odd.

When I arrived in the office, both Carl and Mike and a somber man in a dark suit were already there. I soon found out he was the manager from the bank. Carl's small office was filled with three adults holding administrative positions... and me. This was going to be a serious meeting.

Carl asked me, "How did it go at the bank?"

"Fine."

"Did you get the change as I requested?"

"Yes."

This conversation was too serious in nature, with three gentlemen looking directly at me and asking monotonous questions. I was nervous and realized they must be questioning the total amount in the bag.

"Is there a problem?" I asked.

I knew there was a problem without asking.

"I sent you to the bank with one thousand dollars and you came back with two thousand dollars," Carl said.

The three men waited for my reaction, which was a shrug of disbelief. I didn't know any more than they knew about how I'd received an extra 1,000 dollars. I was getting a little uncomfortable as I was the only one in the room answering the questions.

It was obvious Steven had put the extra money in the bag, but the three of them didn't know Steven had waited on me. It was odd they didn't ask me if I knew anyone who worked at the bank. Eventually, Carl told me I could go back to work, so I happily left. They obviously realized the money was not intended for me if I'd returned it to them.

The bank manager must have asked his tellers who had done the transaction for the kid with the 1,000 dollars. If he did, and found out it was Steven, he might have thought it was an honest mistake. Or he did nothing since he got his money back. As we know, banks don't like to take credit for their mistakes. The manager let it go. From what I heard from Steven later, he was not accused, and it was accepted as an accident.

I never heard any more about it, so I forgot the extra 1,000 dollars existed. I never asked Steven how he ended up putting the extra money in the bag in the first place. The truth is, I wanted to move on.

I don't know whatever happened to Steven Jackson, but if he continued to do his arithmetic in the same manner, the bank wasn't going to stay open too long.

Finally, there was Donny Kienle, who lived up the street. His father owned the music store in Tillamook. Donny was angry at his parents for ignoring him while working to be successful. His brothers, father, and mother were much older than him, since his parents had already raised a family by the time he was born. He always broke the rules set by them.

I was with him often, so I was guilty by association. He got us in so much trouble my parents wouldn't allow me to play with him anymore. My worst beating by my father, which I can vividly remember seventy-five years later, was for allegedly participating in one of Donny's worst rebellious "shenanigans."

Donny took the chicken eggs from a neighbor's chicken coop and broke them. It caused the neighbor to lose the opportunity to increase his flock with new chickens. Plus, it was unacceptable behavior for anyone to do such a thing. It was the last straw for all involved—his parents, my parents, and me—and my final lesson in how to choose my friends.

Earl Llewellyn Goldmann

The Hathaway Meade gang covered the gambit of memorable children anywhere in rural America in the 1940s. We had a creek to fish, a forest to play in, and World War II to keep us cognizant of the outside world. The members of the gang moved on as we became older and pursued other interests than hanging out looking for our next adventure.

LEROY VANOVER

Leroy Vanover and I were college students home for summer break in 1954. He was working in the Coast Range Forest as a logger north of Wheeler, in Tillamook County. Working as a logger was the most dangerous job in Oregon. Leroy earned a considerable amount of money because the work was difficult as well as hazardous.

He was earning money to finance his education at Western Oregon State University, where he was the catcher on the college baseball team. I, on the other hand, was working in a safer situation at a lumber mill located in a blimp hangar on the decommissioned Tillamook Naval Air Station south of town. The hangar served as the home for the World War II lighter-than-air blimps, a.k.a. dirigibles, used for early warning detection of possible Japanese submarine attacks over housed lumber mills.

Jobs in the lumber industry in Oregon were easy to find in 1954— as easy as falling off a log. The cities of San Francisco, Los Angeles, and San Diego were building houses for the new influx of ex-servicemen and their families following the World War II years. Many of these men, who came west to the coast during the war, experienced the pleasant weather of America's western cities and decided to stay. When they found the absence of any snow to shovel in the winter months, the decision was easily made. With the vast amount of lumber being shipped south, the forest product business in Oregon boomed.

Earl Llewellyn Goldmann

Many towns in Oregon had baseball teams sponsored by lumber mills. Usually, college baseball players would be assigned an effortless job in these mills and play on the town's ball club. In Oregon, the teams were called semi-pro because some of the teams would have a player or two who played professionally. They no longer played professional ball but still could play the game. Some of the players, especially good pitchers or hitters, were subsidized with under-the-table money from fans, the team sponsors, or the team itself.

Leroy and I were going to college in the fall with some extra money to add to our baseball scholarships. We were playing baseball together during the summer of 1954 for the Tillamook Elks Lodge semi-pro team. Our home field was the Fairgrounds Ballpark, located where the Tillamook Community College stands today.

We played games on Sundays, mostly because the players on the team held down full-time jobs during the week. The team was also made up of some local players from around Tillamook. Our team had players from all around the county.

We had Jocko Armburst from down south; Donny Dedman from Bay City; the Kellow brothers, Merle and Forrest; and Bud Johanson from the Cloverdale area. Both Jim Cooper, who played first base, and Bobby Riggert, our pitcher, hailed from Tillamook. Bobby Estes came from Garibaldi. I played second base and, of course, heralded from Tillamook as well. Other college players such as Lenny Farrell and Jigs Jakelski came from the University of Portland.

The next summer, 1955, Lenny signed a contract with the Atlanta Braves for 50,000 dollars, a hefty sum for that era. He was one of the "Bonus Babies" of the 1950s, a Major League Baseball practice between 1947 and 1965 of signing young amateur baseball players to large contracts. The player was required to go straight to the major league team without playing in the minor leagues.

Leroy and I played American Legion baseball together in the summer of 1953, then graduated to the Elks Lodge team in the summer of 1954. We became good friends through baseball, even though Leroy went to Garibaldi High School, and I attended Tillamook High. The schools were separated by ten miles and across Tillamook Bay. It was an exciting time in our lives. We were young and directly involved in America's national pastime. Life, it seemed, couldn't be better. Everything was new and wonderful.

We planned Saturdays together to see if we could meet some girls in Rockaway. At that time, it was the hot spot for tourists on the Oregon Coast north of Tillamook. In the summer, there were always girls coming down to the beach on holiday. One Saturday, we danced at the Pavilion in Rockaway after meeting some girls from Grant High School in Portland.

On Sunday we played baseball against a team from Tongue Point Naval Station on our homefield at the Fairgrounds. They were a good team, but we prevailed with a 4–3 victory. Leroy made the hit that won the game. The team celebrated our victory with Leroy getting a lot of adoration from his teammates and his fans.

Leroy's life ended Monday morning in the forest above the Pacific Shore of Oregon. No one noticed the large villainous log above him, precariously hanging to the hillside. The large log broke loose and rolled swiftly down a sharp incline. It picked up speed and trampled the vine maple and elderberry brush in its path as it moved toward Leroy. He was setting a choker on another log at the bottom of the ravine and didn't see it come loose above him. It rolled toward him until it was too late to escape.

He was crushed between the two large logs. The other loggers, I imagine, looked on in shock, then in silence. Some turned away, heads bowed. They knew Leroy was gone. His fellow loggers were amazed at how quickly death came that beautiful Monday morning above Nehalem Bay as the fog lifted into sunlight above the forest.

The foreman shut the job down for the day. The loggers returned to the jobsite the following morning, understanding the danger that took Leroy from their midst. It wasn't that they were unemotional, cold, or unfeeling toward a fellow logger. They were just loggers in a sometimes-harsh business, trying to cope. It was just unusual for it to be a twenty-year-old college student with his entire life ahead of him.

Life at the time seemed so normal. That's what made Leroy's death so tragic and confusing. He was instantly removed from my world and vanished like he hadn't been real. We were starting to be good friends. Then he was gone. I didn't know what to feel. It was so sudden.

After I attended Leroy's funeral, the remainder of my summer passed, subdued and unclear. I spent an abundance of time reflecting on the sudden loss of my friend. I missed him not being on the baseball team and sharing adventures with me on Saturday nights at Rockaway. I felt a larger loss than the others because Leroy and I had developed a camaraderie with each other.

Following Leroy's death, our summer team played games, but it wasn't the same without him. He was our catcher and the vocal leader of our ball club. He was missed by his teammates, but none of us expressed our grief. Counseling wasn't available in the 1950s when someone dealt with a difficult loss. Many times, people didn't want to talk about someone after they'd died. Everyone reconciled death on their own path to peace of mind, which usually involved silence.

Leroy's parents continued to attend our ballgames and wanted very much to talk to us about Leroy. The conversations were difficult. I felt sorry for them. They had lost their only child who was on his way to a college degree and a future in professional baseball. His dream of the Atlanta Braves was gone.

It was a summer I never forgot, one where time stood still. I came to realize as the years went on that there are more important things than baseball… that a person's life is momentary. I remained in shock at the end of the summer, uncomfortable with Leroy's memory until I enrolled again at Oregon State University. I felt a closeness to him since I was doing something he would understand: returning to school, waiting for baseball season to begin in the spring.

Leroy will never be forgotten. It's an honor to remember my friend and the summer of 1954.

JIM SCHROEDER

My parents left our house on Evergreen Drive for a meeting at the Redeemer Lutheran Church in Tillamook. They told me to stay home and not go anywhere that evening while they were away. I was bummed because many of my friends were going to be in downtown Tillamook "hanging out" at the Fern Café.

After my parents left, I hurried out the door to go into town and see my friends. As a fifteen-year-old, my friends were more important than my parents. Disobeying was something I didn't do very often. I knew, if they caught me going against their demands, an excessive amount of grief would be bestowed upon me, such as doubling my chores or grounding. This time, that didn't stop me. The church meeting took three hours, so I had until ten o'clock before needing to be home.

I left the house, crossed the railroad yard near our place, and walked briskly by Hanson's Lumber Mill, where my father was a lumber grader. I headed west on Third Street near the city park. It would take me a half hour to walk to the Fern Café.

As I passed Chuck Lamb's and Bill Loftin's houses, just across from Wilson Elementary School, I received a welcome surprise. A friend from Tillamook High School pulled his car up alongside me. It was Jimmy Schroeder in his parent's royal blue, 1940 Ford coupe. I was glad to see him and jumped in next to Jimmy in the "woman's seat," a phrase used in 1951.

I needed a ride but, more importantly, I was at the age when riding around with friends in a car was important. It felt free and independent. The 1950s was a time when young people would "drag the gut," interpreted as driving your car up and down Main Street in your hometown. You may know this activity as "cruising." Carloads of guys spent hours doing this. To keep things going, other young people on the sidewalk would yell loudly at them. One of the more popular cars to drag the gut in was a 1956 Chevrolet, or "Chevy." It represented "coolness."

I was going to be a sophomore at Tillamook High that fall, and Jimmy was going to be a senior, so it impressed me an upperclassman picked me up. Later that year, in the winter season, we would be on the varsity basketball team together at Tillamook High. Jimmy was a great guy.

This day, we drove into town and stopped at the intersection of Highway 101, or Main Street. If we went straight ahead, we went west toward the ocean beaches. Jimmy suggested we drive out to Oceanside and see who was skating at the roller rink. We drove over bridges at the Trask and Tillamook rivers, past McKinly's Boat Moorage, and headed toward Netarts and Oceanside, two small hamlets at the Pacific Ocean.

It took us around twenty minutes to arrive at Oceanside, one of the prettiest spots on the Oregon Coast. As we stopped in front of the small roller rink, it started to rain. To our surprise, the roller rink was closed. We forgot it was open only on weekends. The rain added to our disappointment as the weather became even more dreary. I thought for only a moment about getting home before my parents returned from their church meeting and asked Jimmy to head back to town.

Jimmy agreed and turned the car around to head back to Tillamook. The summer had been unusually warm, and it hadn't rained for a couple of weeks. This left a coating of oil from the warm macadam of the roadway. When oil mixes with rain, the street becomes slick. We drove past Netarts and approached the big hills on the highway just before the turnoff to Whiskey Creek. Jimmy drove up the first hill with exceptional care because of the rain and slick surface of the highway.

Intestinal Fortitude

As we neared the top of the hill, the car started to slowly spin. The front of the car spun us as in a dream state. His car turned so we were now sliding headfirst back down the road. It then went over and down the next hill. The vehicle rotated around again because the tires were bald and the road like glass. Between the tires and the road's hazardous condition, we were out of control except for Jimmy's determination to steer the car to a safe outcome. Though sliding backward created a perilous situation, I felt confident in his abilities.

Jimmy swung around in his seat so he looked out the rear window and steered the car down the road backwards. He showed some impressive driving skills in doing this maneuver. His ability to not panic and show nerves of steel helped him navigate the car. He looked like a professional, and that calmed my nerves.

We slowly went back over the hill and slid down the other side backward. I wasn't afraid because of Jimmy's calm demeanor and control of the car, even though we could have flown off the cliff as the vehicle appeared to have a mind of its own. When we reached the bottom of the hill, we went into another quick spin and crossed the opposite lane, just missing an oncoming car. Then we spun through the gravel on the side of the elevated road and became airborne only to land in a roadside ditch. It happened so fast I didn't have time to panic. When the car landed, I realized I wasn't injured, and it could have been much worse. I shuddered at the thought.

The car landed in the elderberry bushes below the side of the road, right side up. We came to rest softly as the thick vines broke the fall of the car. I was surprised and thankful the car never turned over. It sat below the road and was hard to see because the dense brush formed a wall. Jimmy and I quickly jumped out of the car, surprised at the nonexistent damage to the car. The two of us scrambled up the embankment to the highway above us.

Cars stopped and people asked if we were okay. They appeared amazed the car hadn't turned over and we weren't injured even after going airborne into the brush. The people in the vehicle following us saw the accident take place, stopped, and offered us a ride to Tillamook. It was growing dark as the evening sun dropped below the crest of the Pacific Ocean. I arrived home just ten minutes ahead of my parents' return from church. The timing couldn't have been better to keep me from getting into trouble.

It was certainly an interesting few hours, leaving my house without permission, being in a car accident, and getting home just in time so my parents didn't know. I didn't tell anybody. Tillamook is a small town and something like a car wreck could get back to my parents very quickly. Fortunately, the car was not totaled. It was difficult to keep the secret of the accident to myself. The longer I kept quiet, though, the easier it became.

I felt a little like the priest who skipped Mass and slipped out for a game of golf, made two holes in one, and couldn't tell anyone of his improbable feat. The entire ordeal reminded me to obey my parents. I had already used up my luck.

We never know if there will be an unexpected glitch in our blueprint. I worried for two weeks after the car wreck somebody would ask my parents how I felt after the accident I was in with Jim Schroeder, but that didn't happen. I came away from it all with an appreciation of Jimmy's nerve and ability to drive a car. He drove a car backwards up and over a hill, keeping it in the correct lane as we slid along the highway. I imagine he was just what the Air Force was looking for when he showed up for officer's training and became a fighter pilot.

HOWIE

In 1985, I taught social studies and coached girls' golf at Canby High School in the small town of Canby, Oregon, south of Portland. I also had several rental properties in Oregon City, where I lived. Managing them took up some of my time but, since I had owned them for twenty years, they were easy for me to take care of.

Over the years, the properties were profitable to the extent that I accumulated a modest amount of cash. My wife, Karen, had an outstanding position working for the Morton Zulutsky law firm in downtown Portland. We were doing well financially, and it seemed like a suitable time to venture into the bar and restaurant business. I always wanted to own that type of establishment. My best friend, Howie Fritcher, with whom I played cards and golf every chance I could, was in the profession of listing and selling businesses, often to first-time owners. We knew each other from growing up in Tillamook in the 1950s.

Howie peddled smaller-type establishments such as bars, taverns, cleaners, and minute grocery stores. A few years before, he owned a bar and restaurant in Oceanlake, down on the coast. The name of the place was "Just Howie's." It did a good trade in the summer, but when winter came, it was slow. It was seasonal, like the entire Oregon Coast.

Howie sold "Just Howie's" and bought a bar in nearby Detroit, up in the Cascade Range on the highway to Central Oregon. The bar was a large log cabin-type building that had stood for years in the small town, but it mysteriously burned to the ground. Though some of the town's citizenry wanted to blame Howie for this unthinkable event, no evidence pointed to him, so the insurance company paid off the policy.

Howie took a settlement of 10,000 dollars and moved up the highway to the central part of the state near Sisters, Oregon. He landed at Black Butte Ranch, a resort near the town of Bend, and played golf for six months. He thoroughly enjoyed his insurance settlement with a carefree attitude.

Since Howie was free at the time and knew the bar and restaurant business from the ground up, it seemed like a good fit for us to go into business together. That was what I always wanted to do. We decided to be partners in a sports bar and restaurant on Burnside Street in Portland. We called it "Triples." Howie agreed to manage the place and not take a real estate sales commission on the transaction he put together. I, in turn, put up 20,000 dollars for working capital to get the bar up and running. I also paid off the previous owner with the idea I would be paid back though our future success.

I'd finally made it. I'd always wanted to own a bar, even though I knew it was demanding work to run one, meet the public, and do the books for profit. Unfortunately, it was even more work than anticipated. Our arrangement put too much pressure on Howie's shoulders and was a bit unfair. I usually dropped by the bar after teaching school all day to help as best I could, but I was little help. My lack of time and business experience were factors in our failing.

We trudged along for about a year with Howie getting increasingly more tired since he was there for long hours each day. I too started to feel the effects of teaching during the day and helping Howie during the evenings and on weekends. We tried to boost the dinner sales, which were sluggish, by advertising dinner specials. I was often frustrated with the results.

Within our first year, I also discovered something about Howie I was not aware of before. He liked to gamble, and he was not a person who put a bet on something and let it go. He was addicted to it. He sought the rush of emotion while winning or placing a bet that only these wagers brought him.

Intestinal Fortitude

I discovered the depth of his gambling issues when, one night, someone shot the front window out of our bar with multiple shots from a high-powered rifle. Howie told me the police said it was a drive-by shooting that missed the other car and blew out the window, as this type of criminal activity was a popular pastime in Portland at the time. The police were not fooled. They knew someone was communicating with Howie using deadly means to send a message. The police did an investigation of the attack on our business and were certain someone was sending a warning but ended up drafting their report as an accidental shooting.

On the inside of the dining room, we discovered bullet holes in the walls which we later filled and painted. Howie's son, who was in the glass business, replaced the large front windows. A few days later, when I was looking at our company checkbook, I noticed a check written for 6,400 dollars the day after the window was shot out. I asked Howie what the money was for, and he said it covered some business expenses. I had just paid off his gambling debt but was more concerned about his well-being. Since we were friends, I let it go and never brought it up again.

I was on a merry-go-round for more than a year with a bar not making a profit and a partner with a gambling problem. But I continued to teach and coach at Canby High School, took care of my rentals in Oregon City, and followed my children, Eric and Annie, as they played sports in school.

In all this chaos, I also ended up in the hospital for a couple of days. My heart went out of rhythm, diagnosed as arrhythmia. While I was teaching one day, my heart started palpitating with a rapid pulse, and I had shortness of breath. I was transported by ambulance to Willamette Falls Hospital in Oregon City. The problems with the bar and my busy school schedule put me over the top. I had a heart attack at fifty-six years old. It scared me into making some big decisions.

We kept Triples going for several months longer, while Howie looked for a buyer. He was able to find one quickly. Roger Johnson was interested—a friend of ours who played golf at Arrowhead Golf Course where we were all members. The ex-football player from Oregon State University became the new owner—another sports guy yearning to be in the bar business.

Howie sold the bar and restaurant for a small profit, so I did not get hurt financially from my adventure. We split the few thousand dollars with a handshake. The approximately 7,000 dollars I lost to Howie's gambling was the price of saving a friend and a friendship.

Following our sale of the bar, Howie and his wife, Annie, divorced. The business and his gambling took a toll on their marriage. The bar business provided too many opportunities to misplace one's moral compass. It was a tragic event for them, helped along by our failed attempt at entrepreneurship. Howie's union to Annie was the best thing that ever happened to him. Sadly, I do not think he ever recognized that fact. Annie was a diligent worker, smart, and pretty. She had a nice personality and loved to play golf. He had been married several times before and had children with each of them. He dated many women after the breakup with Annie, but none compared.

In the end, my first adventure into owning my own business did not end quite like I had hoped it would. I did not have the success I envisioned, but I had no hard feelings. Dreams are what a person must have during their lifetime if they want to be happy. I failed, sure, but how many people get to live out their fantasy? All those times sitting around a golf course talking about trying to get into the bar business was not a delusion that vanished into the clouds. I did it. The experience and the friends I made along the way were worth the trip. My aspiration fueled the effort to succeed, no matter how small the success was at the time. Sure, the heart attack was not pleasant, but it was part of the journey.

Following our failed business attempt, I took Howie to two U.S. Open golf tournaments at Pebble Beach Golf Course on the Monterrey Peninsula in California. We saw Tom Kite win the Open in 1992. Howie was always a great traveling partner. Brian Bailey and Tom Geinger, two other high school friends, went with us to the Open in 2000. We played cards and golf, and saw Tiger win the legendary 100th U.S. Open.

Tiger was twelve under for the tournament and won by fifteen shots as no one else was under par. His Open win was also the first leg of the "Tiger Slam" holding all four major championships in a calendar year. We felt like we were on the forefront of golf history.

Later in life, Howie would gamble for days. Like a binge drinker takes to alcohol, Howie took to gambling. Often when he came to Arizona to play golf with me, he would disappear into a casino for a couple of days and nights. The first time he disappeared, his friend Lance Oliver and I called the police and several hospitals, in fear he was in some danger. We seriously checked on his whereabouts but eventually realized that, with his addiction, he must have been gambling at a casino on the Pima Reservation near Scottsdale. From then on, we let it go.

Howie and I remained friends until his heart gave out and he died in Kent, Washington, a suburb of Seattle, about a year after we'd enjoyed our trip to Monterey. He was waiting for another needed surgery to add to his previous bypass, but his carelessness didn't allow that to happen.

Howie was fifty-nine years old at the time he died in 2001. It was too soon for him to go. We had more golf and cards to play, and many more laughs yet to uncover.

With the passing of Howie, I realized deeply I'd lost a unique companion who was a big part of my life. As time went on, I never filled the loss his death caused for me. He is missed in so many ways. I continue to learn about grief.

Rod Carrier

I worked as a rod carrier during the summer of 1954 in Northern California, following my first year at Oregon State College. Not a rod like a gun. but one seen on a surveying crew. A rod, also known as a sight level, is used by a surveyor to zero in on his target with a theodolite instrument using a rotating telescope to measure vertical and horizontal angles. The company I worked for was rechecking an earlier land surveillance in Northern California. Prior to this opportunity to work out of town, I was home in Tillamook, Oregon, where most people found work in lumber mills and on dairy farms.

The first year was a great couple of terms as I served as captain of the baseball and basketball teams. I was coached by Paul Valenti, who was my friend until he died in 2014 at the age of ninety-four. As a member of the Sigma Chi Fraternity, I fit in athletically and socially. They also leaned toward professionalism, something I wanted to know about and practice. I was growing in the right direction and gaining confidence. It was the first year of my nine-year journey to pursue an undergraduate degree, an odyssey that took me to three places of higher learning in Oregon and countless hours of classes. Besides OSC, I made stops at Oregon College of Education and Portland State College before graduating. All are universities today.

While home for the summer in 1954, I didn't know I would take a lengthy academic journey. As I've mentioned, I wasn't in any hurry to get my degree. Obtaining a degree carried the connotation of responsibility, even possible permanent employment, something I wasn't ready to do. I was going to work the rest of my life and felt fun was needed before settling down with a job and a family.

I started the summer with a job at Diamond Lumber Mill while playing baseball on the Tillamook Elk's semi-pro team but, like many other people in Oregon, I was hit with a massive surprise. When the American Federation of Labor's (AFL) workers went on strike, jobs evaporated in the lumber mills. For three months, the 1954 Timber Strike in Oregon touched a lot of people. The walkout shut down the loggers in the forests of the Coast Range and Cascade Range, as well as all the sawmills, planer mills, and truck drivers. Lumber was the leading industry in Oregon at the time, so it affected the entire economy of the state.

Summer jobs for college students were scarce or nonexistent. Out of work, with no job in sight, I caught a break when Chad Gilzean, a Sigma Chi fraternity brother from OSC, called me. He lived in Dunsmuir, a town in Northern California at the foot of Mt. Shasta. Chad had a job for me if I could get down to Dunsmuir in a day or two. I enthusiastically accepted and headed that way immediately.

He had two jobs on a surveying crew in his locality. The crew I worked on was checking the elevation data from a previous geodetic survey for the United States Department of Commerce. I spent the summer in the employment of the federal government, feeling secure because of the money. A lot of aspects about the job were good: it was interesting, and I was outdoors in unfamiliar territory that didn't rain a lot, but my paycheck was the most noteworthy. Thanks to Chad, I had a rewarding summer job, and a great feeling about it and myself.

I contacted my friend Zeke Smith about going with me. Zeke needed a summer job for college money, too. Since he had a car, he drove us to California the next day. He was always a little edgy, so our expedition had the promise of being unpredictable at times. Zeke was known around Tillamook as someone who rebelled against authority. He usually did not conform and that sounded exciting at the time.

Zeke's latest episode was a big party he threw at his parents' house when they were away. He stole all the beer and food for the party from Westwood's Market, where he worked. He hosted the entire party. Zeke thought it was a suitable time to get out of town because the market was onto him. So off to California we went on a new adventure.

We drove the 400 miles to Dunsmuir in eight hours and went to work the next morning. We were employed and able to rent a cabin in Weed, California, at the foot of Mt. Shasta. When we signed the short-term lease with the property owner, it was for something we could afford and still have some money left over for college.

The cabin butted up to a rugged rock cliff that rose straight up behind it. This cabin was rustic and an old wood structure. The motif was western shabby and needing some tender loving care by the property owner. We didn't notice the train tracks between the cabin and the cliff, the Southern Pacific main line between California and Oregon. The first night, a train came roaring through, the noise echoing and shaking the cabin so thoroughly we thought it must be shelling or bombing and we were under attack. If someone handed us a peace treaty, we would have signed it. Now we knew why the cabin was cheap.

The surveying crew was made up of three men plus Zeke and me. One was the boss who ran our team, and one carried the tripod theodolite used for the surveying. The boss looked through the instrument while the third guy recorded his findings. Zeke and I carried the foot long rods with the directional symbols on them.

The crew members were nice guys, which was important since we had to do everything with a degree of coordination and teamwork while working closely together all day. We surveyed along the Southern Pacific Railroad tracks from Lake Shasta to Weed while going around the base of the mountain. We checked the topography recorded years before to give ourselves a baseline. We determined the survey was either extremely important or a government boondoggle. I never came to any conclusive answer to that observation.

Our supervisor monitored our time from the moment we started until we finished. Since we were working in the Sierra Nevada Mountain Range and at the base of Mt. Shasta, we were working somewhere around a 3,000-foot elevation above sea level during the day. When we arrived for work at dawn next to the snowcapped peak, it was damn cold. Zeke and I couldn't pull on enough jackets to stay warm. The snow level was not far above, so a dry brisk air awaited us every morning. The numbing chilly air felt like it passed right through us.

As soon as the bright orange sun rose in the morning and popped up over the mountains to the east, it grew extremely warm, and we quickly removed our shirts. We went from freezing to sweating in seconds as the sun made the back of our necks and foreheads glisten. It always amazed me how the temperature changed so quickly. We rode to work in a long nine-passenger van with side windows. At noon, the men of the crew sat in the van and ate their lunch while Zeke and I found a tree for some shade. Lunchtime stretched out, on some days longer than others since the crew liked to play cards and drink bourbon.

Zeke and I worked in Northern California the entire summer and enjoyed the communities of Dunsmuir, Mt. Shasta, and Weed, which were just a few miles apart. We went to dances and took girls to the movies. We even tried out for the local baseball team, which didn't go well since our ability to play the game intimidated the local players. They couldn't allow themselves to be replaced by any out-of-towner unless it was Babe Ruth!

The cool fall climate began to transpire, and the local boys tired of us dating the neighborhood girls, so we left town at the end of the summer. It was time to go anyway since college was about to start. Besides, getting into a tussle with those "townies" was not on our radar.

I knew a couple of those same guys who were with me at OSC the previous year. They pulled a mean-spirited prank toward a young lady they knew from Weed, which they devised to send me a message about dating the girls of Weed while in California.

Zeke had worked out a date for himself with the prettiest girl in Weed. She, in turn, fixed me up on a movie date with them. We arranged to meet the young women in front of the New Weed Movie Theatre.

When we showed up, I saw that the gal I was paired with was unattractive and not the kind of date I looked for in school. Her face was pockmarked, and her facial structure was off-center. She was socially challenged and could put people off.

In addition to the two young women, about ten guys from Weed stood nearby, chatting a little and waiting to see the look on my face when I was introduced to my date. They stood there grinning as

I met the young woman. I was a little perplexed but paused and showed no emotion one way or another. After I saw all the guys on the sidewalk in front of the theatre trying not to laugh out loud aloud, it became obvious what was going on.

I thought the best thing to do was to act ordinary and take the girl to the movie. I beat them at their game and showed her an enjoyable time by having fun myself. After the movie, we took the girls out to our cabin and danced. As the night progressed, my date relaxed and became quite a cut-up, joking a lot and showing a humorous side to her personality. I was caught off guard by her positive attitude. It taught me a couple of lessons: don't judge a book by its cover, and don't be quick to form an opinion of someone.

It puzzled me even more when I realized the pretty girl who arranged the date for me must have been in on the prank as well. It was embarrassing, mean, and cruel to my date—and to me too.

I've never forgotten the incident and the variety of mixed feelings from that evening in front of the New Weed Movie Theatre. This life lesson on how to treat people prepared me for my college social life and was the payoff for my time in Weed.

We officially ended our employment as a bitter freezing wind came off Mt. Shasta and it snowed. We could barely hold the rod that last morning we were so numb. It was a struggle, but we finished the day and headed back to Oregon.

The rod-carrying job was a life lesson in adapting to others in a memorable and beautiful mountainous region. The experience of being on my own and making my own decisions every day gave me confidence. It was the first time I had lived and worked on my own, and it served as a valuable lesson in taking care of myself without some supervision. I was far enough from home I couldn't rely on my parents. My interactions with other people and the gamut of emotions that took place in Weed, from highs to lows, left me with an overall good feeling.

The month-long lumber strike ended in Oregon with the workers getting a small pay raise. Strikes rarely succeed to the delight of the workers, and this one wasn't any different.

I sent my checks home for safe keeping but, as it turned out, my parents spent the money for living expenses as my father was out of work due to the lumber strike. I never saw the money again. I deserved a small thank you for keeping them afloat during the strike. They acted as if I'd never really gone to California. No one asked if I enjoyed the job or my time there. I didn't mind they used the money to get through a tough time, but to act as though my job there never existed or the money wasn't for my education was disrespectful. The irretrievable paychecks put a damper on an otherwise marvelous time as a rod carrier.

When I asked about the money, my father grew upset with me. It was just one more example of his disregard for my feelings with an attitude of no concern for me. This push and pull with him and the money played out for me throughout my life. More than once, my parents spent my money to get by. At this time, he couldn't accept the fact that his youngest son had supported him. He couldn't admit to me or himself I was capable of something favorable. I believe his frustration and his harsh treatment of me as a child was coming back to him in the form of guilt. Our relationship was doomed by those beatings that took place many years before. They would always stand between us.

Since the money I sent home was spent, I returned to Tillamook broke. My baseball scholarship at OSC wouldn't cover the total cost of the school year, but I didn't stay bummed for long. I worked in the lumber mill for a year to get back to OSC and earned a basketball scholarship from Coach Gill for my future.

The main reason I attended OSC was to play basketball, even though I had a baseball scholarship. The basketball team was loaded with talented players who won the conference championship. I couldn't compete with them and make the basketball team as a sophomore. So, I stayed home to work and earn some money, and I decided to go back to OSC after the team graduated their entire squad. I made what I thought was a logical choice based on playing basketball and tackling my money problem. It made sense at the time.

My friends Jerry Bushy, Don Dental, Cliff Ebert, Jim McConnel, and a few others hung around Tillamook with me that winter, working in the re-opened lumber mills. We had an excellent group of guys. Jerry was preparing to enlist in the Army and ship out to South Korea. McConnel was still in high school. A few of the guys were recently home from the Korean War. We killed time working in a lumber mill, drinking beer, and checking out the girls all the way up the coast from Tillamook to Astoria. Of course, all work and no play, wasn't cool.

     Although I spent a year in Tillamook with a notable crew of young guys contemplating our next moves, I never lost sight of my goal of returning to OSC. In life there are obstacles you must overcome to be successful, and this was one I met with zeal.

ROGER

During the mid-1950s, I was employed at the Meier & Frank Department Store in the wintertime in downtown Portland, Oregon. Located on Broadway in the center of the city, it was a destination store when you visited Portland.

My good friend Brian Bailey, from Tillamook, Oregon, and I roomed together on Flanders Street in the Northwest part of the city up from the Columbia River. We lived just below 21st Street in a nice neighborhood filled with large stately apartment houses only a block away from Burnside, the original center of Portland. Brian also worked at Meier & Frank with me in the same high-fashion shoe department. We shared the same boss, a young sandy-haired individual who was always smiling, and we rode the same bus to work.

Our boss's name was Roger Smith, a bona fide character in the high-fashion shoe department at M&F. He wasn't a company man any more than Brian and I were dedicated M&F employees. In a manager's job he was overqualified for, Roger was bored. Brian and I weren't planning to sell shoes for a living, and retail sales wasn't our life's work—we were treading water with college in the back of our minds.

We enjoyed living in the big city, meeting some new girls, and drinking a little beer. Roger, Brian, and I became good friends—a triangle of friendship, of sorts, built on the premise that we didn't take the whole selling thing too seriously.

Brian and I lived on M&F wages of just more than forty-two dollars a week. I lost a lot of weight during my stay at this job as food wasn't a priority, but beer could be. Brian stayed with the store until fall when he returned to Oregon State College.

After Brian left, I moved to a one-room flat on Broadway, across the street from Portland State College. I lived in the Broadway flat for fifteen dollars per week and had a lot of fun on the twenty-seven-some dollars left.

My friend Howard Fritcher tended bar at the Multnomah Hotel, a few blocks from M&F. I knew I could always go by, see Howard, and get a free drink or two. There usually was some nice lady there, too, who wanted to take me home for dinner. On occasion, I accepted the invitation.

With Brian gone, Roger and I grew more tired of our jobs at M&F. After I checked in on the time clock in the morning, Roger often took me downstairs and across the street to the basement of Rich's Cigar Store. We played pool instead of selling shoes for M&F. Roger and I, as you can see, weren't dedicated to sales.

We both left M&F at their request, which wasn't a major surprise. Roger ended up traveling the country for a sizable shoe company, and I went home to Tillamook to take a job in a lumber mill.

I did go back to college for about six more years at Oregon State, then Oregon College of Education—now Western Oregon State University—and finally Portland State College. I enjoyed moving from school to school to earn a more well-rounded education.

After graduating from Portland State, I spent five years teaching geography seven periods a day, five days a week to ninth graders at Estacada High School. I used the same lesson plans from year to year and class to class, which made my teaching monotonous. Ninth graders can offer up discipline problems as much as learning problems. Eventually, my teaching assignment drove me right out of education. I often couldn't remember if I'd said something to the class the last period or five years earlier. The monotony and repetition I found maddening.

This story does come back to Roger Smith, so hang in there.

My good friend and fraternity brother Lou Zarosinski from OSC and the Sigma Chi days was working for a school textbook company,

Intestinal Fortitude

the American Book Company out of Cincinnati, Ohio. He caught wind of the fact that I was tired of teaching and wanted a change. Lou offered to set up an interview for me with his boss, Mike Worthing.

My interview was scheduled for a meeting at the Portland Airport. Mike flew up to Portland from San Francisco. We sat down at a booth in the airport cafeteria to talk about me taking a territory with American Book Company in Eastern Washington, Western Idaho, and Northwest Oregon.

While discussing salary and other conditions of the job, Mike was handed a napkin by the waitress. He opened it up and read the note inside.

A funny look immediately crossed his face. He pivoted in his seat and looked around the cafeteria for something or someone. He showed the note to me.

It read, "Fuck you."

I was a little stunned and began looking around myself.

At the cafeteria's counter, with a big grin on his face, sat Roger Smith. I had last seen him eleven years before, yet he'd sent a rough and direct note to my potential future boss.

Mike was a nice guy, to a point. He saw Roger with the big grin and realized the note was supposed to be handed to me, not to him. Even though Mike was surprised, he hired me anyway.

I haven't seen Roger Smith since. That's a good thing.

LOU ZAROSINSKI

I met Lou Zarosinski in Medford, Oregon, one summer evening in 1954 in the front room of Nancy Brown's house. When I arrived with my friend Bill Briggs, Lou was sitting on the front room sofa, talking to Nancy. I knew Lou's brothers, Don and Ed, from my just-completed first year at Oregon State College. We were fraternity brothers in the Sigma Chi house.

Don and Ed's tall and charismatic younger brother had just graduated from Klamath Falls High School in Klamath Falls, Oregon. He was heading to OSC in the fall as a first-year student. He told us he planned to pledge Sigma Chi.

Lou came to Medford to visit Nancy, who was extremely popular. She was pretty and liked boys. We knew this by her charm. Bill and I drove up from Yreka, California, a considerable distance, for Bill to see her. Then we drove back home that night. Lou made a date with Nancy for the next weekend, then said he had to drive back to Klamath Falls, about a hundred miles away. Nancy was a popular girl to glean that kind of attention.

She had to be sought after if Bill and Lou would drive more than a hundred miles each to see her. I never saw Nancy again after that night as she accepted a scholarship to Michigan State and stayed in East Lansing for her education.

Lou and I became good friends since we both had an interest in real estate. Also, Lou later lived in Oregon's Canby School District, where I taught at the high school. All of Lou's children took U.S. history from me as they went through Canby High. Aaron, Alison, and Caan were all diligent students and great kids.

In 1970, in Oregon City, Lou encouraged me to get started investing in real estate. He helped me see the benefits of owning rental property and the advantages of having someone else help you pay for your investment. He explained the advantages to me of a tax write-off when you own the property and rent it out, and the money you earn when you collect the rent.

Lou helped me with advice in buying my first rental. He assessed the value of the property and gave his insight. He answered a lot of questions for me over the years about real estate. By introducing me to the rental business, Lou played a key role in my family's prosperity.

He had an impact on me, my family, and our revenue stream for a period of thirty years.

We stayed lifelong friends. He later helped me attain a sales position with American Book Company when I needed a break from teaching, another story in another chapter. I will always be grateful for his friendship and good advice.

Lou and 13,000 Dollars

One day, I needed 13,000 dollars in a big hurry. I was late on a "balloon" payment on one of my properties and about to be sued. I didn't have that kind of cash, and loans were not only hard to get but expensive as well. I called my real estate advisor, Lou, for some advice.

He came by my house, picked me up, and drove us about fifteen miles toward Molalla, out into the farmland near Arrowhead Golf Course. We made a few turns and then went down a narrow gravel road, full of potholes, and stopped at a trailer house. The trailer looked greenish because of the damp moss and algae growing on its roof and walls. The moss was partly covered with old leaves and fir boughs fallen from the spruce trees overhead. The trees and brush were about ready to overtake it.

The two of us exited the car and approached the trailer, though Lou still had not given me an explanation. He knocked hard on the trailer's door. When an old man opened the door, Lou said simply, "This is Earl. He needs thirteen thousand dollars."

The man in the trailer looked like he was about seventy, short, with a bald head except for a patch of hair in the back. I wondered if he might have worn the same blue crew neck sweater every day.

He smiled, nodded, said, "Fine," and walked back into his trailer only to return with a check for the amount requested.

I signed a note for the money, agreed to the repayment-in-full date, and we left.

I was amazed. I'd just met this man, and he'd given me 13,000 dollars without any questions asked, only on Lou's word. I never found out how Lou knew this man. He didn't like to divulge all his secrets.

At the time, the 1980s, in the United States, interest rates had risen to eighteen percent. As I recall, the man with the money didn't charge me the highest rate and gave me plenty of time to pay it back.

To produce a quick infusion of a lot of money, Lou knew where to go. That was Lou. He'd help you if he could and helped me more times than I can remember. He was a faithful friend.

LOU AND THE DUMP

In approximately 1974, I looked at an old two-story house to buy in Oregon City, Oregon. My friend Lou Zarosinski took one look at the place and said, "This is a gold mine. Buy it."

It didn't look like a gold mine. In fact, it looked like anything but to me. But, with Lou's urging, I purchased the place with the idea of turning it into a rental property. Lou, who also had rental property, was all for it. He wholeheartedly encouraged me to make the buy.

I was skeptical of this house at first because of the condition it was in—not good. The Municipality of Oregon City had condemned it since it was practically abandoned. The front door was nowhere to be found. Hippies and hobos used it for a crash pad stopover when traveling through town. They never picked up after themselves.

The house was filthy and filled with outmoded stoves and refrigerators, which didn't work, and numerous old broken tables and chairs. There were enough old car tires lying around to fill a dump truck. I hired the man across the street who owned a dump truck to take the junk to the landfill. I carted the stuff down the hill in front of the house to his truck, filling the bed to the top, twice.

The toilets of course didn't work because the water was shut off, but that didn't stop the hippies and the hobos from using them. The odor was unmistakably dreadful. Since the toilets were out of commission, the tenants eventually started using the closets as toilets. Remember, though, Lou labeled the house a gold mine, and I believed him.

The railroad tracks of the Southern Pacific Railroad passed by often, so it was a handy layover for any bum on the road without a place to stay. The noise from those trains arrested your concentration from whatever you were thinking.

Every window was broken out or cracked. I became an expert glazier by the time I fixed all the new panes. Just for starters, I went through a gallon of putty in two days.

The place earned a name from the viewpoints of my son, Eric, and my daughter, Ann. Upon seeing it up close for the first time, they named it "The Dump." In the beginning, I will admit, the building took on the name. The horrendous condition of the property when people were using it for a stopover made the name seem perfect. Even though I would bring the house back to life, the name stuck.

As I neared the end of the exhaustive cleanup, I started to see why Lou was so excited about me buying the place. It was still a sturdy two-story building solidly built in the early 1930s that featured a large porch that ran across the front of the house. Though not the Taj Mahal, The Dump was rented continually for the next thirty-five years.

The renters weren't members of the middle class. Some were just off the street, trying to get their lives in order. They were living in their car and had just found work. All were below the poverty line. Some were out of work, getting housing aid from the county. Most were good people struggling to make a go of it each day.

I leased The Dump for a small move-in fee and kept the price low. I had a soft heart for a sad story, and I believed them when it came time for the rent to be paid and they didn't have it. My wife, Karen, on the other hand, was always telling me to raise the cost or to evict someone late on their payment. She didn't understand the advantages of this property or the fact that no one called me to come immediately to take care of some repair. My tenants did not want to upset the good deal they had with me on the low price for lodging.

Intestinal Fortitude

I always fixed everything that needed attention but was busy teaching and coaching at Canby High School, which took up a lot of my time and was in another town more than thirty minutes away. Eventually we purchased other properties. They needed to be taken care of, too, and none of them were easy. So sometimes it took me a little time to get back to The Dump, but no one complained.

Sometimes a renter sublet a room to someone who was homeless or down on their luck, unbeknownst to me. One time, a renter had fifteen people living in the upstairs unit. Of course, when I discovered that, I reminded my tenant, nicely, of the occupancy rules of our agreement on the unit.

When I bought the property, I paid 6,400 dollars. I went immediately to a savings and loan and obtained a mortgage against the property for fifteen thousand dollars, which included funds to fix it up. I put 8,000 dollars into the property and took the remaining seven thousand to make a down payment on another property. Nobody at the lending institution checked up on me.

The city had condemned the property at the time of purchase, mostly because the water line to the house from the street did not hold water. Not a good thing for a water line. So, I hired one of my students at Canby High School to help me dig a trench to install a new water line. I bought a meter from OC Waterworks Department and installed it at the street. With a few repairs to the house, the OC Inspection Department relented on their condemnation decree. Putting a front door on the place and fixing all the broken windows might have also had something to do with their decision.

I worked on The Dump a lot, always fixing it up so it was livable. It was also fun to try and do some overhaul I hadn't done before. The Dump was an adventure. I painted it tan a couple of times, put a new roof on it, and fixed the stairs leading up to the front porch. I proudly did all the repairs myself.

Electrical work was one skill I didn't possess. One day, I caused fire to shoot out of the fuse box and had to turn off the switch with a broom handle. That day marked the end of any more of my electrical experiments.

Even though I didn't have great skills while doing the restorations, the place looked good in the end. It showed well from the street at time of inspection and the roof didn't leak.

After owning the building for decades, I practically knew every board and nail in the house. After painting the entire house—inside and out—a couple of times, roofing it, working on the water supply, and taking care of myriad repairs, I understood that house. I could walk the place blindfolded.

The greatest thing about The Dump was writing off the property on my income taxes. We generated a good profit from my teaching and coaching and from Karen's salary managing the law office in Portland. Without the write-off from the work done on The Dump each year, the Internal Revenue Service would have hit us hard. So, it was truly a star asset at tax time.

My tenants included good people living paycheck to paycheck. One woman stayed twelve years, so the place wasn't a revolving door with renters coming and going. I met a lot of interesting people because everyone had a story. I enjoyed learning about these people's interesting lives, which many times surprised me.

I sold the property once to two men, in the 1980s, for 50,000 dollars. They wanted to get into the rental business, and I wanted to invest elsewhere. They liked to work on houses and turned the house into a duplex, along with repairing the wiring. They came to me with a contract offer, which I immediately showed to Lou.

He said, "Sign it as soon as you can."

The two new owners of The Dump wrote the contract themselves, and I "carried the paper" by acting as the bank. Unbelievably, their monthly payment called for sixteen cents to be applied to the principal and the remaining money was all interest. This was an amazing transaction for "the bank" in the world of real estate.

They kept the property for two years while continuing to make improvements. Then they gave it back to me for assorted reasons. I paid the two years of back taxes they'd somehow overlooked and instantly had The Dump back in my possession. I rented it out to various people for quite a few more years, then sold it for 105,000 dollars. I "carried the paper and became the bank" on that sale, too, for a few more years before being cashed out for a nice profit.

I had Lou to thank. He was right. That old house was a gold mine. In some ways, it was hard to let it go, but I made money off it for almost forty years.

My real estate mentor was a great friend to me and everyone else. Whoever said about Will Rogers, "He never met a man he didn't like," could have also had Lou in mind.

Lou, Mike, and Joe

After graduating from Portland State University, while teaching those seven monotonous geography classes every day, five days a week, I was also coaching junior varsity basketball. Our win-loss record usually weighted on the loss side of the ledger. I was having a challenging time looking at teaching as a lifetime endeavor. It frustrated me at every turn.

My wife Karen ran into my old friend and OSC Sigma Chi fraternity brother Lou Zarosinski. Lou taught school for a few years, then gave it up to sell textbooks for American Book Company. She and Lou talked a bit that day and he spoke of an available sales job with his company, a territory in Washington, Oregon, and Idaho.

Karen told Lou I was tired of my teaching assignment at Estacada High School. Their meeting transformed my life from a teacher to a traveling textbook salesman. Quite an adjustment for me coming from the classroom, with its rigid bell system, to almost total freedom of movement.

First though, I had to be hired by the Western sales manager of American Book Company, Mike Worthing, Lou's boss in San Francisco. Mike had been a minister in Maryland before becoming a sales manager. I don't know if being a minister helps selling textbooks or not, but Mike knew the business. The interview went well, and I accepted the position.

Intestinal Fortitude

Mike gave me a company station wagon, an expense account of 300 dollars a month and a salary of 1,000 dollars per month. I quit teaching at Christmas, and Karen and I—with our children, Tony, Eric, and Annie—moved to Spokane, Washington. That salary was great in 1965 for someone thirty-five years old. Plus, the city of Spokane proved a beautiful and inexpensive place to live.

The job of traveling in Washington, Oregon, and Idaho was a lot of fun at first. Seeing new and beautiful country, meeting a lot of teachers and administrators, was exciting. I also had an extremely popular elementary school English series of books to sell. To any salesman making sales, that life was sound. School principals were calling me to come and make a sales pitch about my books. I was in a good place.

The problem was I traveled every week because of such a large territory. I was never home enough in Spokane. I enjoyed traveling in a beautiful part of the country but sleeping in motels and hotels every night became old and lonely. My children were young and growing up without me.

I thanked Mike for all he had done for me and headed back to Oregon. In those short two years, I traveled to sales conferences in Texas, Ohio, and California. I learned a lot about managing a territory while traveling and meeting people. I grew up a little, and the job gave me a lot of confidence.

Lou did me a huge favor and I was always indebted to him for it. Years later, when I moved back to Oregon City, Lou introduced me to the apartment rental business. In doing so, he changed my life once again.

Upon my return to Oregon, I went from selling textbooks and traveling in the wide-open spaces of Eastern Washington, Oregon, and Western Idaho to managing a golf course in Vernonia, Oregon. I went from motels every night, eating out, and driving many miles to working at the golf course and being at home with my family. It was a substantial change and a nice one.

All was good with the golf course except for one important aspect. The course was only nine holes. It was far from a population center and didn't make enough profit to sustain our family. I remained at the golf course for almost two years, then called Mike Worthing in

San Francisco. I learned of the Los Angeles territory opening from my old friend Lou. Mike needed a representative to work in the California social studies adoption.

Every five years, the state acquires all the available textbooks pertaining to social studies and decides which one the California schools can use. Being picked number one was worth a lot of money to a book company. I was hired to make presentations to the selection delegation.

Mike hired me again and I left to sell textbooks to the Californians. I received a nice salary, expense account, and a new car. We lived in sunny southern California, and all looked good until a glitch in the scheme of things became known.

We moved to California, bought a house in the San Fernando Valley, and were looking forward to our latest adventure. But the State Department of Education in California called off the social studies adoption program. Exactly what I had come to California to promote was no longer a reality.

I quickly faced the uphill battle of trying to sell books to individual school districts who received their books from the state for free. It was a ridiculous situation. Schools weren't buying books, so I was doing public relations work for my company. It didn't take long for me to get bored in such a dead-end situation.

I took a second job working in new home construction and earned two salaries because I didn't give up the job with American Book. I worked a lot of hours trying to keep up with both jobs. My plan was to save up enough money to move the family back to Oregon. It didn't take me long to put together the funds for the move.

California wasn't the ideal place for my children to attend school. My son Tony was verbally abused during his junior high school years, and I didn't like the future arrangement for Eric and Ann. They were about to enter school for the first time.

Life in the Los Angeles area was an adventure. I'd always wanted to go there and see it for myself. I would later miss the Dodgers' baseball games, USC and UCLA football, the Lakers, and the beach at Santa Monica. But my roots grew in Oregon.

After accumulating enough money for the move, I got a bit lucky, or was it serendipitous? Another book company, Laidlaw Brothers of Chicago, hired me to take over their Oregon territory. I was able to move back to Oregon on their dime and buy a house in Oregon City using the extra money I had accumulated as a down payment.

Mike Worthing understood my boredom with the California situation and wished me well. In Oregon, I went to work on the social studies adoption which I considered a little more than ironic.

In about four and a half years' time, I moved our family to Spokane, Washington; Vernonia, Oregon; Los Angeles, California; and back to Oregon City. We moved so many times and so quickly that my son Eric, at six years old, uttered his notable line.

As we drove past a U-Haul truck in Encino, California, he said, "Dad, let's get a truck and move today."

His comment summed up our family's last four years. His words also really hit home and woke me up to the fact that we, indeed, had been moving far too often.

I stayed with Laidlaw Brothers in Oregon for several years, selling textbooks to high schools until being on the road and away from home and my family took its toll on me again. My children Ann and Eric were in fourth and fifth grade and had started playing sports when I decided to separate from the book business for good. I missed my children's games, something I couldn't fathom.

I had not been out of work long when my acquaintance Dick Brown, principal of Canby High School, called and offered me a teaching position and coaching opportunity. I was able to still live in Oregon City and drive the short distance south to work in Canby. I settled into a great life again, teaching, coaching, and watching my children grow up.

After settling back in Oregon, I joined a golf club near Molalla, Oregon, named Arrowhead, with my good friend Lou. The owner of the course and its pro was a friend of both Lou and me and a great guy named Joe Clarizio.

A few years after Lou and I joined Arrowhead, Joe and his wife, Jean, took a trip back East to see Washington, D.C. While traveling through Maryland, they stopped for the night at a motel across the street from a small nine-hole golf course. Joe decided to go over and play the course. Since he was alone, he asked the person behind the counter of the golf shop if anyone was around who would want to play with him.

Earl Llewellyn Goldmann

The person at the counter pointed to a man in the lunchroom who said he would like to play, and off they went. They, of course, got to talking and Joe said he was from Oregon. He asked his playing partner if he knew anyone in Oregon.

The player replied, "I know two people in Oregon, Lou Zarosinski and Earl Goldmann."

Joe of course was dumbfounded by the man's replay. His playing partner that morning was Mike Worthing, our old boss from American Book Company days. What were the odds of such a chance meeting? Joe could hardly wait to get back to Oregon and tell Lou and me what had taken place in far off Maryland.

DEER HUNTING

I worked for the Goff Brothers Roofing Company in Tillamook, Oregon, during the summer of 1960. To the Goff brothers, Clyde and Glenn, and me, the idea of work was sometimes an illusion. We looked like we were going to seriously engage in some degree of work by making a lunch and getting into the company truck, but we rarely followed through.

Once our crew settled in the truck, the conversation turned to other topics unrelated to work. It didn't matter who mentioned an alternate activity, all the side steps were discussed, scrutinized, and considered. The first consideration was looking out the window of the truck to see if it was raining or if it looked like rain.

Clam digging was Glenn's first choice. He hurriedly looked in the tide book to see if the day's tide fit into our schedule. Sometimes he returned this information back to the glove box, dejected that we had missed a good clamming tide. Golf was always a backup because it could be played rain or shine. If nothing caught our fancy, there was always a liquor store nearby to purchase a bottle of bourbon. These choices came around often.

One fall day, we came across another work-free endeavor that received a unanimous commitment from the crew. The decision from the cab of the company truck was given a resounding vote with a rousing, "Let's go hunting." We soon realized it was the first day of deer season.

I encountered a problem with deer hunting. To do the activity, I needed a gun and a red flannel shirt, neither of which I owned. Clyde and Glenn were avid hunters and owned all the gear a huntsman needed. Clyde came to my rescue. He had a son about my size and had bought him all the deer hunting gear required. His son never shot the gun nor wore the red shirt. Both were new.

So off we went, the three of us, up into the Coastal Range on Highway 6 along the Wilson River. As we neared the Jordan Inn, featuring a bar and restaurant, we left the highway to head north over the Wilson River and into the mountains. We drove the logging roads for a while but didn't see any deer. We decided to park the truck and hunt on foot along a slope below the road.

Clyde and Glenn were below me and I was on the top of the ridge. They were tracking in the brush of an old logging site. Sure enough, as they had thought, it was a good spot to flush out a deer. A buck snuck out to a spot behind them, and turned right toward me, without seeing me standing still on the top of the ridge. As this incredible creature came up the hill toward me, he jumped over an old log. To my amazement, I shot him in the chest while he was in flight.

I didn't like to kill animals, but had just shot a nice-sized buck, a beautiful animal. Thinking I'm a great hunter, I felt a little proud of myself. Yet I was sad the animal was dead. I was confused by my mixed emotions.

I had just shot my first deer, so Clyde and Glenn were excited for me. They didn't know it, but it was to be my last. I never went deer hunting again.

Betty

The brothers wanted to play a joke on Clyde's wife, Betty. When we arrived back at Clyde's house, he parked the truck so she couldn't see the deer in the Ford pickup's bed. While they gutted the dead animal, they cut off its testicles. The scene was bizarre. I wasn't too sure I enjoyed killing a deer in the first place. Then they castrated the beautiful creature and handed the cut over to me. I wondered if it was a ritual that took place when you shot your first deer.

Intestinal Fortitude

My friends instructed me to hold the animal's balls for Betty to see as she came out of the house and say we hadn't brought down a deer but came close and only shot its balls off. The point of the humor was based on her knowing what was in my hand, but she didn't have a clue what I was doing or what I held. The joke bombed.

Even if Betty wasn't sure what was so funny, Glenn and Clyde still had their laugh. I explained the whole thing to her, but she still didn't get the humor of her husband's prank. I'm sure, to this day, she thought I really shot the balls off a deer. You must be an actual deer hunter to get "deer season" humor.

How unique. I downed a deer in flight with one shot, the first and only time I hunted. Glenn and Clyde were good guys and wonderful people. I appreciated their friendship even when I questioned their thinking and actions.

SAN FRANCISCO AND PEBBLE BEACH

At the end of the summer of 1955, Bob Stevens, Brian Bailey, and I decided to go to California. We were wide-eyed and young, not yet twenty-one years of age, and had experienced truly little of life outside of Tillamook. We wanted to go experience something new before enrolling for the fall term in school at Oregon State College in Corvallis, Oregon.

We worked during the summer at a lumber mill job in Tillamook and accumulated some money for college. We decided we could afford a trip to San Francisco to see the famous city and continue to the beautiful Monterey Peninsula. Our goal involved playing golf at the celebrated Pebble Beach Golf Course before we started classes.

Pebble Beach opened in February of 1919. It has hosted six U.S. Opens in the last fifty years. The first major played there was the 1929 U.S. Amateur. In the early years of golf, the American and British Amateur Championships were considered "majors." Bobby Jones was a medalist in 1929, and his celebrity helped open the eyes of golfers across the country. The combination of a true test of golf and the stunning beauty of the course along the Pacific Coastline beckoned golfers and tourists alike.

Pebble Beach was a well-known and intimidating course to play even in 1955, a superior choice for golfers from around the world. People voted the course as America's first-rate option in the

Intestinal Fortitude

western United States, and serious golfers considered it a stunning must-play course.

Before we left for California, some of the golfers at Alderbrook Golf Course, our home course, and Babe True, the owner, told us we were foolish to pay five dollars to play Pebble Beach, which was our game plan. At that price, a lot of money in 1955, it was the most expensive public course in the western United States. Even back then, Pebble Beach commanded a high price for green fees. Today, the price for a round of golf there is close to 550 dollars for eighteen holes, still one of the most expensive courses to play in the West.

At the time, we paid seventy-five cents to play at the Alderbrook Golf Course in Tillamook. We paid a dollar and twenty-five cents at Alderbrook to play all day and did that often. Hence, the reason the local golfers at Alderbrook gave us such a tough time about the excessive cost of the green fees at Pebble Beach.

Tom Baily, Brian's dad, gave us money for gasoline, and we were off on our great adventure. Brian's brother, Ron, had a new 1954 white Ford coupe, compliments of his dad, the mayor of Tillamook, who owned the Ford dealership in town. Ron loaned us his car to make the trip.

What breathtaking sights we took in as we arrived in San Francisco. The City on the Hill, the Golden Gate Bridge, the cable cars, Kezar Stadium where the 49ers played football, and Union Square... with palm trees no less. When I saw those landmarks for the first time, I knew for sure I was a long way from Tillamook. It was like driving through a foreign country.

When I think of San Francisco, Union Square still comes to mind. I smile to myself and think back to a time when life was simpler, easygoing, and carefree. Life is never that uncomplicated, of course, but I was young and thrilled to be in the City by the Bay. I went back to Union Square many times over the years and remember fondly the exciting first time I visited there in 1955.

We checked into an amazing hotel, the Handlery, located in Union Square. We paid fifteen dollars for our room... living large. Dinner was near our hotel at Bob's Steakhouse on Bush Street. It was, according to our bellman at the hotel, the "hot spot" in San Francisco, and he highly recommended dining there. We had filet mignon steaks for five dollars. You could cut them with a fork.

We met Bob the owner, a nice guy who introduced himself immediately and began chatting with us. He knew early in the conversation we were from the hinterland by our eager demands. We were a long way out of Oregon, and it showed by our rousing exchange about the golf seen and anticipated. We did not care. We were having fun in the Golden Gate City.

The walls in Bob's restaurant were covered with large, signed photos of all our favorite Hollywood movie stars. They were faked by him and signed by anybody for effect, but we did not care. We were impressed, whether Bob knew them all or not. We paid close attention to him, mesmerized, as he told stories about each star. If the truth be known, we had come to San Fran to meet someone like Bob—a larger-than-life character not like anyone we knew in Oregon. He was just a part of the greater scene of being young and in San Francisco that summer in 1955. It was terrific.

The next morning, Bob, Brian, and I left San Francisco and traveled south to the Monterrey Peninsula by way of Santa Cruz. We traveled with eyes wide open along Monterey Bay, the Ford Ord Army Base—now closed—past Seaside, and into scenic Monterrey.

Historical Monterey is one of the oldest cities in California. The Spanish first settled there, and it became part of the United States in 1846 following the Mexican-American War and the signing of the Treaty of Guadalupe Hildalgo. Their constitution was written in Monterrey in 1849, the same year the California Gold Rush started. It became America's thirty-first state in 1850. Monterey played a key role in the Golden State's early history. We came to enjoy playing golf, not only at Pebble Beach, but at the seat of the state's initial birth.

Back on that memorable morning, we drove through town, past the famous Monterey Aquarium, to Pacific Grove, and pulled into Borg's Motel. We stayed a short distance from the north entrance to Seventeen Mile Drive. This picturesque ride took us to the Pebble Beach Golf Course and the quaint town of Carmel. The drive was not only breathtaking, but one of the most well-known roads in California and beyond. The Monterey Peninsula also has another small town, Big Sur.

Intestinal Fortitude

Our motel room, located on the Pacific Ocean, presented an impressive view of the rugged coastline. We played golf on the pretty Pacific Grove Public Golf Course the next day. The course lay near the ocean shore and was known as the "Poor Man's Pebble Beach." It is called that because of its distinct location, though the green fees were very reasonable. It was a city course where a lot of local golfers played. We golfed it in preparation for our big challenge, the arduous course we came to conquer.

In no way could amateurs such as us prepare for a course as incredible as Pebble Beach. The degree of difficulty, such as deep traps, high rough, and lengthy holes created challenges. The wind blowing in off the Pacific Ocean from different directions on various holes was unbelievable. These encounters made the course for me just shy of falling into the "monster" category.

There was also a mental force working against a golfer of my ability, especially traveling the distance we did, in playing this type of course. It settles in your head. I remembered the barbs from the golfers back home at Alderbrook referring to my foolishness as beyond the realm of reason. As I thought about the course so much, it became bigger and harder by the hour. Pebble Beach occupied my mind, or at least lurked just under the surface, waiting for me around the clock.

By the time I finally walked up on that first tee at Pebble Beach and attempted to hit a proper shot, I could hardly take a back swing with my club. I reached down deep into my character to find out what I was made of and tried to get my head on straight. I remember once I was off the first hole with a shaky tee shot, I overcame the intimidation of the course. When I hit a decent three wood to the first green, I knew not to get too anxious. I had seventeen more holes to go.

Much of the enjoyment of playing Pebble Beach Golf Course was the spectacular vistas seen when walking along the rugged coastline of the Monterey Peninsula. I recalled standing and gazing at the enchantment of the coastline and golf course, looking south toward the towns of Carmel and Big Sur and beyond, and thinking how marvelous it was to be in this special place on Earth. From the first time I saw the Monterey Peninsula, it has always felt like a place

I belonged. The salt sea air, the pine trees, and the old Spanish City were inspiring and relaxing at the same time.

When we headed out on the course at Pebble Beach, a light breeze blew in off the ocean in typical seaside fashion. It reminded me of Alderbrook golf and the Oregon Coast, and playing golf at home in Tillamook, Seaside, and Astoria. We were familiar with a breezy afternoon wind. One of the biggest challenges there for us was the high thick rough—in several spots, we visited these too often. The adverse conditions and deep foliage prevented us from hitting a solid shot.

I found playing Pebble Beach painfully fun. Though a struggle, but I can remember enjoying the fun of being there with Bob and Brian. It was also satisfying to know we were golfing on the storied Pebble Beach Golf Course and achieving something few young guys our age back in Oregon had accomplished. We were at the most prestigious golf course in the West, and no golfer at Alderbrook Golf Course had even attempted it. Pebble Beach was unique in many respects with a combination of difficulty and beauty. We walked the course and carried our bags. Real golfers did not take a cart.

I remember making par on just one hole of the eighteen. It was the ninth along the ocean, going south toward Carmel. I managed to stay out of the rough with my tee shot, hit a fairway wood to the green, and two-putted for a par of four. I'll never forget that one. The ocean crashing on the rocks a few feet away added the perfect touch to my only par.

By the time we started making the turn near the town of Carmel and proceeded to come back toward the clubhouse on twelve, we were growing a little tired from walking the course's sizeable 6,828-foot length. It took us more than four hours. At Pebble Beach, the ninth hole was about as far away from the clubhouse as you can get. Most golf courses are laid out so the ninth hole returns to the clubhouse. Not so at Pebble Beach.

The holes that parallel Seventeen Mile Drive were long and problematic because of the small greens. Not to say the other holes on the golf course were easy.

Brian started hooking his shots to the left and couldn't stop. He "snap hooked" his tee shot very quickly on the par-three twelfth hole to his left. That means the ball flew toward the adjacent green of the eleventh hole. It continued to roll between the legs of a woman golfer on the green as she putted. Brian apologized to her, and she took the incident in good spirit.

Despite the disruption of her golf game, she gave Brian his ball back. On the one hand, we were playing the most celebrated golf course on the West Coast while, on the other, Brian hit a most embarrassing shot. That scenario would not soon be duplicated by any golfer in the world since we all try to avoid doing anything that resembles that shot.

Brian grew frustrated with his game and the golf course. He had enough golf by the fifteenth hole. He decided to walk back to the clubhouse and not finish the round. As Brian strode over to Seventeen Mile Drive, he marched across the front of the fifteenth tee just as another foursome began teeing off. The golfer who was ready to hit his drive stood frozen in disbelief as Brian hiked in front of him. Brian was so upset he either didn't see the golfer or didn't care.

The guy, exacerbated as Brian passed in front of him, said to his playing partners, "I can't believe it. I'm playing a bet for five dollars per hole and some guy walks right in from of me as I'm trying to hit the ball."

Brian, obviously distraught with his game, just kept walking. He stepped over a fence, jumped the ditch, and strode up onto Seventeen Mile Drive. Carrying his golf clubs on his shoulder, he continued hiking back to the clubhouse. Golf can be a humbling game but, even more so, a maddening one.

Bob and I finished our round at the famed par-five eighteenth hole. We found Brian sitting in the sun at the clubhouse with a smile on his face as he drank a cola. The sun shone brightly, and a light breeze still blew in off the ocean.

I had just played Pebble Beach. I was elated when I walked off the eighteenth green and knew I would never forget this occasion. Life was good in the summer of 1955 on the Monterey Peninsula.

We told Brian we were sorry he'd encountered the "snap hooks" and couldn't finish his round of golf. Brian just wanted to forget about it, so the topic was dropped from further conversation.

The next morning, we headed north to Oregon to our classes at Oregon State College. On our way home, we traveled on the old Golden State Highway, U.S. Route 99, which was used before Interstate 5 was built. To save time, we took the "winter's" cutoff, north of Vacaville, that bypassed Sacramento.

We bought a case of beer in Red Bluff, and I drove. After a couple of beers, Brian, from the back seat, said he wanted to stop so he could urinate. Just to hassle him, Bob said we weren't stopping. We needed to get home on time, and it was a long drive. Brian decided, since we were going straight through, he would urinate into an empty beer bottle. He had to be extra accurate and careful because of the small opening of the bottle. While driving, I turned around and pushed Brian with my right hand so he would urinate on himself while attempting to fill the bottle. As the jokester, I thought it seemed like a funny trick to pull to snap our friend out of his grumpy mood.

I wasn't watching the highway closely enough as we came to a right curve in the otherwise straight highway. I looked back at the road as we were crossing the other lane of the two-lane highway filled with traffic. At high speed, we crossed in front of a big semi-truck.

With the truck's large grill staring us in the face, we heard a loud air horn blast. I spun the steering wheel to the right which put the car into a spin. We slid across the highway, turning around once. What a bizarre sensation to see the hood ornament seemingly circling around you. It felt like a high-speed fairgrounds ride that you couldn't get off.

We missed the truck, spun out of control, and hit a gravel area next to the highway while sliding to a stop. I was lucky. I avoided the oncoming truck and another car behind it. Our car did not flip over. Instead, it had stayed upright, skidding to a stop in the large gravel space. Fortunately, that was the right place for us to find refuge. The experience was enough to make us believe someone was watching over us. We had looked squarely at death and knew it but somehow escaped.

In apprehensive voices, Bob and Brian blurted out how we had come so close to a smash-up, noticeably marked with a little agitation about my driving.

As I vacated the car, my knees wobbled. I stood by the car and shivered, trying to comprehend what had just taken place. As the car

Intestinal Fortitude

had rotated on the hard concrete surface of the highway, it had ground the left rear tire to shreds and filed off a portion of the tire rim. I inspected the lacerated tire's alarming condition. As I changed the tire, I felt fortunate and lucky at the same time.

We decided Brian should take a turn at the wheel as my capability, if not challenged, was in serious question. With his pants drying, he carefully drove back into traffic on U.S. Route 99. We drove in silence for a few miles as we headed north once again to Oregon, until we passed Dunsmuir, California, at the foot of Mt. Shasta. The three of us relaxed more then and the conversation started to emerge again about golf and all the fun we had over those days in Monterey. With 400 more miles to go, we realized we needed to settle down and enjoy the drive.

I felt a lot of uneasiness the rest of the way home, as if I were on a cloud suspended in space. I still heard the loud air horn of that huge semi-truck. It had profoundly frightened me. I concentrated on remembering the fun of the trip to calm my nerves.

Eventually, Brian pulled the car into my driveway back in Tillamook after our one-week adventure. We had seen new sights and fresh territory for the first time and enjoyed it together as friends. And we avoided a fatal accident!

When I sat down to dinner that night, my father said to me, "I bet you don't have one dime left!"

I reached into my pocket, pulled out a solitary coin, and laid it on the table next to my dinner plate. It was a dime. I came home with a ten-cent piece after my week-long trip to California. I do not recall what point my father was trying to make, if any, but that remaining dime surprised me as much as it did him.

With one hundred dollars in my pocket when I left Tillamook for the one-week trip to California, I figured it was enough money to make the journey. One hundred dollars went a long way in 1955. Times have changed a lot since then, especially the influence of inflation on the dollar. It would cost a *lot* more to go to California today, spend a week, and have the amazing time Bob, Brian, and I had. Our one-night stay in downtown San Francisco in Union Square, the filet mignon meal at Bob's Steakhouse, and our travel to Monterey

Peninsula to play golf amounted to the best one hundred dollars I ever spent. Our safe arrival home made it all worth it.

Thirty years later, with my friend Howard Fritcher, I attended the 1992 US Open at Pebble Beach. Tom Kite won the tournament, shooting even par on the final round on Sunday in a windstorm. Howie and I about froze not death, as well as being bothered by the wind, as we watched from the bleachers at the eighteenth hole.

By coincidence, we met the celebrated golf pro John Daly in a local establishment. He had missed the cut and was ready to party. He took us out on the town in Monterrey and paid for all the merry making. It was a night I would never forget.

Howie and I returned eight years later in 2000 to see Tiger Woods win the Open by fifteen strokes, with a record twelve under. The 2000 win was the one hundredth anniversary of the tournament. My friends Brian Baily also returned in 2000 along with Tom Geinger. The trips to Pebble Beach and the Open were filled with golf, fun, cardplaying, and partying with my good friends from Tillamook.

I've been back to San Francisco and the Monterey Peninsula multiple times since my infamous 1955 trip with Bob and Brian, and each time I return, I still feel the same exhilaration.

Years later, Brian was the best man in my first wedding. He lives today in Milwaukie, Oregon, and still plays golf three times a week. Bob is in Atlanta, Georgia, confined to a home for those with dementia. I no longer play golf but follow it closely and am blessed with good health. We are all eighty-seven years young.

ALCOHOL AND DEPRESSION

Even though several people have tried, no one has yet
found a way to drink for a living.

Jean Kerr,
Irish American author and playwright

INTRODUCTION TO ALCOHOL

When I first started drinking beer with my friends during high school in Tillamook, I discovered something astonishing. Alcohol altered the way I felt and thought before a conversation took place.

Before the age of fifteen, I never drank or used a drug. When I started, alcohol gave me confidence and a feeling of being faster and funnier. I felt included and part of the group. Other people liked me. I attributed these feelings to alcohol. I loved it.

Drinking was "sensual" for me: the taste of the first beer, the aroma that came after the cap clicking off the bottle, the shape of the cold bottle in my hand, the coolness of the beer going down my throat. It all exhilarated me when opening a new can of beer.

The entire picture of drinking enticed me. It was an environment I wanted to be part of throughout my life. For me, drinking was associated with friendships, camaraderie, and fun.

From the time I drank my first beer at age fifteen to consuming my last cocktail at age sixty-five, my odyssey with alcohol was a love-hate relationship. My life was challenged by people, places, things, and alcohol. Drinking played a substantial role in my life. The perils of my alcohol use are well documented. While alcohol's virtue was misconstrued as okay, it was damning on the other hand. I advocated the understanding that alcohol is better until it is worse.

ALCOHOL

After teaching four and a half years at the high school in Estacada, Oregon, I left for the new adventure in Spokane, Washington. At this point in my life, my alcohol intake meant a few beers on Friday nights at a teachers' get-together following football games, and drinks at my in-laws' house on the weekends. Since my mother-in-law was a bona fide alcoholic, according to me, the drinks flowed when she invited us to join her. My intake of alcohol escalated exceedingly. It wasn't long before alcohol took on a more significant role in my life.

Then I found the job with the American Book Company (ABC) textbooks as a traveling salesperson. Spokane was the largest city in my territory and my home base. The move was also the first of our family's four moves in five years to three different states.

ABC expected me to be highly organized and take initiative. That was one reason Mike Worthing, my manager, hired guys like me from the coaching ranks for sales in the book business. Work was always a priority to me. My parents had taught me to respect my superiors and the job I was involved with at the time. I was to show up on time and work a full shift—well, except for that roofing job.

A company car and an expense account came with the position. With my manager away in San Francisco, I was on my own for most of the time, which felt empowering. The only drawback was traveling every day. But I liked being able to stay out in the bars at night. My alcohol intake increased tremendously with my newfound freedom, and so did the loneliness that came with it. I wanted to be able to manage the pitfalls that come from being on the road without supervision. But in my thirties, I had too much freedom and money, and not enough common sense.

Many in Spokane referred to the region around that area as the Inland Empire, and our family had a marvelous time living there. We took advantage of the many outdoor activities in the northeast corner of the state of Washington. We water skied on Lake Coeur d'Alene, played golf amongst the pine trees at Manito Country Club, picked blueberries on Mt. Spokane, and snow skied at Schweitzer Mountain near Sandpoint, Idaho. All the physical activity and healthy habits helped me focus on my family on the weekends, when I rarely drank.

Our personal car was a black 1956 Volkswagen Beetle, not a growing family car and the only color available for the early VW. One Saturday, while out driving with my family—Karen, Eric, and Annie—in downtown Spokane, we came upon the Ford dealership. As we traveled up Monroe Street, high in the air we saw perched on a large pedestal a 1967 silver-blue Ford Mustang convertible with a black top and interior. It was spinning around on the display and calling my name. It was beautiful and dropped from the heavens.

I took one look at the Mustang and said to Karen and the children, "I'm buying that car!"

"Oh, no!" The concern tinging Karen's tone, told me she knew I was buying the car and nothing she could say or do would stop me.

It was one of those moments when I made a hasty decision based on emotion, what I now refer to as my alcoholic behavior. Acting irrationally happened on occasion with or without a drink in hand. Convinced I couldn't live without the blue convertible for my personal life, I drove into the dealership, jumped out of the VW, and bought the Mustang on the spot. To the dismay of my staring wife and children, the dealership made me an offer I couldn't and wouldn't refuse. Ford practically stole my VW from me and charged me too much for the Mustang, but the car was a beauty and I never regretted buying it. Every time I think of Spokane, the blue Mustang story comes to mind.

As a textbook salesperson covering parts of three states—Oregon, Idaho, and Washington—I quickly made friends with the local bartenders. On the road, alcohol and women became a way of life for me. The alcohol enabled me to cross my moral boundaries and develop a separate life from my family. This behavior labeled me a daily "problem drinker," one without control.

I flirted at times, and other times, I was in pursuit.

If I wasn't picking up the women, they were picking me up. I remember returning to the Owyhee, my hotel in Boise, Idaho, after selling all day. The pretty woman working behind the front desk in the lobby said, "Mr. Goldmann, Ron Robbins called and wants to have dinner tonight."

"Did he leave a number so I can reach him?"

"I told him you were busy tonight," she said.

"I am?"

"Yes," she said.

Then I got it. I said, "Oh, I am."

So, it would go from day to day. Being on the road was at times a lot of fun. But I had to get up the next morning knowing I had cheated on my wife, which caused a feeling of guilt. And if I felt too much guilt, I always drank alcohol to quiet the feeling. Alcohol I found could always help me to lower my morals and values. And so, it went like a merry-go-round with me at the bar the next day to start over.

The women I met on the road triggered my love addiction caused by insufficient nurturing as a child. The abusive treatment of me by my parents and their indifference to love and affection in my childhood hid in me like a disease. I sought tenderness and adoration in my life, often in the wrong places and with the wrong people. Only my aunt Corrine, when she came to visit during my younger years, showed any love or affection when she gave me hugs and kisses. I always functioned as if I didn't like it, but that was far from the truth. I looked forward to her coming to visit.

We stayed two years in Spokane and the interior of Washington state. During the week, I traveled for work from Spokane to Boise, Idaho. I had a chance to see a beautiful part of the country. The problem with seeing all that gorgeous country was I saw it alone. I missed my family. My lifestyle was a very lonely place, the reason I navigated each evening toward the bar scene. Traveling alone, eating alone, and sleeping alone were the hard parts of being a traveling salesperson. I felt disassociated and forsaken.

It was exciting for me to meet new people across a broad swathe of America, but I really wasn't a part of their lives in any intimate way. My relationships at home with my family were necessary. As an imposter to both my family and social associations, I had little connection to either. I feared the loneliness would reach despair and lead to excessive drinking.

Before I could jeopardize my family life any further, we moved back to Oregon. Again, my family accepted my decision. Making a geographical move to save me from alcohol and women was not the answer. I continued to feel detached from my family because of my obsession for alcohol and another life. I needed to change.

I accepted the position of manager at the golf course near the small town of Vernonia, in the foothills of the northeastern side of the coastal range. I was home every night, and my drinking simmered again because I deprived myself of it. It felt painful.

My friend Dave Gambee, from my OSC basketball days and fraternity life, had given me the opportunity to run his golf course, something I always wanted to do. He had no knowledge of my drinking history and, like a good alcoholic in denial, I did not mention it. But it was the reason I moved back to Oregon. I wanted to prove to myself I could function without drinking. I did whatever it took in my new adventure to make it work, accepting the positions of greenskeeper, manager, and anything else to keep me busy and away from the alcohol. I didn't want anyone to think of me as a problem drinker. Drinking was the problem I attempted to solve every day, without discussing it with my family.

I enjoyed the outdoor work and the golfers who came to play but avoided any extra time in the bar by staying busy and too tired for temptation. My preschool children loved the experience of running on the fairways in the morning, since we lived in an apartment in the back of the pro shop. Our standard of living had decreased several notches from our home in Spokane. The good salary, expense account, and company car were also part of the past. I earned a small salary from the golf course profits, which were thin after covering overhead.

Even with its downside, that life was for me. By living my dream of running a golf course, we learned to live with less. This life offered me a chance to stay off the road, but I was delusional to think my addiction to alcohol had cured itself.

Karen and I worked the golf course sunup to sundown, seven days a week. During the summer months, it was late into the night, restocking and cleaning for the next business day while balancing the books. For as busy as we were, there should have been more profit since I wasn't drinking it up! There was little time to stop and have a drink between mowing the greens and fairways and taking care of the customers at the pro shop. The stress of the situation almost caused me to go back to my old habit of daily drinking.

It was a wonderful time for as busy as we were, until, for me, it wasn't anymore. No matter how much I was involved with the golf course, I was not getting centered emotionally no matter how hard I tried.

Also, being far from a metropolitan area meant the golf course needed support by the small town of Vernonia. Some golfers who played lived quite a distance away, so they didn't play often enough to support the course. Karen and I managed the course for two years, but eventually came to the sad realization the course couldn't support our family. With much reluctance, we moved again.

With the end of my golf course dream, it was time to look elsewhere for employment. Even though being in the golf course business and making friends in the small town of Vernonia was enjoyable, I had to leave and take good memories with me. This adventure was a blessing for me, a time away from drinking regularly, though a "white knuckle" time as I held on. It was not a time I committed to sober up for good, but a time to pause and reflect on how drinking was impacting my life and had done so for a long time.

Immediately upon leaving the golf course, a couple of options opened for me. The first choice was to teach again, and the second was to go back to selling textbooks. I wasn't ready to go back into the classroom, so I returned to American Book Company and my former manager Mike Worthing. My "alcoholic thinking" again imagined things would be different, with expectations that led to

Intestinal Fortitude

disappointment the second time around. I should have remembered something I had heard: "Things don't change if things don't change."

Insanity, someone once said, is repeating the same thing over again and expecting a different result with no plans for change. That was me and my drinking. Vodka night after night to feel faster, funnier, and more charming.

I rationalized that I could always go back to teaching and make a good living at it, but this wasn't the time. I wanted another shot at earning a better-than-average income. Mike, my former manager, had a territory for me in Los Angeles. Since I had never been to LA and it held an air of excitement, temptation pushed me to accept the position. My family was game to see what all the talk was about California. So, I rented a U-Haul truck and left for Southern California with a sense of adventure. My territory covered the counties of Los Angeles and Ventura. We bought a lovely home in the San Fernando Valley, north of the Hollywood Hills. We could afford relocating with the money saved from the sales of our homes in Estacada, Oregon, and Spokane, Washington. Plus, the California housing boom of the 1960s was just beginning and you could purchase a genuinely charming home for 30,000 dollars.

I prided myself on the fact that my drinking subsided while home at night managing the golf course. For a while, the "plug in the jug" idea of pushing away the bottle continued in LA. My territory size allowed me to have only an occasional drink at home at night—a form of drinking I saw as "normal," since most people I knew drank. During the four years I lived in Vernonia and Los Angeles, I kept my drinking on the back burner. In LA, I made a considerable effort to control my alcohol consumption, a personal victory for me and my "alcohol problem."

Our stay in California proved to be an exciting two years. Our jaunts took us to many of the well-known tourist locations and ballgames. We went to the beach in Malibu. We saw the Dodgers and the Lakers play ball, including seeing my old friend and golf course owner, David Gambee, on the basketball court. He played for the Detroit Pistons against the Los Angeles Lakers, a game we attended. Dave and I were a long way from our basketball days together at Oregon State College.

Though we weren't in California exceptionally long, the family enjoyed living in the San Fernando Valley. The biggest drawback to the LA area was overcrowded schools. My two young children, Ann and Eric, were ready to begin kindergarten and first grade, and this unfortunate situation contributed to my decision to terminate my employment with American Book Company.

Disenchanted with ABC's outdated product and the company's attitude about my future, I decided to move back Oregon. With fewer problems associated with drugs and truancy in the state, its schools offered a better situation for my children. In LA, we met with the children's future teachers before school started. They looked tired already from the prospect of having forty or more students in their classroom. My alcoholic thinking, to "do it now," convinced me another geographical move would make my desire for alcohol go away and help solve my employment dilemma.

Before we left California, I received a lucky break by Laidlaw Brothers Book Company of Chicago who hired me to be their representative in Oregon. My new employer paid for our move back to Oregon, a nice benefit. At thirty-eight years old, I worked for them in an industry I knew extremely well. It felt good to be back home where I had spent most of my life, and to be away from the chaos of LA. I was more relaxed, doing well, and not going to the "drink" solution to any great degree.

I traveled to Chicago twice a year for sales meetings held at the Older LaSalle Hotel in downtown Chicago. A "city of broad shoulders" as depicted by Carl Sandburg in his work, *Chicago Poems of 1916*, "The city is like a giant man, hardworking and ready to take on any challenging task."

I loved the city of Chicago, its aura, and its character. It differed from Los Angeles as it had a hierarchy of Midwestern strength. Both sides of my family had emigrated from the Dakotas to the West Coast. I had Midwestern roots and liked Chicago's comfortable sensibilities, as well as the bars on Rush Street, downtown. Alcohol once again crept back into my life. My employment with Laidlaw became a perfect alcoholic storm.

At a sales meeting there one Christmas, I drank so much Scotch it wouldn't stay in my stomach. The Scotch went through me in minutes or even seconds. It didn't stay in my body long enough to extract the alcohol into my system. I was physically an alcoholic with the cravings, but I didn't know or understand what was happening to me.

By the end of the week, I couldn't get drunk on Scotch. I may as well have poured the Scotch in the toilet and forgot about being the go between. I didn't get sick or stagger; I was a "functioning alcoholic" with my drinking out of control. I didn't get alcohol poisoning or end up in the hospital, but I gave it a stellar effort. Some water might have surprised my liver, but I was addicted just the same.

I felt constantly bored. One of my excuses for drinking so much was my job with Ladlow Brothers. My position was effortless and not enough of a challenge. It was difficult for me to leave because of the good salary, expense account, company car, and personal freedom in doing my work. But even though I had those "perks," I couldn't stay mindful. I lowered my golf handicap as I traveled around Oregon.

My drinking increased tremendously when I worked for Laidlaw Brothers, and then it virtually exploded. The bars in Oregon might have awarded me their "top drunk" tribute for increasing their business. My alcohol consumption was a prominent problem, but not recognized outwardly by me. The people around me were oblivious at first. I hid it well, able to keep it a secret because I wasn't in one place for long. I traveled from town to town and drank only after four o'clock, never during the daytime.

While I was busy with my sales and practicing discipline with my alcohol intake by forcing myself to say no, things appeared "normal" to me. But most of the time, I performed as an alcoholic to others, such as my wife or manager. Whether admitting anything to anyone or even to myself, I was getting worse by behaving erratically. Nobody confronted me out of fear of what was happening.

This "perfect storm" ignited when my manager in San Francisco revealed himself as an alcoholic too. He enjoyed coming to Oregon and traveling with me, which was mostly an excuse for him to get out of the office and drink. We traveled around Oregon selling books during the day and consuming high volumes of alcohol at night. We weren't good for each other. We were a couple of alcoholics in denial, even wrecking the company car by running off the road, when I was sober no less.

The scenario kept repeating itself as we spiraled downward. Laidlaw Brothers fired me within two years. This was the final nail in the coffin for me and them. A classic alcoholic story played out in real life, all too common amongst those who drink to excess. Only this time the story was personal. It was about me and my selfish and immature behavior regarding my job and my family.

I admitted my fears about my alcohol to no one until I cleaned out my company car to return it to Laidlaw Brothers and made a staggering discovery. Amongst the many books in the trunk lay eleven half-filled bottles of vodka, Scotch, bourbon, and wine—bottles I didn't know existed. My situation appeared normal to me at first, but I finally admitted only to myself I had a genuine problem with alcohol. The thought of being an alcoholic was my main concern, but I had yet to embrace any fear or urgency to seek help. I wasn't ready to take the big step. I felt I could take care of myself. In my view, admitting I needed help meant I was a failure.

All those shiny bottles staring back at me prompted a revelation, but I was living in an alcoholic state of denial, the first hurdle one must jump to change. To run from the truth that went deep and a fear I could not face, I drank another drink. I started to feel lethargic and out of shape, a little flabby, with less muscle tone. I let my healthy habits slide and began feeling listless apathy. As an alcoholic, I played the part of being okay, including ignoring the physical side effects of serious hangovers and disorientation. With no control over my drinking, I sensed someone else was living my life.

By acting out with so much deception and drama, I won the Oscar for a leading role in deceiving others, but more importantly myself. When Laidlaw Brothers fired me, it proved to be what I needed. It got my attention. Though short-lived, it gave me a change in environment and life away from being on the road, but I was still dealing with myself and my drinking. Although there were no more bars, motels, or drunken co-workers in my life, I still had to deal with my deep-seated trauma from childhood, and the accident in college, that continued to haunt me.

My drinking problem had more than one reason to exist. I struggled all my life with love addiction. I chased adoration at every age. My childhood home was void of affection or, as I interpreted it, an antipathy toward favor. Love addiction is real and fosters in many homes such as the one I grew up in.

As a child, I needed more adoration and passion than I experienced. Love addiction for me wasn't about sex. It was more strongly associated with my need for love. Many times, though, sex is the outcome of seeking acceptance and love. In my case, alcohol became an enabler in lowering my moral code and taking that route against my values. Alcohol blunted my conscience so I could bypass my guilt and virtue.

In a big way, my firing was a blessing. It started me to thinking about my poor decision-making with work and family in relation to alcohol. What was going to be my future with my so-called "minor" problem? In the beginning, the firing was fortunate for me as it happened so quickly. It was like stepping through a door into the sunlight. This change allowed me to leave an unmanageable life of living on the edge that included lying to myself and keeping secrets of trysts and affairs. At home, this undisciplined life was ending. There was now a chance to straighten out my thoughts and behaviors, and to climb out of the crevice I had dropped myself into.

During that time, it felt like I had escaped alcohol and could get my life back together. By no longer assaulting my moral compass with alcoholic behavior, my life came in to focus. The question was what to do about it all. A firing from myself, in a way, made me happy. I now had a chance to improve by accepting my alcoholism. I was grateful for the end of my Laidlaw Brothers tenure.

Things happen for a reason, and there are no coincidences in this life. Within a week, Canby High School principal Dick Brown, who knew me from previous coaching assignments, called and offered me an excellent job. This meant a lot to me and my future. Dick coached basketball at Mt. Angel High School when I coached at Oregon College of Education. We coached against each other, so he knew me—or thought he did at the time

The city of Canby was a few miles south of Oregon City, where we were living. It was a good fit for me teaching United States government, U.S. history, and physical education. I happily accepted the position as a stabilization to my life. The quick opportunity, again, totally changed my surroundings, from traveling on the road to walking into the classroom. Believe me, this was a substantial change in occupations but, just as important, a critical change in lifestyle.

Going from total freedom of movement on the road with a hefty expense account to the confines of the classroom and a tight budget required quite a leap. From taking full care of myself and tending to my customers to being concerned about a classroom of overcharged hormonal adolescents all day was a big step in another direction. It could hardly be more different, but the opposites worked for me. I loved teaching and mentoring the students with their schoolwork and, in many cases, their lives. It felt good to be back in the classroom. It was exciting and fun and where I belonged. For a while, alcohol took a back seat. My head cleared of the fuzzies, which helped my outlook and attitude toward my family and teaching. I began to exercise to get my body back in shape. My family became a welcomed priority in my life.

My move to the classroom brought on another change as I reflected on my daily alcohol consumption. It bothered me. Those eleven bottles in the bottom of my car's trunk had gotten my attention. I couldn't shake the memory. That small event in my drinking life stayed planted in my mind and annoyed me. Through that incident, I admitted to myself my drinking was not a minor occurrence.

The environment of school, the teachers and the students, and being involved with activities and sports allowed me to function in life and move forward. Improving myself was an important concept to me. Because I managed my responsibilities at Canby High School, no one except my wife knew how much I was drinking at home in those last years of teaching and coaching. I desperately needed help to change my situation and prepare for retirement, and to stop hiding my drinking. My wife and my children began to see me for who I was, but we were all busy. Discussing my drinking problem with my family did not happen.

My children eventually knew I often drank to excess because I didn't hide it anymore. They grew up around alcohol, watching their grandmother Smith drink a fifth of Seagram's bourbon every day.

Their grandfather and their mother also drank. Eric and Ann saw a lot of alcohol consumed in our home and at family gatherings. That scene had to change, but how much effort would there be on my part was unclear. All my friends drank, so my effort wasn't too obvious. I desperately wanted to be a good example for my children, but they did not know that would happen. With this type of thinking going on in my head, I attempted to be a prudent drinker, but I fooled no one. I was trying to show good judgment and restraint with drinking. It wasn't easy, but it was a positive start mentally to move toward recovery.

I didn't really want to quit drinking, and no one in my family was threatening me to quit or suggesting I seek out a treatment program in the recovery world. There were a lot of them in the Portland area, including ads on television. After considering counseling, I didn't see the necessity to be that radical in my approach to curtail my drinking. Because of my denial, I pitied those disheveled drunks on the street with a bottle in a brown paper bag. I thought they needed those meetings in a church basement much more than I did.

At this stage in my life, my misconception of what recovery was all about failed to show me that alcoholics came from all occupations. There is no one typical alcoholic. One aspect of my drinking, at that time, was that I didn't hit rock bottom. My elevator never hit the basement, but no one gave me an ultimatum to leave my home. My family stuck with me, and I did not upset our financial security. Even at this late stage in my drinking, my job and the look of respectability and responsibility existed. This is what people in recovery call a "high-functioning alcoholic," one who appears normal and contributes to society.

My excessive drinking didn't lead me to crash and burn like many others who took that path. I somehow kept my life in acceptable order while knowing deep inside it was just a matter of time before the storm would hit. Most alcoholics, like me, do function well in society and hide their drinking. The idea of a downtrodden bum walking the streets represents only a small percentage of alcoholics in America, according to the National Council on Alcoholism.

My life was in chaos at the time Laidlaw Brothers fired me, even though the comeback at Canby High School happened. Many bridges were burned on the road and needed some repair. My taking advantage of people had to change.

The Canby teaching position, with the hope of making a sober return to teaching, was helpful to me. I coached every sport offered by the school, primarily, the girls' golf and boys' basketball teams. Canby was a good school and offered me credibility with teaching and mentoring and showing leadership as a coach with the students and teachers. They were supportive of my teaching and coaching decisions, even though we had a young staff with terrific personalities who did an abundance of socializing. I went to school many a morning with my head beating like a bass drum in John Phillip Sousa's marching band. The secret to my being a strong disciplinarian in the classroom was starting my teaching day with a hangover.

The drinking wasn't because of unhappiness teaching at Canby or being disgruntled with my students. There wasn't a day I didn't become excited when entering the classroom. The influence of the student's eagerness added purpose to my teaching. The classroom was my domain, an arena of activity for knowledge and influence. My happiness with my teaching assignment and classes was due to them being lifelong interests of mine. By doing a proficient job in the classroom, per my reviews, I hid what was going on inside of me and rattling my brain. For a while, the urge to drink stayed at bay and I partook only on occasion.

Canby High School received a good return on their money. I coached the boys' basketball team into the state tournament a couple of years during the 1980s, as well as winning a league championship. These two accomplishments had not happened before in the school's history. I coached the girls' golf team for twenty-five years; I had fun doing it and took the girls to a lot of tournaments. Along with being so involved with school, I also served a stint as president of the Canby High School Teacher's Association.

By helping with negotiations for the teacher benefits contract with the district's school board and going before a school board to ask for more money, I assessed my resolve but enjoyed it, too. This lasted for a few years, and I came away with no noticeable scars. As the saying goes, "He who pays the piper calls the tune," and the board was calling the tunes.

Intestinal Fortitude

My drinking was under control during those years at Canby High School. I stayed terribly busy, but the obsession was there. I could feel it as if it were another person in my skin. Being highly engaged in teaching and coaching, the students, faculty, and support staff made the school a marvelous place to teach. They all helped a lot to distract me from my secret life. There were many times I was involved at night with basketball and other school activities that kept me away from drinking.

After twenty-five years at Canby High School, in 1995, I retired from teaching and coaching there. It was my last employer.

Today, I know alcohol abuse is a progressive disease. It grows worse over time, physically eating away at your body, mind, and spirit. Alcoholism never gets better on its own without major changes in all aspects of your life. The physical, emotional, and spiritual aspects of my life were in jeopardy. In the back of my mind, I was keenly aware teaching school would not cure my alcoholism or necessarily exacerbate it. While teaching gave me a chance to abstain to some degree and confront the temptation to drink because of my responsibilities, but that was as far as it went. I still did not quit until five years after I retired.

My first five years of retirement turned out to be unsettling with alcohol again playing a key role in my life. After twenty-five years as a teacher and coach, I embarked on a five-year career of serious drinking. I could not stop, nor did I make any attempt to quit. At the climax of my first few years of retirement, I changed my life in a big way by divorcing my wife and moving to Arizona on a full-time basis. I had finally had enough and saw that I was not satisfied with my life and killing myself. I had to risk hurting my wife and my children for peace of mind and a happier life. It was a big decision, and not a quick one, because we had been married for forty years. Although we often lived apart during the marriage, I struggled for a long time about leaving.

There in Scottsdale, Arizona, I met a wonderful woman who supported me to stop drinking by being an example for me. She helped me understand alcohol and addiction, make a commitment to a sober life, and not look back with a lot of regrets. Patricia Brooks and I have now been together more than twenty years and married sixteen of those years. She is a long-time success story, thirty-eight years sober. By participating with her in recovery, I have not found it necessary to take a drink in twenty-plus years.

The nondrinking life was not always a charmed existence for me. There were many bouts of depression and times of craving alcohol, but it has been a good and happy life. I am grateful for my recovery from alcohol, for the support of my wife and others, including therapists, and for my own fortitude to live this life, to live at all.

MORE ON ALCOHOL

I tracked time by certain events. One was when my wife Karen and I paid off our twenty-five-year mortgage in 1990 on our historic home in Oregon City and then divorced. We had lived there for thirty years.

We retired in 1995. Karen stepped down from the Portland law firm of Morton Zalutsky, where she managed their phenomenally successful downtown office for close to twenty-five years. After twenty-eight years in the profession, I moved on from teaching high school and coaching.

We lived near Karen's parents in Oregon City, just outside of Portland, where her father was a doctor. They didn't come any better than Dr. Smith. He was a terrific person who liked to play golf and bridge and relished a cocktail in the evening. He and I enjoyed these pastimes tremendously during the forty years I was married to Karen.

Her mother was a different story. Every day, she entertained drinks starting at four in the afternoon and demanded the center of attention along with her bottle of Seagram's bourbon. My family, including Karen, Eric, Annie, and Tony, were each influenced by her drinking. She had an adverse impression on each of us, the most glowing was her belligerent demeanor toward us when she drank. None of us wanted to be near her. The truth is one gift we gleaned from her was the knowledge of what alcoholism was and looked like.

She sat arrogantly in her big chair in the living room, daring anyone to suggest even changing the channel on the television. She was the "elephant in the room" as we all walked around her on eggshells to avoid her rude, hurtful behavior and caustic tongue.

After Karen and I turned fifty, and our children were no longer living at home, I drank consistently. I developed my own progressive dependence on alcohol with four or five drinks each evening. At age sixty, the drinks went down smoother than other years. I'd pour one, then another, and soon was half a bottle deep.

Karen's drinking wasn't as serious as mine. She might have a couple of drinks with me, more than likely just one. Most of the time, she fell asleep in her favorite chair in front of the television after just a single imbibe of wine. She drank extraordinarily little, juxtaposed against my act of frequently "bending the elbow."

After Karen fell asleep, I went on pouring drink after drink until I had "cheered my inner man" and alcohol became my best friend. The problem with that was the friendship only went one way. Alcohol always let me down. I never had just one drink—you could take that to the bank. And, as time went on day to day, we both found it increasingly difficult to connect with each other about anything. After decades of marriage, we didn't find a new freedom in retirement, nor more happiness in our golden years.

We drifted apart after only a brief time into retirement. I started spending the winters alone in Arizona. Alcohol wasn't the only cause for our divorce, but it played a critical role because it changed who I really was and had been. As a notorious solvent, it dissolves careers, families, and marriages.

A bottle of any kind of alcohol felt like a friend to me, one I could rely on. I even felt good about it sitting in my kitchen cupboard. I drank to be glad, to drown my troubles, and for every occasion in between. I indulged in the drink to find my "off button" to ponder my life or, when alone, to escape my situation.

I could never stop dwelling on the car wreck that took place when I was twenty-one and a student at Oregon State College. I felt guilty because of the senseless deaths of my roommate, Al Smith, from the Sigma Chi House; and Alice Rampton, a Corvallis High School student. The loss of them haunted me all my life. There wasn't a day that went by that I didn't think of them.

Alcohol blanked out the world, helped me forget about my past, and convinced me to disregard my future. I was severely depressed because of my failing marriage and the loneliness it produced.

After forty years, many of my friends asked, "Why bother to get a divorce?"

I told them, "I want a loving relationship every day for the rest of my life. Since I only get to go around once in life, I want to take the chance of finding true happiness."

When my children stopped playing sports, our relationship went downhill, then crumbled. We found we didn't have more in common beyond the children. I drank to cover up our dying marriage and was certain nothing would ever be as good as it had been. That feeling of cooperation that Karen and I established between us had dissolved. Our relationship had died and felt cold. After forty years of marriage, it felt like I was living in a void.

Our marriage suffered even more after Eric and Annie were out of the house and on their own. We had functioned as a family when they were living at home. We built a good life while following our children's school and sports activities. As good athletes, our children were the bond to our family throughout their school years.

They went on to play sports in college. Eric played football at Western Oregon State University, and Annie played softball at Portland State University. Karen and I watched them play sports from grade school through college. It was a wonderful time in our lives. We found something in common in supporting our children.

Being a nonconfrontational person, I found the inevitable decision to leave difficult to make. I didn't know what life was going to be like on my own after four decades of marriage. It was a big step.

One day, like an omen or a light coming on in my head, I knew it was time to leave Karen. Somehow it made sense to me that it was time to go. After I'd given Karen and our marriage an abundance of deliberation, my path was clear to me. There was little between us as a couple. We were hardly friends.

Our divorce held few dramatic moments. The process went quickly and amicably. We both had good lawyers.

When I left Karen in 2001, at sixty-six years old, I told her she was killing me. The truth was I was destroying myself, and alcohol was the assassin. If we had stayed together, it wouldn't have been a healthy life, or a long life, for me or for her. I was frustrated with my drinking and my marriage, and being entangled in a life of liquor and loneliness. My behavior continued and would have killed me sooner than later. The National Council on Alcoholism will tell you, on average, for both men and women, death will come twenty years earlier if one depends on alcohol. That knowledge got my attention.

It sounds so melodramatic but going through a divorce is difficult at any stage in life. The end of our marriage came in 2002 with the finalization of our divorce settlement. I had been retired seven years. Every time my drinking had begun before, it escalated like it was last call in a bar at closing time. It skyrocketed after retirement. If Oregon City needed one more drunk to meet their quota, I had volunteered. The lifestyle was detrimental to my health.

I created that environment where alcohol makes everything better, until it makes everything worse. At age sixty and until I turned sixty-five, my drinking intensified to a pint of vodka and a bottle of wine every evening at dinner time. I developed my own ritual toward alcohol consumption. The perfect formula was to just get drunk. There's no attractive way to say it. Alcohol no longer let me BS myself that I was taller, faster, or funnier. Each day blurred into another. It became more important for me to have my daily drinks.

I no longer liked to hang out in bars to drink. I had no interest anymore in meeting women or talking to other drinkers. It became too expensive, and the bartenders didn't pour a stiff enough drink for me. I also didn't want a driving under the influence (DUI) arrest on the way home. I worried about getting into a car and killing someone or myself. Drinking at home alone was the best option.

I appreciated good vodka and wine over the years and knew the difference between a smooth Merlot and a tasty Pinot noir. I knew the best vodka to buy and how to describe its nuances. By the time I was sixty-five, I bought Gallo wine by the half gallon from Safeway and told myself it was the best my money could buy. Now that vodka was all the same, I purchased the largest bottle in the discount barrel at Walgreens.

By the time I quit drinking in 2001, it didn't really matter to me what the fine points of vodka were or the subtleties of a Zinfandel.

It was the feeling I had from alcohol, the cravings in my head and my body that mattered the most. That "high" embodied what I would have to overcome to conquer my dependence on alcohol.

At this point, I should have admitted myself to, at least, an outpatient treatment center or joined a recovery program with daily meetings. It did not happen because I didn't see myself as an alcoholic or ask for help from anyone, and nobody suggested I seek help, either.

Karen and I never talked about attending any counseling that might have saved our marriage. It had no foundation; it was inevitable it would dissolve and have only been a sham any other way. I wanted it to end. Once I said those words, there was no turning back, and Karen knew it.

Still drinking heavily after the divorce, I moved permanently into my condominium in Scottsdale, Arizona, to ponder my future. My alcohol consumption was in the forefront of my mind as I considered changes for my new life. I felt depressed and that I was missing life.

My neighbor Patricia was soon to enter my life and help me realize I had to rescue me from myself. She showed me by her own example there is a way to live without alcohol and how to do it. She had what I wanted, and I was willing to do anything to live a sober and happy life without alcohol.

DRIVING DRUNK

On a July Saturday night, while attending Oregon State College in 1954, I drove drunk in my father's new Mercury sedan, speeding and swerving on Highway 101 north of Tillamook. Two hefty state troopers, armed and determined to keep the peace in the beach town of Rockaway, pulled me over in that "hot spot" for young people on the Oregon Coast. When the police officers approached me, they appeared agitated, showing me their clubs. They were ready for me because of what had gone on that evening, partying with friends.

That small town had a large auditorium where big bands played music for dancing on Saturday nights. Rockaway was a place inundated with older types, ages fifteen to twenty, looking for fun on the weekends. The more juvenile members of the troupe kept the police busy with underage drinkers not yet twenty-one.

I had left Tillamook earlier in the evening as the sun set over the Pacific Ocean and headed north to see what was happening at Pirates Cove Restaurant north of Garibaldi. Margie, the owner of the bar, usually had a band playing to bring in business, and that night was no exception. The place was popular because of her outgoing personality and the Benny Goodman–type music she played.

On my way to Margie's, I stopped for another beer at Monty's Tavern in Bay City. I was in no hurry and talked with Donny Dedman, a local, for a brief time. Donny and I played baseball together on the Tillamook Elk's semi-pro team. He suggested I return to Tillamook and get off the highways since I had already had a few beers. In no mood for friendly advice, I went on to my destination.

Driving through the next town, Garibaldi, I saw a police car sitting in a parking lot, looking for speeders or people driving under the influence. They watched me as I drove past them. I thought they might follow me. I felt a little paranoid for drinking and driving but still not motivated enough to turn back, even though I knew the consequences of drunk driving in Oregon. The alcohol overcame any clear thinking I might have had that night.

While passing the Coast Guard station and going north up the hill and around the corner, I spotted the same police car again, this time in my rearview mirror closing fast, surely after me. I gunned the Mercury up the hill and immediately found the parking lot at Pirates Cove, my destination. Lucky for me, there was an open space between two cars, so I quickly spun into the spot and shut off the lights. The police sailed past Pirates, not seeing me. With their lights flashing, they were gone in seconds. We were just shy of Rockaway.

This would have been a suitable time for me to head back home to Tillamook. But instead, since I'd eluded the police so craftily, I stopped into Pirates Cove to say hello to Margie. Downing another beer seemed like a promising idea. After my beer, I jumped back in my car and made a huge mistake by heading the Mercury north toward Rockaway. I should have gone home but instead made an alcoholic decision.

It wasn't long before the police spotted me, put on the flashers, and pulled me over. When the state trooper opened my car door and told me to get out, I made another alcoholic decision. I planted my right foot on the Mercury's brakes and came out swinging.

I was too drunk to hit either one of the troopers, so they grabbed me and slapped the steel cuffs on my wrists. I thought about punching them but hated to fight. I just reacted. Alcohol caused me to do dumb things, and trying to take down a state trooper was about as dumb as they get. Fortunately, the police stopped me on the road driving drunk before I killed myself or somebody else in a car wreck. They put me in their cruiser and drove me to the Tillamook County Jail at the courthouse.

The next day, I called my father to get me out. He was not pleased but said nothing of consequence at the jail. He thought back to his own youth and shared a story of his wild escapades in Elko, Nevada, when he was a cowboy on the Buena Vista Ranch.

When I went to court, the judge said, "Your sentence is one week in the county jail and a hundred dollars for DUI. I am not charging you for threatening an officer."

That one hundred dollars in the 1950s was a lot of money, but it was the week in jail that had me worried. Of course, the sentencing was nonnegotiable, so I spent my time in jail, courtesy of the county amongst thieves, other drunks, and even a couple of felons.

The physical layout of the Tillamook County Jail offered a cell at night to sleep in with two other detainees. During the day, we stayed in a large open holding area called the bullpen. This was where we ate and spent the day with the entire jail population. The felons mixed with the DUI types. I spent the entire week on high alert for any trouble or danger. It was incredibly stressful with all fourteen prisoners in the same space.

In the bullpen, I stayed away from the others and kept quiet. If one of the prisoners wanted to talk to me, only then did I enter a conversation. Two felons were going to the state penitentiary following their trials. They had nothing to lose, so I timidly walked around them all day. The bullpen mimicked an oligarchy with the two felons acting as judge and jury if any difficulties arose amongst those of us in the jail. A den of thieves with a hierarchy. It reminded me of the chickens on our farm with the rooster overseeing the pecking order of the coop.

The first night, my two cellmates started trouble with veiled threats and derogatory comments toward me. There was nothing else to do but challenge them to a fight to end the problem, certainly not my first choice of action. Surprisingly, they backed down and I had no more issues with them for the rest of the week.

I didn't relax for a full week. After my release, I wanted to wear only white clothes to feel clean, and I continuously attempted to wash the jail off my mind and my body. I went home and took a long hot shower day after day. This taste of incarceration showed me the desperate feeling of being in custody.

Alcohol fed my breakdown to socially unacceptable behavior. Alcoholism, for me, was a cunning disease. It pulled me in again in my early twenties when I had a tough time looking at myself in the mirror. It wasn't enough to make me consider stopping my drinking. Eventually, I overcame the denial and questioned how or where I was going if I kept drinking, but still didn't seek help.

It's lamentable, but I didn't stop drinking until I was sixty-five years old, after many more alcohol issues had cropped up along the way. With the help of my wife, Patricia, I saw clearly that I must quit. We could only be together and have a good life if I didn't drink. Patricia had been in recovery from alcohol for twenty years at that time.

If I'd continued drinking in 2001, I would have lost her before our relationship even began. Now that we have been together for more than twenty years, I recognize that initial smart and healthy decision we both made, and haven't looked back.

MYSTICAL WHEELS OF JUSTICE

When I was thirty-five, working for the Laidlaw Brothers, I went on a trip to Medford, the county seat of Jackson County, to meet with teachers for an upcoming textbook adoption. One evening after selling all day, I stopped at a bar in a shopping center in downtown Medford. I met two nurses who were also just getting off work. We each had two drinks. I make the point of saying two drinks because I seldom had as few as two drinks in any one sitting in my life, as my friends will attest.

We had an enjoyable conversation as the nurses were great fun. They were cute, young, and blonde. In football vernacular: "triple threats." We talked about their work as surgical nurses at Providence Medford Hospital and their lives in Medford. My experience has been that nurses, as a rule, are great people. They are a down-to-earth group of people who look at life squarely and don't take kindly to someone trying to pull the wool over their eyes. These two nurses, out of sheer kindness, became witnesses in my upcoming trial for driving under the influence or DUI.

I left the bar, climbed into my car, and started to return to the nearby Holiday Inn, where I stayed in Medford. I came to the first stoplight and saw red lights flashing in my rear window. A Medford detective in an unmarked auto was behind me. I pulled my car over and he pulled in behind me along the street. It was obvious the detective had been watching the back door of the bar, waiting for any unsuspecting drinker to emerge.

The detective came up to my car window and asked for my driver's license, which I gave him. He went back to his car, turned on an overhead light, and examined my license. He sat in his sedan with the driver's side door open. He observed my license for quite an extensive amount of time and continued to sit in his car.

We were parked in sight of the Holiday Inn where I was staying. As time passed, I grew agitated by the detective and the delay. It seemed an exceptionally long time for him to be checking my license. I'd had just enough to drink, the two highballs with the nurses, to cause me to not think things through clearly. I kept getting more provoked by the minute. My temper was about to get me into trouble.

After what seemed like a half hour, I'd had it with the detective. Looking back on the situation, I now know the detective was baiting me to do something stupid. Without even thinking about what I would do next, I became reckless. I stepped out of my vehicle and went back to the unmarked squad car where the detective sat holding my license up in his left hand, still pretending to examine it. I reached into the car and grabbed my license out of his hand.

"If you're going to arrest me, get on with it. I'm on my way over to the Holiday Inn where I am staying," I said.

With that line, I practically begged the detective to arrest me. My temper and the two drinks collided in my brain, and I was up a creek without a paddle. Through my foolishness in begging him to arrest me, he did.

Without too much of a surprise to me, the charge was driving under the influence or DUI. Of course, he put me in his police car for a ride to the station. The detective also had a young student police officer riding with him. This trainee became especially important to me that night, virtually saving my bacon.

After we arrived at the police station, the officer I'd grabbed my license from gave me a breathalyzer test. The steamed detective said the result of my test was 2.2, ten points over what is considered drunk in Oregon: 1.2. At 2.2, I would have been staggering drunk. I heard him tell the young guy tested just ahead of me on the breathalyzer machine he had rung up a 2.4. That guy was plastered. He was barely able to stand and was incoherent.

It didn't register with me that the detective had raised my number to 2.2 for his convenience. It was my first breathalyzer test, and I wasn't paying close attention. I also didn't think the police were dishonest, but this detective was trying to cover his own behind and stick it to me by jacking up the number on the machine. He let his anger get the best of him as mine had earlier. He'd arrested a citizen who was not drunk.

Here is where the student police officer did me a huge favor. He watched the whole procedure and corrected the detective who was still mad at me for grabbing my license out of his hand.

"That's not 2.2 but rather 1.2," the young police officer said.

The next day, after being booked and spending the night in jail, I returned to my car and headed to breakfast, mad at myself for getting into such an ordeal. I felt a little embarrassed too. At breakfast, I ran into Johnny Jarboe, an old friend. He had played on the varsity basketball team at Oregon State College while I'd played on the first-year team. Having played against him in practice many times, I knew him well. I told him about my big night. He listened to my account of what transpired and gave me some sound advice on what I should do next.

"You should get as good a lawyer as you can lay your hands on, someone local in Medford," he said.

Running into Johnny that morning after getting out of jail was a blessing. His support, after the previous night's encounter, was priceless. I took his suggestion seriously. I asked a friend of mine, Jerry Evans, who owned the popular Jacksonville Inn there in southern Oregon, whom he thought was the best lawyer in Medford.

Jerry said without hesitation, "Averill Harrelston."

I was familiar with his name. Harrelston was a state legislator and well known throughout Oregon. I also had the distinct impression that Jerry had found it necessary to hire Harrelston in the past. I immediately went to see if I could convince him to take the case.

He said he would represent me when I came back in a month for the court date. As I drove out of Medford that morning, I felt a lot better.

Intestinal Fortitude

In the back of my mind, though, it did seem a little strange that a big-time lawyer, even in a small town, would take on a jury trial about driving under the influence. The case seemed mundane to me but was being treated as an essential case, beyond driving school.

Another thought that popped up in my mind was the possible uncertainty of a jury trial. Who would be on the jury? What would happen during the deliberation of the case if someone had a grudge against alcohol? If one of the jurors had been in an accident with an intoxicated driver and suffered a loss, my case could easily have been in jeopardy.

Since he said he would represent me, I headed back home to Oregon City to wait out the month. By hiring a respectable lawyer, someone I trusted to do a bang-up job, I felt good. But I had reservations because you never know how things will go when facing a jury in court. Personalities and dress and body language can all play a role.

The date of my case came up and I headed back to Medford, ready to meet up with Harrelston, my "go get 'em" lawyer. When I arrived, I went directly to his office, next door to the courthouse. We needed to discuss my case, scheduled for that afternoon.

When I arrived, I received some news that about floored me. My high-powered lawyer was out of town and wouldn't be representing me. The office secretary ushered me into another lawyer's office. It was as if my arrival was choreographed, and I was a character in a play. My part was played by a guy who was frantic as he was being led to the gallows.

The office was paneled with dark mahogany wood, and a typical green desk lamp threw a dim light on the situation. Sitting behind the desk was a young kid who looked like he had just graduated law school that morning. As I sat down, I told the young lawyer in a matter-of-fact tone that I knew what was going on.

I said, "The big guy, Harrelston, who is supposedly out of town, but probably on the golf course, didn't want the case. He knew he couldn't win it, so the big fellow is now throwing me and you to the wolves."

I was testing the young lawyer and wanted to see his reaction. He sat straight up, looked me in the eye, and spoke to me in a fired-up voice. Any good coach rallying his team before the big game would proudly do just that.

"We can win this case," he said with enough conviction to make me want to put on the cleats one more time.

I said, "Okay. Let's go."

I found the young barrister to be a real competitor first and a good lawyer a close second. I admired him and knew we now had a chance.

My trial before the jury would turn out to be remarkable, to say the least. The news of the decision of the jury would come from the most unexpected source. I never would have predicted it.

My young lawyer turned out to be very skillful and was bent on winning my case come hell or high water. He attacked the breathalyzer machine itself. He got the detective, whom he put on the stand, to admit the machine really was not all that accurate. The detective admitted the machine could be off a point or two, and my reading was 1.2, exactly on the Oregon state law for being drunk. My lawyer also persuaded him to admit it could be possible I wasn't drunk at all. I began to love my young lawyer; he was on a roll.

The two nurses with me at the start of my adventure with the detective came to court to testify I'd had only two drinks and had not appeared drunk to them. In a curious manner, Oregon law allowed them to sit in on the trial before they took the stand. They listened as the detective squirmed in the witness box from my young lawyer's questions. These two women were well prepared to testify for me in an unquestionable style. It was something I thought unusual, but I wasn't going to look a gift horse in the mouth. I was more than happy to take advantage of what came my way.

Being exact on the illegal number on the machine was what my attorney attacked during the trial. He pointed out the steamed detective had tried to sabotage me by raising my number to 2.2 when it was really 1.2.

In another odd point, the prosecution allowed a woman schoolteacher I knew to remain on the jury, not disqualifying her. Who would have thought that could happen? The final incident that almost guaranteed my victory happened at recess when the jury went out for deliberation.

Intestinal Fortitude

I left the courtroom to stretch my legs and work off a little anxiety by walking the halls of the courthouse. I also went to use the bathroom, and I was standing at the urinal when an elderly gentleman came in to use the one next to me. He was tall and a little unkept, and he surely hadn't shaved since the previous week. His disheveled clothes hung on his tall, slender frame.

He said to me, "You're the young fella who is on trial."

"Yes, I am," I said.

"You're going to get off."

"Really? How do you know that?"

He said, "My wife is on the jury and yesterday she bailed me out of jail in Eugene for being drunk on the street."

With that said, we parted company. Sure enough, after the court reconvened, the jury exonerated me. When I think back on my trial, the tall man at the urinal always appears in my mind, and thoughts arise about the wheels of justice moving in mysterious ways.

My young lawyer and I walked out of the courtroom where he had done such an outstanding job. While heading down the steps of the courthouse, he asked me if he could buy me a drink to celebrate our victory. I thought his invitation for a drink was a little ironic since a couple of innocent drinks had landed me into this mess in the first place. I kindly declined his offer and thought the idea was just shy of insane.

I realized that morning that losing my temper when drinking had put me through a lot of unnecessary aggravation. I would always look back, knowing next time there likely wouldn't be another tall gentleman at the urinal with a wife on the jury.

MAKING AMENDS

I returned to Oregon State College for my sophomore year after a summer working at home in Tillamook. I immediately met and dated a wonderful blonde girl named Taylor. We enjoyed each other's company and had a lot of fun together. She liked the things I liked, was a true sports fan, and enjoyed that I played on the basketball team at OSC. We had grown up near each other on the Pacific Coast. I'm sure, from our conversations, she was smarter than King Solomon.

Even though our high schools played each other in sports and I ventured often to Seaside in the summer to meet girls, I never met Taylor until my college days. Seaside was the beach town young adults from Oregon and Washington descended on in droves in the summer.

Three of my Sigma Chi fraternity brothers and I played golf at the Corvallis Country Club on Friday morning and then headed to Philomath for lunch and a beer. My golf partners that morning near Corvallis were Johnny Frederick, Wally Zwingli, and Bob Walker. We joined the same fraternity at OSC in 1953 and often spent time together.

We were all under twenty-one years of age but knew a place that would serve us. The Chat and Chew Tavern was popular with OSC male students, especially jocks, so we fit in. Pictures of Oregon State athletes covered the interior walls of this establishment. After lunch there, we stayed on for more beer and storytelling. Bob Walker had made a hole in one that morning, so we were having a fun time celebrating his feat.

Taylor had a new Oldsmobile coupe at school. She came by The Chat and Chew that day and surprised me when she announced we were going to Newport on the Oregon Coast. I thought to myself that things were getting serious. There I was feeling good on beer, a tasty lunch, and a decent game of golf, and a pretty girl wanted to take me to the beach for the weekend. How exciting was that? Some days, things just went my way.

I insisted on driving, but my condition almost got us killed as I swerved close to another car. Taylor didn't know how much beer I drank before she picked me up. Had she known, she would have never let me get behind the wheel of her car. We miraculously arrived in Newport unscathed and checked into a Best Western Motel overlooking the ocean and an incredible view of the beach. Amazingly, Taylor had no comment about my driving to break the spell of what was to be a special night.

The beautiful setting provided a view of the beach and the blue water lapping up to the shore. With the last rays of the day's sun illuminating the tips of the waves to a glisten, it was magical and set the tone for romance that evening.

It wasn't long before we were in bed for the first time. I'd looked forward to making love with Taylor since we had met. My expected performance did not happen. Sadly, I was unable to perform all evening. The more I tried, the more frustrated I became.

My response was an unbelievable and uncharacteristic outburst of a temper tantrum, a fit. I attacked Taylor by slapping her in the face. She vaulted out of bed in horror, hurriedly dressed, and left the motel room sobbing and scared. The night ended before it even started. Having endured enough of my drunken behavior, Taylor quickly left in her car to return to Corvallis. I was too drunk to stop her, acknowledge my actions, or even know how I felt about it all.

I was not able to rise to the occasion and became totally agitated. Her beautiful body should have aroused my passion for her and the satisfaction of my desire. But my mind was in a frenzy, gravitating to anger, as I lost control of my perception. I rolled over and fell asleep until morning, not in any frame of mind to care one way or the other.

"The first loss of a drinker is his dignity. The second loss is his sanity." I had read or heard those words once, and they kept flashing through my mind the next morning. Along with my pounding headache and slow-moving body, feelings of guilt and shame settled in for the long haul.

To her credit and my surprise, she returned the next morning and picked me up. She had a big heart and a kind nature to come back for me. We discussed nothing on our drive back to Oregon State. I felt terribly embarrassed and too hungover to have the good sense to apologize.

My drunken actions ended our relationship. I wasn't man enough to call her at the Kappa Kappa Gamma sorority house, where she lived, to express my regrets for my behavior. Once again, I'd ended a bond due to my drinking, this time in quite a fanfare.

Over the years, that night in Newport haunted me. I felt ashamed. I grew a bit more responsible about my drinking episodes with age and overcame my denial about the truth of that Friday night. Later in life, I no longer denied what took place or my part in all of it. In my conscience, I knew I had to do the honorable thing and own up to my behavior from that fateful night.

Twenty-five years later, I played golf at the Astoria Country Club in the Oregon Coast Invitational. I heard from friends Taylor had returned to Seaside, a town I passed through on my way to and from the golf tournament. She had been a schoolteacher in Lake Oswego and then moved back to Seaside with her husband to start a business.

On that trip, I stopped by her business in downtown Seaside, made amends with her, and apologized for my drunken behavior that night in Newport. I did this in person for closure, as well as to face my alcoholic behavior so I could go forward. It was difficult for me to grow if I didn't start to confront my past.

Taylor was genuinely surprised to see me and exceedingly grateful I had stopped to see her with good intentions.

"Thank you for coming. I've never forgotten that night," she said carefully.

"You're welcome. I needed to do this for both of us," I said. "I'm happy I'm here."

She gave me a big hug and cried as we both had a weight removed from our shoulders. Why wouldn't she? I had remained sad, too, after the initial shock of that incident. It was as though she had been waiting those twenty-five years for my apology.

It was an emotional encounter. I had the feeling we would have married had that fateful night never taken place. She had grown older but looked incredibly beautiful. I swallowed hard and thought about what I might have missed because of alcohol and my blunder so many years before. Taylor needed an apology to let go of that infamous night in her life. I felt better knowing I did the right thing.

I never saw her again, but that was not my motive. My only desire that day was to set things straight and apologize for my actions that hurt both of us when we were young. I'd ruined that special night but forgave myself that day.

Taylor forgave me. The incident was now etched in our memories.

William Faulkner once said, "The past is never dead. It isn't even past."

ANXIETY

I lived in Scottsdale, Arizona, when I turned seventy-seven years old. Married to my wonderful wife, Patricia, I was playing golf and cards with friends from Oregon during the winter months and wrote my first book. I loved my life.

We lived in Old Town Scottsdale off Camelback Road. We resided in a high-rise condominium, on the seventh floor, with a magnificent view of Camelback Mountain. Fashion Square Mall and the movie theaters were close by. Pat and I had a good life, enjoying the many cultural events and restaurants of the downtown heart of the city. With no warning, this wonderful existence abruptly changed for Patricia and me.

I was stricken with anxiety. I was drop-kicked into a world of fear that lasted three years, until age eighty, and it completely altered our lives. It was the worst time of my existence. I was so overcome with angst I became emotionally paralyzed. The fears I experienced were menacing and never ending. As a result, my fears impacted our daily routine.

Anxiety was my companion at various times and as early as high school, but at age seventy-seven, I needed to put my life on hold as it became so severe. Sometimes I experienced panic attacks and felt helpless, scared, and out of control. These bouts were triggered often by my phobias and occurred while at the movies, playing golf, or taking a car ride.

Intestinal Fortitude

    I had played golf since I was fifteen and played well all during my life, but that mattered little as my fretfulness overcame my golf game. In my mid-seventies, my ability to play the game of golf started to wane. My poor play and anxiety co-existed, so my game deteriorated. I was doomed as my nervousness escalated and became debilitating.

    I couldn't hit the ball as far as I did when I was younger, and my game was inferior. Of course, my thoughts about everything in life became negative. Most people who play golf and love the game as I did adjust their expectations and keep on playing. Unable to do that as I grew physically and mentally older and weaker, I suspect my worry and uneasiness played a key role in the demise of my game.

    Patricia tried to help me to adjust my feelings about the game, but I couldn't accept her advice even though it made good sense. Playing golf and being overcome with fear is a miserable combination. I started fearing shanks, the nemesis of most men golfers at some time in their golfing lives. A shank is when the ball squirts to the right of the clubface for a right-handed golfer. They just pop into your game. It's a puzzle as to why they take place without warning. I believe it's more mental than physical.

    I also started to fear hitting bad shots during a round of golf, which is classic anxiety, the dread of anticipated events. I couldn't compel myself to take the bad shots in stride and remember that all golfers hit poor shots even the professionals on the Professional Golf Association (PGA) Tour.

    I was afraid to putt, fearing the ball wouldn't roll straight off the putter's face. All my old playing partners agree, even before anxiety set in, I wasn't a particularly good putter in the first place. But now I was below par and developed the "yips," a sorrowful affiliation identified by your hands shaking and jerking as you try to putt the ball into the hole.

    If I had a golf game scheduled with my foursome, I feared playing days in advance of our tee time. The feeling of dread overwhelmed me. I had been a good golfer for more than sixty years, yet the anticipation of golf kept me immobilized for days. I was in such a state I felt oppression from a superior authority.

    It took all the fortitude I could muster up to go to the golf course to play one last time. Patricia pushed me out the door and into the car. I thought about turning the car around. Getting out of the car, in the parking lot at the course, was my last chance to escape. I knew it was my final round. In the end, I was so afraid of golf with the stress overpowering my life I gave it up. The feeling of dread became too much for me to bear.

Even though I feel better today, I haven't played the game I love for a decade. I enjoy golf on television and occasionally hit a few balls at the PGA Store. Today, now that I'm feeling better and in my mid-eighties, I still can't get over how stressful the game became to me at that time. I couldn't tell my playing partners about my anxiety concerning golf. It was embarrassing to me and hard to admit to anyone but my wife. I felt they wouldn't understand, even though I had known them for many years. I felt very much alone at the golf course.

During my free time, when my mind was not concentrating on a daily activity such as walking with my wife, I worked crossword puzzles. The reason I chose the teasers was because solving them took my mind off the fear that persisted in everything I did or thought. Focusing on the puzzles gave my mind a rest or a diversion from the dread of being alive. They relieved my torment during these three difficult years. By fixating on them so often, I was showing another side to anxiety, obsessive compulsive behavior. Even though my conduct was insane, I'm thankful I had the crosswords to concentrate on.

I became good at doing the puzzles, even if they were the path to Obsessive Compulsive Disorder (OCD). I completed the *USA Today* crossword in record time. I also had a stack of puzzle books on hand so I wouldn't be without one. If I didn't have a brainteaser to work, it would be a disaster and cause a panic attack. These word riddles helped me escape disaster.

Driving from Scottsdale to Carlsbad, California, became another terrifying event. Pat and I made the trip sometimes twice a year by car to visit my son Eric, his wife Sherri, and my two grandchildren, Sofia and Jordan. Usually, it was for a family event such as Thanksgiving or a chance to go to the ocean.

The drive triggered another episode of fearing an anticipated affair. There wasn't any reason I feared the upcoming trip but, for a month before we left, sometimes longer, I became fearful. My mind was preoccupied with a corner in the road along our way. The bend was in California just after leaving Palm Springs. At that specific spot on the freeway I feared our car would crash.

This dreaded corner might have stemmed from an auto accident I endured during college, north of Corvallis, Oregon, in 1956. That crash altered my life and killed my best friend, Al Smith, and a young lady named Alice Rampton when I was twenty-one years old. The excessive terror triggered by the car trip that was coming into my near future was connected to that old memory I still carried with me. I lived most of my life with survivor guilt.

The delusion of the corner was lunacy. Its imagined threat of danger intimidated me beyond reason and held me captive. When I finally approached the corner that haunted me, I made sure Pat drove the car. When we finally made it around the corner, my alarm disappeared. A rush of relief and a calm came over me.

Going to the movies also stirred the fear inside me. I was preoccupied with sitting in the same seat in the theatre every time I went to the movies with Pat. If I couldn't get the same seat, I had to sit as close to that specific seat as possible. I was suffering from OCD. To secure my favorite seat, Pat and I left an hour early from our condominium to get to the theater in time to connect to my important seat. We lived ten minutes away.

I was also afraid of violent or sad movies, which reduced the number of choices. Most films have either one or the other element, or both. The movie obsession was based on irrational thoughts effecting my behavior. It was maddening, but I couldn't control it. Pat and I enjoyed the movies and attended often, but my anxiety interfered in one of our favorite pastimes.

I went to five psychiatrists during this period before I found someone who prescribed the correct medications for me. Some wanted to cure my problem with "big time" powerful drugs that would have me "spaced out." I would have been back to square one when they wore off. I always refused to take those drugs because they would have "doped" me up and caused addiction.

I fought through the tough times on my own and with Pat's love and support. Eventually, I was fortunate to survive the unending rough days. Today, I take a combination of four drugs that took a lot of trial and error to get exactly right.

My journey through anxiety, due to the seclusion I maintained, was a narrow glimpse at myself and others suffering through an irrational time. It gave me an appreciation of those who suffer with mental issues and the frustration they go through in finding the correct dosages of drugs. Some never find relief due to weak or nonexistent healthcare programs. They often give up before finding an answer, which can be devastating.

My unreasonable fears popped up and overcame me for no apparent reason. I was continually telling myself not to be frightened. I look back now at some of the terror I experienced and try to laugh about it. But it wasn't funny at the time, and it's not funny today. I lived through those anxiety years, but sometimes I wonder how I did it so long because each day was an ordeal. There was no way I could escape the daily torture except by working crossword puzzles.

I now know why some people commit suicide, something approximately 50,000 people in the United States do each year and 800,000 people in the world. That's one person every forty seconds who loses hope and gives in to their desperation. The loss of hope is the last bastion before suicide.

As French author Albert Camus said, "It takes more courage to live than to kill oneself."

I feel a bit prideful I had the courage to keep going day after day for three years. Today, I can't conceptualize how I fought against the mental anguish during that overwhelming time of fear. It was just meant to be.

Today, I am symptom free. I will always have a warm spot in my heart for Dr. Roefe, the psychiatrist who, finally—after many years of seeing a lot of others and taking various medications—secured the correct combinations and dosages for me. In a sense, it liberated me enough to go back to much of my previous life with a renewed interest. No more obsessions and fears with movies, roads and their corners, crossword puzzles, and the golfing "yips."

I feel better today with the proper medications to overcome the anxiety. I could forget about those three years and choose not to reveal my story to anyone, but this is my memoir, and I am portraying the truth about my life. Maybe publishing my journey through anxiety will help someone else to understand and face their own uncertainties.

Mental illness is tormenting and hard to live with. It's not something people discuss in bars or around the dinner table. Each year, it affects one in six people in America. Too many thousands of people die by suicide each year in the United States due to psychological issues. I'm grateful to not be one of them.

Religion

I've noticed that, among religious people, many are cold, and a few are frozen.

Charlie "Tremendous" Jones,
author and editor

CHURCH AS A KID

My first memories of religion were events surrounding our family attending the Redeemer Lutheran Church in Tillamook, Oregon. I was six or seven years old. The church on Third Street, a small structure of white stucco, featured some stained-glass windows, a cross on top, a basement below, and a "sticker bush" in the front yard. This shrub is also called a burweed or a "jagger" bush in other parts of the country. It was considered dangerous.

I do not know why anyone would plant a sticker bush in a yard. My bet was it had a parallel to Jesus wearing the crown of thorns, put on his head by the Romans before the crucifixion. The thicket could have been a symbol of the pain caused by the wretched crown. I would not put it past the austere Lutherans to believe the congregation needed a tender reminder every time they brushed up against the tortuous undergrowth. I had a clever idea of Jesus' hardship since I always encountered the wicked hedge.

When you are young, small incidents define the time you participated in the bigger picture. These tiny events stayed in my memory and, in many cases, were later remembered as humorous. When I attended Sunday school and was later confirmed in the Lutheran church as a teenager, these events came to mind. They reminded me of what was supposed to be religious training and participation in the redemption of my soul, yet they loomed on the edge of being bizarre.

Looking back into the face of the minister I knew while attending the Lutheran church in Tillamook, I concluded he was depressed. Reverend Schmidt, a lifeless man in a black robe, seemed to me not any crazier about being in church than I. He was without passion for the ministry of the Lord, making the correct moves to fool us sinners. Our pastor was going through the motions of what the congregation was supposed to see as religious leadership.

When I was a child sitting below the pulpit looking up, this was my first real introduction to boredom.

As W.C. Fields said, "It's hard to fool kids and dogs."

This pastor did not convince me he had reached his steadfast calling. He was tired. Of course, I was young and restless, and he represented the strict and rigid word of God. He was the supreme interpretation of the Bible for our congregation. He was not that popular to a squirming youngster looking for any avenue to overcome boredom. As far as I could tell, everything unacceptable looked like the most fun. I saw more opportunity for wrath in my life after listening to him.

Sunday School

Sunday school was where it all started to go wrong. The teacher had a habit of assigning a Bible verse for us children to memorize during the week. When we returned the following Sabbath, we recited it to the teacher and the class. Sounds easy, but all week I wouldn't put any time into memorizing. Then, on the Lord's day, I could not recite it. I have never been good at learning by the rote method. Besides, I was six or seven years old at the time, yearning to play with my childhood friend, Bobby Montgomery, back home on Evergreen Drive.

Sunday school was my first opportunity to fail academically, and I did so with regularity. Following my dereliction of duty to the Sunday school class, I was supposed to feel the guilt of letting down the Almighty, my teacher reminded me. I was having an issue with God and religion.

After Sunday school's depressing failure, I sat through an hour of church, sandwiched between my parents on the hard wooden pew.

This was highlighted by the minister looking down at the congregation from his tall pulpit, tossing verbal threats like hand grenades, and admonishing the congregation to show a small amount of repentance for their sins. I am not sure how other churches gather parishioners to repent for their sins, but the Lutheran method was based on a simple premise: fear.

If you sinned, you were going to Hell, simple logic as far as the Lutherans were concerned. We were being scared into Heaven.

I do not know how many times my mother told me, "If you don't straighten up and behave, you're going to Hell."

After hearing that line enough times, I thought I could not be good on a sustained basis, so why try? I just decided to have a fun time.

I could never get it straight anyway with the three different sides of God, the three levels of consciousness: the Father, the Son, and especially the Holy Ghost. Omniscient, omnipresent, and omnipotent really threw me for a loop. "God is love" was a Bible verse I could grasp, but on the other hand, I was headed to Hell according to my mother. It might have been her last straw trying to quell my hyper misbehavior. I was a young child trying to understand the holy writ to move upward. I was riding a creaky elevator.

Sunday Clothes

When I was young, I had twenty-two aunts and uncles, so I had a lot of cousins. Our entire family practiced the theory of "hand-me-downs" when it came to clothing. We would pass on clothes from the oldest to the youngest cousin as we grew out of them. My oldest brother, Charles, would get them first from an older cousin, and then they would work their way to my brother, Almon, who was just two years older than me. Eventually, the clothes would come to me when he grew out of them. It was a good system to save money on clothes that still had some wear left in them. When Charles and Almon came by these clothes, I also received them, but not right away.

Sometimes Charles was given a handsome jacket, and I felt good knowing I would wear it in the future. The best hand-me-down that came my way was a cashmere sweater our cousin Bud Remus passed on. When it did not fit either of my older brothers, I ended up with a beautiful, gently used, light-beige sweater. I'd never heard of cashmere, but I wore it to junior high school in 1949 to the envy of my teachers. The sweater was the best piece of clothing given to me during our family's hand-me-down era.

Not all the clothing I received from my brothers and cousins fell into the same comfortable clothing category as the cashmere sweater, which brings me back to Sunday school. I received a pair of classic-style slacks from my cousin Wendell that were as scratchy as steel wool. Since Wendell was slightly bigger than I, they came directly to me. The pants were my first visit to physical and mental anguish in clothing. Even when I stood perfectly still, they itched. There was no downtime with the discomfort. They made my hands itch when I touched them.

When Sunday morning came around, I had to put on these pants to go to Sunday school and church, a period of two hours of agony. My mother, at first, told me they did not itch. Then she told me to pretend they did not itch. Eventually, she told me to just wear the pants and quit complaining.

After a few Sundays of this treatment, I finally, out of desperation, decided to lie and say I was sick and could not go to Sunday school and church. I wiggled out of wearing those scratchy pants. I took a chance God would see it my way, by forgiving me my lying, knowing my situation demanded an unholy solution. My parents let me stay home as they went off to church, which increased my belief in the usefulness of the "good" lie.

God heard my prayers to not have to wear the pants again and let the lie slide that once. When my father arrived home from church, he told my mother to get rid of the pants.

Money

The church services were boring to a child who could not understand what was going on, except knowing it was not much fun for the congregation to be told they had better repent or suffer the consequences. Occasionally, something would happen that reminded everyone the congregation was made up of people with actual lives.

Intestinal Fortitude

Mr. Hartman was a great guy, a jokester, always trying to have fun. The elders of the church collected the offering in wooden bowls they passed down the pews from one person to another. The church also had wooden floors. One Sunday, when Mr. Hartman was passing a money bowl to the next person, he dropped the bowl full of dollars and coins.

No one in attendance ever forgot the noise it made in the quiet church as the bowl and the money hit the hard wooden floor. Besides the noise, the sound woke up the congregation, and the coins rolled under the pews in all directions. The churchgoers were all bending down, looking for coins that had rolled under their feet. It took a while to collect all the money again.

Mrs. Hartman was upset, but the look on her face seemed to say she had seen this sort of thing before from her fun-loving husband. It was comic relief from yet another relentless sermon delivered by the black-robed bionic man of doom above us in the pulpit.

When the elders counted the offering in the basement of the church, some of my young friends and I would go downstairs and watch. Mr. Lacasse, an immigrant from Albania with a strong accent, did the counting. When he got to the number thirty-three, he would say "terdy terd" and we would get a snicker out of it. Saying "terdy terd" around a seven-year-old in 1943 was heady stuff. I would have been, once again, told by my mother I was going to Hell if I tried it.

Hymns

During the sermon, some gentleman would invariably fall asleep and start snoring, until his wife gave him a poke in the ribs. Not particularly unusual in a warm church filled with men who worked hard all week to keep everything together for their family's wellbeing. They seemed a lot like me, acting up a little during the week and then getting put back on the road to redemption with a well-placed reminder from "you know who" in the pulpit.

Attending church always seemed to me to be an exercise that was unnecessary. Couldn't a person attend once a year or never? Wouldn't they get as much out of going just once, as a person who goes every day or weekly? I liked the idea of having a shrine of sorts, like they do in Asia, and visiting it once in a lifetime.

There was one redeeming condition that made the church service enjoyable, and that was when Mrs. Christianson attended. Not only was she young and pretty, but she had a beautiful, strong singing voice with a clearer quality than I had ever heard before. She sang the hymns in a way that led the others in the congregation along in strength and melody. When she was in church, the place had a radiance to it missing when she was absent. She caused me to follow the hymns of the service with a whole new interest. I've always liked hymns, even to this day. The minister scowling down from his pulpit could not dampen my enthusiasm for church on those Sundays when she was with us. She made the sanctuary a glorious tribute to the Almighty.

Sticker Bush

Reverend Schmidt had two daughters, Carol and Ethel, who were a few years older than me. I thought they were pious and well behaved since the minister was their father. I figured they might be different from the rest of us, having to live under the same roof of a man of the cloth. It was a real surprise one Sunday when we were all playing around the sticker bush on the lawn beside the church. The girls moved a little too close to the sharp stickers. Carol ran off a string of cuss words that would make an Oregon logger proud! This was the first time I heard a girl use such words, let alone a preacher's daughter. She was a match for any of the boys in my neighborhood when it came to cussing. I must have looked comical standing in awe with my mouth wide open in disbelief.

Confirmation

When the children of the congregation families reached their teens, they had to go through a ceremony called confirmation to grant them the privilege of membership in the Lutheran Church. We studied tenants of the church's doctrine. Then, while we sat before the congregation, the minister asked specific questions. If enough correct answers were given, some vows of acceptance were offered, and you were in. I do not remember anyone being turned down, no matter how many questions they answered. What would the minister say if you could not answer enough questions?

"You blew the quiz. Go see if the Catholics or Baptists will take you?"

It was a scary event. Who wants to look like a numbskull in front of his parents and the church members? When Almon and Charles went through the ritual of confirmation class, they joined a large group of aspiring teenagers seeking affirmation. With time being a factor with such a large group, they were asked only a couple of questions, as the minister wanted to keep it moving along.

When I came to the class a couple of years later, I had to answer every question from the minister. I had the misfortune of being the lone aspirant in my confirmation class. I gave a couple of answers correctly and botched up the rest, but the minister gave me his approval and I was accepted. The procedure was like a tribunal, I received a reprieve from the pontiff and the gallows of lost souls.

I just could not perceive the habit of transgressing sins during the week and then showing up to church on Sunday seeking atonement. With the Lutherans, there was too much manipulation using guilt and fear. The confessions did not hold any relevance and became redundant. As I grew older, I was able to understand the procedure and the custom.

That was the Lutheran church in Tillamook when I attended during my youth in the 1940s and 1950s. I may be a little tongue-in-cheek about religion at times, but I am a hundred percent serious about determining my comfort level of commitment on this topic.

GOD: A SKEWED LOOK

As I write this second memoir, I am thankful for my life and how it has transpired. I am at a good place, with a peaceful existence alongside my wife, Patricia.

There are some things, however, I have not settled in my mind. One involves never coming to a conclusion about the existence of God. Whether there is a God has been on my mind for longer than I can remember. Since I am getting close to the end of my life, the answer to this question is more urgent. I believe a God would want me to have a firm idea of what I believe. On Judgment Day, standing before God, I do not want to stutter and stammer and say, "Gee, I am not sure if you exist."

Existence of God

If there is a God, how will I react to such an entity whom I assume rules the universe? God has such unimaginable power. It does not seem possible to be on a first-name basis with such a creator and ruler. This cannot be a casual relationship. A mere Sunday morning church service is hardly enough praise for such a supernatural being.

Do I worship God with a blind faith as if He does exist? I believe people who worship the sun have an easier time believing there is a Divinity. The sun is in plain sight and always looking down on us. Even in cloudy weather, I know it is there somewhere. There is no mistaking its power. The Aztecs in Mexico call themselves the People of the Sun and have four different sun gods in their history, the first being Tezcatlipoca. The Aztecs were not taking any chances worshipping the incorrect god. If you have four different sun deities, your chances are better that one of them is the true God.

A Sign

Do I worship God with blind faith because He is metaphysical? I believe it would be better for everyone if God let us all know for sure He or She exists. A concrete sign from God would help. I feel we might behave better if we knew for sure God is really watching our daily lives and is going to make an important judgment in the future because of our conduct.

Suffering

It is hard for me to believe there is a God considering all the pain and suffering that occurs daily in the world. I puzzle if God exists when catastrophic events occur, such as viruses, fires, and storms. What was God doing while the six million Jews were dying in concentration camps in German-occupied Europe during and before World War II? The Holocaust is just one of many horrible events in the history of our planet. Not to mention the smaller disasters that take place regularly somewhere on Earth. How can I worship a God who allows such pain to happen? God is said to be omnipresent, so He should know what is going on.

I was taught God is omnipotent, omnipresent, and omniscient with unimaginable power. He is present and sees and knows what is going on all over the universe. He is always with us, never taking a break. This belief is hard for me to accept. I keep coming back to the suffering in the world. I cannot believe a God would condone so many of these conditions. Some say it is not God, but the free will of the people.

There is no point in causing pain to defenseless children—or anyone else for that matter. I cannot bring myself to say this is an "imperfect world" as an answer for the pain inflicted on children. That is a copout and lets God off the hook. To me, this is God's world. He is an entity who has the imminent power to embrace total control.

One of the first Bible verses I learned in Sunday school was "God is love," which made no sense. Love to whom? How does a God be a God of love, reign supreme, then condone the pain that takes place every day? How does God explain the Catholic Church and its history of priests preying on young boys and girls?

If there is a God, I believe He would show love to those unsuspecting boys and girls who are caught up in the horrible scenario of sexual child abuse perpetuated for years by priests. It is not as if the priests and bishops were not doing this handywork under His nose and He did not know. He had to know. If God allowed this treatment of choir and altar children by the priesthood, what kind of God would let this behavior take place? This does not speak well to me for God or the Catholic Church.

Correct Religion and Eternal Life

Most people believe they are following a legitimate religion to reach the promised land. Heaven, which many trust to be their final goal, is on most everyone's mind, including mine. But how does anyone really know which type of worship is the true ideology? How do I know what I am doing in relation to God and attaining eternal life is the only path to kingdom come? At one time in my life, it became my concern to pick a church that would catapult me to paradise.

When I was young, children were educated in the religion of their parents. I saw my parents attempt to influence my decision about faith for my entire life. Making a mandate of which beliefs a person follows is a questionable amount of supremacy by one individual over another. My parents raised me in the doctrine of the Lutheran Church. I came away with a fear of God, a belief I was filled with sin and, without praying for forgiveness of my sins, I would go to Hell.

Of all religions in the world, which one is right? I have always been curious about the Lutheran faith and how they stacked up against other teachings by sheer numbers. For people looking for a belief to follow, the number of members of a religion would seem a normal question of inquiry. I was proud to learn that my former faith, the Lutheran religion, the one I grew up with, has eighty-two million followers. It amazed me to discover Hinduism overshadowed it with 1.8 billion followers. Should a disciple take into consideration the number of followers in choosing a doctrine? Does it not matter if one teaching is bigger than another? I wonder, as a former Lutheran, where all those Hindus are headed on Judgment Day.

If my old religion, Lutheranism, is the one true creed to find eternal life, what are we to do about the millions of men, women, boys, and girls who follow Islam, Taoism, Shinto, Sikhism, and Judaism to name a few? It would seem a giant mistake by me to wake up on the day of atonement and find out I had followed the wrong faith during my life here on Earth. I do not believe any God would want that to happen to any disciple of any religion. Everyone on Earth is praying to the same God, only dressed up a little differently from one another. With so many different people following so many different doctrines with the hope of eternal life, the questions remain: Who has it right?

Judgment Day

When I was attending Sunday school, the topic of going to Heaven or Hell was on everyone's agenda. I was afraid of going to Hell and dancing on coals for eternity. When the topic came up of everyone rising from the dead, or Judgment Day, and God's designation for us to go to Heaven or Hell, I paid attention.

Let us say I did not atone for one single sin against one of the Ten Commandments. It took place way back when we were young and we cared less about sin or atonement. When deciding on Judgment Day about whether someone goes to Heaven or Hell, how does God rate us? Maybe He puts us on a point system. Let us say we are a few points shy of going to Heaven. Does God give us the benefit of the doubt? Let us say we get in anyway. It would be a catastrophe to fall one point shy of making the big jump to the promised land. That is why we do not want to die suddenly without the opportunity to seek forgiveness for our sins. That is why we seek absolution, so we are up to date and no sin gets past us to trip us up on our journey into the kingdom of Heaven.

Earl Llewellyn Goldmann

Catholics Versus the Lutherans

I always thought the Catholics felt the Lutherans were illegitimate as a religion because they split off from the Catholic Church. I am sure the Catholics were not too keen on Martin Luther when he nailed the Ninety-five Theses on the Castle Church door in Wittenberg, Germany in 1577. Even though, as a Catholic priest himself, he did not want to break away from the church, he started a movement called the Protestant Reformation.

The Reformation was going to start at some point in the 1500s, and Luther's revolutionary opinions in his Ninety-five Theses are usually given credit for starting the movement. One of Luther's complaints against the Catholic Church was the belief that a priest had to pray for you rather than doing it yourself. The church believed you had to have an intermediary and pay indulgences to the church for them. The Catholic Church was right in the first place, and we do need someone of importance to talk to God.

It does seem a little peculiar to me that a mere mortal can converse with the omnipotent Almighty One. I am sure the Catholics felt bad about giving up the practice of indulgences. It was a real money maker. That is how Bingo Night started.

Attending Church on Sunday

Does a follower of a religion have to physically attend church? Is it important to God that you are present at a church service, religious shrine, or mosque once a week? Since I was a youngster, I thought going to church seven days a week was overdoing it. In Genesis in the Bible, it is reported that God finished creating the universe and rested on the seventh day.

If that wasn't enough to seal the deal of Sunday being the day of rest, along comes Exodus in the Bible. Thought to be mostly written by Moses, it contains the fight song "remember the Sabbath Day and keep it Holy." So, my thinking is that Sunday comes around too often. For me to provoke any change about constant church attendance, I had to go up against a heavy hitter, the Bible. As you can imagine, my desire to change Sunday was not going to fly. So, it was off to Sunday school.

Talking About God

I noticed in my communications with others, they very easily reference God. When a problem arises during a discussion, someone invariably brings God into the conversation. Most of the time, the mentioning of God is meant to make other parties feel good. He is also brought up as a definitive answer to any dilemma, past or present. God's name is referred to for the purpose of soothing over our unanswerable quandary using elementary logic.

If the predicament defies reasoning, some higher force must have caused it. "God still has some work for you to do" is why you were spared from that horrible car accident in college that killed others. Also, "God was looking out for you" would be a standard comment. It would also keep your neighbor from having to say, "He's with God now," when referring to one of my brothers who is gone.

When looking at someone else's problem, they sometimes say, "There but for the grace of God go I." They are reminding themselves to not go down the same road some other numbskull chose, usually a path to trouble. It, however, could have been "God's will." Sometimes a friend will answer a question of an unanswerable problem that has arisen in my life with the comment, "God is testing your faith." He sure is.

Logic and Faith

If I need a concrete sign from God to be a believer, I am in for a disappointment because they do not exist. God does not send me signs, though followers sometimes assume He does. If I use logical thinking to prove my belief in God, someone will come up wanting. Logic plays havoc with religions throughout the world. If I want to believe in a God, it would be better for me to rely on faith.

A discussion about religion of my choice or the existence of God comes down to a clash between faith and logic. A belief in God can only come through my faith. Faith makes it possible for me to accept the specifics of my religion. This would be true of any religion.

I have always been curious about what proof exists, if any, that there is an actual God of the universe. With the written religious tenants and history of the belief, its expressed doctrines are an outgrowth of man here on Earth. Religious leaders and disciples are mere mortals who have lived among us every day and started a religion.

The Philosopher

Confucius, of Ancient China, would be an example. He lived amongst the Chinese people and wrote ideas to live by, called the five Confucian virtues. His teachings are still part of life in China today, known as Confucianism—a tradition, religion, way of governing, or simply a way of life. A peoples' religion fits their culture. Their resources, climate, food supply, and lifestyle dictate the doctrine of their religion.

Times can change through the years and beliefs often adjust to their doctrine. A good example of this process is when the Mormons in Utah gave up their belief of having more than one wife to get to Heaven. The United States government informed them, for Utah to become a state in the Union, their followers could only have one wife. The Mormons changed their ways and Utah was admitted as a state in 1896.

My points in all this? First, man forms these religions of the world, and we all know man is not without blemish. Second, millions of people become followers of said religion founded on a deity of superhuman powers and control over a part of life—think Poseidon—or the world. The people give the deities names such as Allah, Almighty, Jehovah, Supreme Being, and so on. The whole scene does not sound very holy. A believer has faith in a superhuman being brainstormed by a prophet who might as well be his neighbor for all the divine wisdom he possesses.

Some worshippers profess a religion because of the jitters about the unknown. They are worried about whether there is a Heaven or Hell. Many like to turn to a higher power that is bigger than they are in times of trouble. It gives them comfort to pray to a God for our old uncle Harry who is on his last leg. How many times have I heard,

"I will keep you in my thoughts and prayers," as a comfort to others or to me?

It has been my experience that a lot of churchgoers like it simple. They do not want to use their imaginations or think. They just want to recite a few creeds, sing a hymn or two from the hymn book, and move on to Sunday dinner.

Do not get me wrong. I have no trouble worshipping a true God. My problem is I do not know any Gods. Sure, there are an abundance of religions, and they all have a God of some sort. That is fine, but they are not my God. Why should I take someone else's God anyway? No one on this planet knows a real live God. I would love to have a God and be a serious worshipper. Until then, I will believe there could be a God and remain an agnostic.

PERCEPTION

**A smooth sea
never made a skilled mariner.**

English proverb

PERCEPTION

During my sophomore year at Oregon State College (OSC), I was involved in a severe auto accident. My life was altered forever, along with other lives, on this day in May of 1956. This is an account of my feelings and reactions before and after this horrendous event. It brought me a seat on an emotional roller coaster from elation down to a lifetime of post-traumatic stress disorder (PTSD). Those involved were Al Smith, a twenty-year-old Sigma Chi Fraternity brother of mine at OSC; two fifteen-year-old Corvallis High School students, Patty Maxon and Alice Rampton; and me at age twenty-one.

Al Smith and I left our basement apartment behind the Delta Upsilon Fraternity house on 23rd Street in Corvallis Oregon on a warm Sunday evening in May. We were OSC students majoring in "trying to grow up, but not too fast." We were always pumped with life and constantly in motion. Al was usually hyped, and I was right on his heels.

I had been informed two days earlier by the OSC basketball coach, "Slats" Gill, he was putting me on a basketball scholarship for my junior and senior years. I had been on a baseball scholarship for my first two years, but things weren't going well with the baseball coach, Ralph Coleman. The new scholarship gave me a welcome option.

"Slats" asked me to play out the baseball season and not get into any trouble with Coach Coleman. I had turned down the baseball coach's request to play semi-pro baseball for Bend, Oregon, the summer before. I missed the ocean, returned home instead, and played for the Tillamook Elk's semi-pro team. Coleman didn't like hearing the word no. By not going to Bend, I hurt my chances of playing more baseball at OSC. If I had a chance today to change that decision, I would go to Bend.

I told "Slats" I would stay out of trouble and left our meeting ecstatic. It was a dream come true. The basketball scholarship represented a lot of effort and arduous work, but I was on cloud nine!

As usual, both Al and I felt great as we planned our Sunday. We were always ready for our next adventure. To him, life was to be lived at full throttle, always moving, always looking for the next escapade.

We were riding around in an older red 1942 Oldsmobile convertible with the top down, and Al was at the wheel. Earlier that afternoon, he had traded cars with Judy Sparks, a girlfriend from Portland. She returned home in his old Ford jalopy, a good trade-off per Al.

As we headed up 23rd Street, Al said, "Lets drive downtown and see what's going on," which was his way of saying, "Let's look for some girls."

As a rule, downtown Corvallis is a dead place, especially on a Sunday evening. But, I thought, this is Al talking. He usually turns up fun somehow. I was filled with anticipation of an enjoyable time.

A slight, warm breeze blew on our faces as we turned on Van Buren and steered toward Jefferson Street. We saw two girls standing in the front yard of a house near the campus of OSC. To my surprise, Al slowed the car and called one of the girls by name. He said hi to Patty Maxon as we came to a stop. She came over to the car. I wondered how he knew her but dismissed the thought. Al was outgoing and knew a lot of people. He asked Patty if she wanted to go for a ride in the convertible. She said sure and asked her friend if she wanted to go, too.

Unbeknownst to Al and me, this second girl, whose name was Alice Rampton, was babysitting for her siblings, three of the Ramptons' other children, whom she left behind in the house. Alice was hesitant to go with Patty, who by now was in the car next to Al and holding the seat back for Alice. Patty soon talked her into jumping into the rear seat of the car. I moved, too, and sat next to Alice. For a while, no more words were said as Al pulled the car away from the curb.

Intestinal Fortitude

We were off for an exciting ride around the block. I don't know who had the idea to take a longer drive along the Willamette River. It was either Al or Patty. Both were so full of energy and eager for fun.

The drive around the block turned into a jaunt downtown and then somehow a turn toward Albany, along the river and going away from Corvallis. It was more of a trip than Alice had agreed to, as she couldn't be gone a long time. Still, no one mentioned young children looking for her or napping and unaware she was gone. Had I known, I would have cautioned Al to keep the ride short.

As he drove toward Albany, Al turned into the decommissioned Camp Adair Army Base through its back gate. We moved about the base, which was empty of life, past the barracks and out the front entrance. After exiting the base, we turned south toward Corvallis and back in the direction of Alice's house. It started to rain, so Al pulled over and stopped the car to put up the convertible top.

Just up the road, in less than a mile, we drove into a dangerous sharp curve. My good friend veered off to escape two cars coming toward us in our lane. They were passing wide on the severe curve and taking up the available span of the highway. Al turned the convertible to the right to miss them and hit the hillside along the street. The car flipped to the left before coming to rest upside down on the pavement. This resulted in the deaths of Alice and Al. They were crushed by the car since they were both on the left side.

Patty was thrown on top of Al as the car came to a stop. She later told me as she lay on Al, she felt him take his last breath and die. Patty realized, amid the calamity, she hadn't been injured while her two friends had died. Like me, later she would wonder "why me?" She too has experienced PTSD from the horrendous accident.

I was pulled from under the car by the police and firemen who eventually came to the scene. I couldn't see because of a film over my eyes from the exhaust fumes. I could hear and tell light from dark as they moved my body. I felt my blood dripping onto my face from my forehead. I couldn't see Alice, but I assumed she was under the car, too, since she had been sitting next to me. I had no idea of her condition, if there were witnesses, or if the other two cars sped off into the night.

We didn't know that this innocent ride was the last for Alice and Al and would forever change Patty's and my life. Within less than a half hour, two lives tragically ended on Highway 99W just north of Corvallis, Oregon.

At the hospital the night of the accident, when the first responders brought me to the ER, I couldn't see, move, or feel. Though I had a broken eardrum from the accident, I could hear the doctors and nurses' conversations in the emergency room while I lay on a gurney.

I sensed Al lying next to me, which was corroborated by the doctor who said, "This one is alive. This one is dead."

I was in an emotional dilemma. If I was alive, Al had to be dead. My roommate and friend had died. I learned Alice was dead when I overheard a conversation with her father and the ER doctor who told him she was at the morgue.

After the doctor put me to sleep, I dreamed I saw an open door with a brilliant light shining through it. I moved toward the light, which I feared was death. I knew I saw the edge of death and, if I passed through the door, I would die. I focused on turning away from it and was able to stop short of the bright doorway and retreat by sheer willpower.

For Alice's brothers, sisters, and parents, she vanished from their lives. Alice was babysitting for her siblings in one instant, then drove off in a car the next moment, and was gone forever, never to return. It had to be terribly difficult to comprehend.

Alice's siblings did not learn the true story of her death until sixty years later when we had a conversation. Her family did not contact me, or me them, for all those years, partially due to survivor's guilt and grief on my part and pure grief on theirs. Until our meeting in 2017, the family knew nothing of the shocking scenario of her death. No one ever came forward to admit to the accident or as a witness. The police report proved incorrect and inconclusive. The investigation was questionable. The police were not able to explain the circumstances. What persisted were rumors and guesswork.

Alice's family didn't contact me because of all the gossip, afraid some of it was the truth. Or they just forgave me and Al and eventually moved on with their lives.

Intestinal Fortitude

That fateful Sunday evening, Alice's parents had been attending a meeting at the Mormon church in Corvallis. Upon hearing of the accident, Alice's father went to the Corvallis Hospital, where the doctor told him Alice was already at the morgue. The conversation was surely brutal. He was being told his daughter did not survive the accident.

The news of Alice's death hit her mother hard. She not only lost her daughter, but also endured rumors that Alice had been in the company of older male college students and alcohol was involved. On the surface, it didn't look innocent. The questions weren't fully answered until I published my book *Bounce Back* and met with the Rampton family in 2019. Sixty years after the accident took place, Alice's brothers and sisters wanted me to explain the accident from my perspective and put to rest the rumors that had swirled around Corvallis for all that time.

Since Al and I were college students, and I was twenty-one, the Corvallis policemen contributed to the rumors by assuming alcohol was involved. It only takes one comment by the police to a single citizen of Corvallis to start the rumors flying. The police themselves were members of the community and had their opinions.

Corvallis police officers came to my hospital room and woke me Monday morning, convinced the four of us had been drinking that fateful day. I was practically in a coma from head injuries when they disturbed me from sleep and endeavored to intimidate me. They tried to badger me into admitting we had been drinking beer at the time of the accident. I repeatedly told them no. They didn't believe me. The police claimed there were beer bottles around the accident scene. I did not appreciate their coercive tactics. I was just trying to cope with the realization that Patty and I were alive, and Al and Alice were dead.

As I lay in the hospital room after the police left, trying to sort through what had happened the evening before, I was consumed with remorse and guilt. I tried to wrap my head around Alice and Al dying. I reminded myself I was alive to try to force the pain of Alice and Al's deaths from my mind. I didn't know how else to handle the magnitude of their deaths that gripped my mind. I was unable to overcome my grief. Only by thinking I was alive and had to go on with my life could I gain control of the loss of them. I couldn't think of any other way to cope. In retrospect, it helped me survive in the beginning, but eventually I settled into a lifetime of PTSD. I thought of Alice and Al every day during my life.

People want to think the worst when an accident takes place, especially when it's as tragic as this one. Corvallis is a small, quiet town and was more so in 1956. The local newspaper, the *Corvallis Gazette*, put Al's and my ages in large, bold print on the front page. This was to be sure everyone saw the age differences between the girls and us when they read the article.

This action accomplished what the newspaper intended to do. It turned the community against Al and me even though he was dead. Since I was the one who survived, the alarming news focused on me. The paper also put a picture of me in my OSC baseball cap on the front page so everyone would know who to disfavor. The accident now had a face to attach to the deception. The newspaper would tell you it was simply good reporting, but printing our ages in larger, bold type was unfair and unnecessary. I did not glean this information until sixty years later when I requested a copy of the newspaper article for my research for my first book. I did not want to read about the accident right after it happened. I wanted to come to grips with it and take on my many surgeries.

Linda Lundy, a longtime friend from Tillamook and a student at OSC, defended me by speaking out early Monday morning in her first class. Her professor, in front of his class, was accusing me of the death of Alice. Linda immediately pointed out to the teacher he was being unfair since he did not know the circumstances of the situation and that the police were still investigating. The professor's feelings were typical of many of those who lived in Corvallis. The students', teachers', and citizens' groundless, negative opinions of me and the unfortunate accident caused a rush to judgment. Linda always stood up for her friends. I will always be grateful for her unyielding friendship.

With no concrete knowledge about the accident and what had taken place, a wave of gossip spread across the OSC campus. Nobody, including the police, seemed to have anything to go on to solve this hit-and-run. The broadcast took on the face of conjecture even though no one knew the relationship of the four of us. There was no way the rumors could be stopped. Even the Corvallis police thought we had been drinking and helped spread the insinuations. They had their minds made up or were convinced somehow Al caused the accident. It also didn't help that I was on the baseball and basketball teams at OSC. It made it a little more sensational since I was known on campus. Very few inquiries took place.

Oregon State College was a tight-knit community, so rumors spread quickly amongst the student body and faculty. Alice's father was a professor at OSC at the time of the accident. He had to endure the implications and questions of his colleagues. Sadly, he didn't have answers for why his daughter died in an auto accident in the company of two older male college students. He couldn't explain why his daughter and her high school friend were there in the first place. He also knew she had a high school boyfriend.

Alice's boyfriend never approached me, nor did her father, after I returned to campus. I did not know anything about them at the time, who they were, or how to locate them. I learned of them sixty years late when I met Alice's family.

The accident also took place at night. Had it happened in the morning, it might have seemed less dramatic. Her father understood how the questions could develop, but it didn't make it any easier. Alice was in a convertible, at night, with her friend and two older college boys in the countryside outside of Corvallis. He couldn't force himself to talk to me about the accident while I was hospitalized, during my surgeries, or upon my brief return to OSC.

I wish now I would have met with the Rampton family shortly after leaving the hospital to explain the innocence of the tragic matter. I'm not sure I was mature enough at the time to handle such a meeting. My parents met with them briefly, but I do not recall what was said. Knowing what I know today, I think it would have been extremely helpful to the Ramptons and to me, too, for that to have occurred.

The knowledge that Al and I liked to drink beer and have fun among some students along fraternity row made it easier for them to believe the insinuations. They had a tough time not believing we hadn't been drinking. It was easy to assume the girls were drinking, too, which was not true, but it fueled the spread of misinformation.

By Tuesday, my night nurse at the Corvallis Hospital began berating me about my role in the wreck and Alice's death. She purported I was to blame for Alice's death. Her sharp tongue continued for two nights. The feeling in Corvallis toward me must have been extremely negative if my nurse felt she could confront me in my hospital room without any restraint. She had to have been asleep in class the day the teacher discussed TLC, tender loving care. Why wouldn't I be blamed? I was a twenty-one-year-old college student, who had miraculously survived a horrible accident. After two nights of her hateful tongue, I asked my doctor to ban her from my room. The hospital accommodated me.

Patty Maxon came through the accident without any physical injury, an unbelievable outcome given the severity of the crash. The convertible had rolled back on the highway upside down, then skidded a short distance. It was a nightmare, but Patty and I lived. We were extremely fortunate. Some people told me it was God's will. I say, if it was God's will, how do you explain the fate of Al and Alice? Two of the nicest young people on the planet were killed because of His will. A God I believe in doesn't kill young people. You say God had a reason, but there is no reason for me.

When Patty came to see me at the Corvallis Hospital the following day, she was suffering. She didn't know what to do or which way to turn for help. She came to see me in hopes I could provide support. She was agonizing over Alice's death and her role in making it happen. She paced back and forth in my room and couldn't calm down. Eventually, she sat down in a chair next to my bed where her anguish turned to tears.

Patty needed therapy to find peace of mind concerning Alice's and Al's deaths. In the 1950s, therapy wasn't as readily available as it is today. You were expected to pick yourself up on your own. No one mentioned physical or mental therapy to me over the next year of my recovery process. I wish I could have helped Patty in some way, but I wasn't in any condition to help anyone. I couldn't see or hear very well and had a fracture behind my left ear and a concussion in the front of my skull. I had the broken eardrum, a compound fracture of my right humerus, and a broken acromioclavicular joint in my left shoulder. I had been bounced around in the car during the wreck and had a few bruises and flesh wounds, but I was lucky to be alive and I knew it. I was hardly aware of my hospital room as I slept most of the time.

Intestinal Fortitude

In the face of what Patty was going through, her parents reacted by taking her out of Corvallis High School and sending her away to a Catholic boarding school in Mt. Angel, Oregon. By doing so, it appeared as though she was being exiled in the eyes of her classmates and the community. It gave the impression Patty's parents were blaming her for Alice's death.

I tried to contact Patty in 2017 by mail and phone. She didn't return my letter or answer the messages. This might be because she didn't want to be found. The Ramptons told us she had a difficult life and left it at that statement. I was told by them the contact information I had on her was good. I was looking for closure for both of us.

The fact remained, Patty was in an automobile accident that killed her best friend. She left town, making it look like she was running way. She was put in an extremely difficult position at an early age. The accident was the focal point of her life, as it was for me. I struggled for years with the guilt of Alice's and Al's deaths. Why should I survive and not them? It would have helped me to have some therapy early on, but the attitude of numerous people was "get over it, we all have problems." My family was as supportive as they could manage, but living paycheck to paycheck, they didn't have the means to send me to psychoanalysis. In those days, it was not covered by insurance or readily available.

I contacted a witness to the accident, Pete Norman, sixty years afterwards and he wouldn't talk to me on the phone. I learned of him through the newspaper article I obtained from the Corvallis newspaper archives. It was as if he knew I was eventually going to call him someday. He was in one of the two cars that passed and forced us off the road. He was a student at Linfield College, just up the road in McMinnville, Oregon, at the time of the accident. He was returning to school that Sunday evening. Ironically, he was a retired lawyer at the time I called him and knew how to handle the conversation. Once he knew who the call was from and what I wanted, he ended the call abruptly.

Not knowing what it was, I grappled with PTSD for decades. Even after years of therapy, nobody clearly defined what was going on with me. It wasn't until I was eighty-two that I was helped by my wife to relieve the PTSD I had been carrying around since I was twenty-one. Patricia felt strongly I should meet with the Rampton family for closure to my stress connected with the accident.

A meeting with Alice's brothers and sisters in 2017 in Corvallis changed all that. My wife researched the name "Alice Rampton" on the internet, hoping to find someone in Corvallis with that last name or named after the late Alice Rampton. We found Alice's brother's wife, coincidentally of the same name through marriage. After following them on Facebook for weeks, we finally contacted them. We decided they were nice family people, and we were right. We made plans to meet with them, their siblings, and spouses, for the first time after sixty years. We were in Corvallis while on vacation in Oregon.

Patricia, together with Alice Henderson Rampton, the wife of Dr. Mark Rampton, younger brother to the deceased Alice, organized the meeting. It was a gathering of the Rampton family, my wife, and I, at their lovely home in Corvallis. Although their home is on the road heading to the accident site, I was comfortable there and able that night to eliminate a lot of the stress that had plagued me all my life. They were very welcoming and offered a lot of information to me, and me to them, but nothing was ever resolved on who caused the accident. No one was ever charged with even reckless driving.

We had a lovely evening sharing stories during dinner. Later, they asked me a lot of questions and recorded them when I answered.

Alice's brothers and sisters conveyed to me that they didn't hold me responsible for her death, and never felt that way. Their expression of sentiment gave me an abundance of relief. During our discussion, I was able to relate the evening of the accident in detail for them, the way I remembered it. It was a significant night for me in relieving a lifetime of stress regarding the accident and Alice's and Al's deaths. The outcome of the meeting was beneficial to me and to them and made plausible by the Rampton family's amiable sensibility. We have stayed in touch since that time.

I came home from our mutually satisfying meeting feeling much better. I'm grateful Patricia put the meeting together and that the Ramptons were receptive to the idea. It helped me cope with my PTSD.

The effect of the accident altered many lives, parents, siblings, and friends. But none more than Alice's and Al's.

Al's parents and his many friends had to take this traumatic event the rest of the way through life without him. He lived only twenty years and was just getting started, but he created a place in his life for everyone when he was here. I'm glad I was included.

Alice was a nice girl. That's all I know because sadly we knew each other for only the length of the fateful car ride we took together. For her to die at such a youthful age, with her life ahead of her, was a loss to everyone who knew her and was going to know her. Sadly, this young woman died sitting next to someone she'd known for only twenty minutes.

Spokane Landing

One late summer night in 1956, I was on board a large Northwest Orient airplane flying from Portland, Oregon, to Spokane, Washington. That airline doesn't exist today; Delta Airlines bought them out in 2008.

The flight was uneventful with only six passengers on board the red-eye flight. So few passengers made me feel like I was flying alone. After about an hour, the pilot put the plane in landing mode. I was looking forward to getting home from a busy sales meeting in San Francisco.

I flew in and out of Spokane enough to know, at that time, the airport offered only one runway that ran north and south. I was also aware the city lay north of the airport. As the pilot readied to land the big jet, I casually glanced out the window to enjoy the sparkling lights of the city. We approached the airport from the west. I could tell by the sun and Mount Rainier. This move made me wonder if the pilot was going to circle to land. If I knew anything that night, it was the runway of the Spokane airport ran north and south. We were heading east and entry here was not typically done this way.

The seat belt light was on, and a pretty stewardess was collecting garbage from the passengers. The pilot's strong voice on the PA system bellowed. He told us to prepare for landing, also mentioning the temperature was fifty-four degrees.

I still assumed the pilot was going to bank the airplane to the right to land because we were going east. It seemed logical to me. As I looked out the window, a quick thought told me we were too near the airport and too low to do such a maneuver. I'd flown enough to know the plane was about to touch down and we were close to landing. As we descended on our "fictional flight path," we continued due east with the city still on my left. This was not a good thing. The plane was on a flight pattern that would cause us to cross over the runway, not in line with it. I was convinced the pilot was going to crash the plane somewhere in the dark near the airport.

Lower and lower we descended in our erroneous flight path and prepared to land. I became a little anxious, but I thought the pilot must know what he's doing. We were down low enough to see the airport's runway lights, but there were none.

Suddenly, without any warning, the pilot pulled the stick back and guided the plane in a serious power climb upward.

I knew it, I knew it, I thought. There was no runway where the pilot was trying to land. A nervous shiver came over me.

I sat back in my seat in a state of anxiety and confusion as the pilot banked the big plane around and landed the jet from the south. I was a little unnerved as I exited the airplane. The pilot stood at the cabin door thanking the passengers for flying with Northwest.

I smirked at him. "Nice landing."

He gave me a sheepish grin. His expression cemented my assumption that he had avoided crashing the plane in a wheatfield. I have heard of pilots landing planes at the wrong airport before. If a pilot could do that, they could certainly approach an airport from the wrong direction and land the plane in a direction not initially expected by the air traffic controllers. My faith in air travel took an uneasy hit that night in Spokane.

PORTLAND LANDING

One winter, I took a morning flight from Phoenix to Portland, Oregon. Not being a very relaxed passenger myself, and one who feared flying, I usually looked at the cabin full of passengers and thought, *So, is this the crowd I'm going to kick the bucket with today?* Not a good attitude for a passenger frequently traveling by air.

I have since developed a little more intelligence about the whole procedure. In other words, the takeoff, flight, and landing for me these days includes *infrequent* white knuckles. In the past, I would grit my teeth, hold on to my seat with both hands, and tense up... expecting the worst, but hoping for the best.

When nearing Portland, coming in around beautiful, snowy Mount Hood, we were about to touch down. The pilot, without any warning, aborted our landing by tilting the plane in a steep climb. The plane was so low we were down between the runway lights and could almost feel the tires hit the runway. He put the pedal to the metal and poured on the juice to the jets. We abruptly ascended skyward.

When the pilot turned the plane skyward at about a thousand feet, aborting the landing, the pretty lady next to me screamed and threw her arms around my neck. She held me in a "half nelson."

Though she had me by the throat, I gasped out, "The pilot wants to live just as much as you do."

Someone had said that to me once and I thought it was a suitable time to use it.

That didn't seem to quiet her down much. The way the pilot so bluntly maneuvered the plane put a knot in everyone's stomach. His sudden change in direction surprised us all and put prayerful speculation in our heads.

Everyone on the flight was upset. The faces of the passengers looked grim and contorted. The attendant ladies even looked distraught, though they were trying to seem calm and collected. Waves of loud mumbling sounded as passengers tried to come to terms with the Almighty.

As we leveled off and started circling back to the airport, the pilot came on the plane's PA system.

"I suppose you want to know what happened?"

Well, duh. That was an obvious inquiry. All the passengers on the plane murmured so loudly it sounded like a swarm of mad bees. The pilot explained to us that, when he was about to land the plane on the tarmac, he realized the area was iced over and a crosswind was blowing over the runway at high speed. In other words, gusting at forty to fifty miles per hour.

Our pilot said he read the velocity numbers just before touchdown. Technically, if the wind blew ten miles an hour or more across the runway, he couldn't land. The speed of this plane could not manage these conditions without sliding off the end of the runway. He said the size of the plane—we were in a light one—was critical to the whole picture, as a "big bird" wouldn't have a problem.

Our now infamous pilot had taken into consideration the speed of the plane, the icy runway, and the wind at the last minute before landing. He explained that if the wind blew under ten miles an hour, he could safely land. Eventually, he said. "We're going to try and land again, and if we can't, we will go to Seattle and get a bigger plane."

The streams of discourse going on amongst the passengers grew intense as he banked the plane around and over the city of Portland for another try. Everyone on board held their breath as the plane came downward on its flight pattern.

Again, we were between the runway lights. The pilot must have been checking the wind speed and found it was more than ten miles per hour because he, again, pulled the plane up and hit the jets.

This time, it gave out a huge roar of power, climbing into the cold blue sky, which suggested we were heading to Seattle.

The lady sitting next to me didn't grab me around my neck this time, but I was ready to embrace the experience. Under different circumstances, I would have been delighted to have a lady put me in a bear hug.

The mumbling in the cabin turned to a few highly explicit comments not on the edge of politeness. A few passengers were ready to form a lynching party and go after the pilot but quieted down when he came on the address system.

"We're going to Seattle."

Cheers roared up and down the aisle as smiles replaced looks of hostility. The pilot had made a remarkable effort to try to land the plane, but the elements were against him. He had done his best, then moved on to Plan B: a flight to Seattle and a bigger plane.

The airplane ride to Seattle was easy and mundane. A "sit back and enjoy the trip" type of flight. As it turned out, I met a nice lady, even though ours was an abrupt introduction. It became a pleasant encounter after the initial surprising attack was over. I agreed with many onboard that the two tries at landing the plane caused some pause.

I didn't lose faith in the pilot as the tension rose around me. I proved to myself that sometimes you must have faith in people to get through a tight spot. The lady who'd practically jumped on me when the plane rose sharply and without any warning caused me to think about her welfare instead of my own. I was surprised how I managed this tricky situation with a great deal of calmness.

We flew to Seattle and boarded another flight back to Portland on a larger plane. In the end, we didn't crash in Portland. We landed safely.

I never really thought it might be the end, although I feared a crash when things first started happening. This episode with the friendly skies did not traumatize me, but I wondered later what the lady's name was who sought comfort from me, and I hoped she was okay too.

Ups and Downs

All of us have experiences in our lives when we've felt good about ourselves, when our hopes, dreams, and achievements catapulted us to the top. These personal accomplishments warmed our hearts when we discovered our peaks. Such a rise to the top in our lives can take many faces. It might be finding God, qualifying for the team, or finding the girl of our dreams. My accomplishments found a height I hadn't felt before while attending Oregon State College as a first-year student during 1953–1954. I enjoyed one of the most satisfying periods of my lifetime.

That winter and spring, while playing basketball and baseball for my mentor, Coach Paul Valenti, I felt self-confidence. A harmony infused my everyday performance and added a hop in my step. It's easy to remember 1953–54 because, even today, I feel the balance.

I had achieved my goal to play on the first-year baseball and basketball teams and, to top it off, was chosen by Coach Valenti as captain of both teams. I had pointed myself toward playing on both teams during my senior year at Tillamook High School and felt ready after finishing my first year to compete for the OSC varsity teams in my upcoming sophomore year.

Many years later, I called Paul when he was ninety-three, just before he died, and told him our year together was one of the best of my lifetime. He played a key role in my life, and I wanted him to know how special my first year at OSC was to me. I am forever grateful for his friendship.

I joined the Sigma Chi fraternity at Oregon State College in 1953, along with my friend from Tillamook, Bud Gienger, who was at OSC on a wrestling scholarship. We were enthusiastic about Sigma Chi because some of the other members were from Tillamook.

I roomed my first year at the Sigma Chi house with a new friend, Johnny Frederick from Tigard, Oregon, who also played on the basketball and baseball teams. The Sigma Chi fraternity was a wonderful place for me. I was tutored by senior members and learned to live with other young men in compatibility and conformity, which became an advantage for a lifetime. Living at the Sigma Chi house was what I needed to accomplish my goals of achieving my monetary and social success. Those experiences instilled confidence and ambition in me.

With the fraternity as my anchor, I returned my sophomore year and played on the varsity basketball team, earning a scholarship from Coach "Slats" Gill. I hit a high, living out a dream since Liberty Junior High School in Tillamook. My peak had been extended, and my elevation rose higher one day in Los Angeles while playing against the University of Southern California. I achieved another goal and was at the top of my game at twenty years of age.

Looking back at the 1950s and my life, I walked on a cloud. My world was a combination of fulfilled dreams and a clear view of my future. Aided by the Sigma Chi fraternity, I set the table and was optimistic of a feast.

Then, in what seemed like a blink of an eye, I fell from the pinnacle I'd achieved. It was as if I'd turned to the last page of the book For Whom the Bells Tolls by Ernest Hemingway, and there I was in a sad ending.

As Hemingway wrote, "The bells toll for thee." The life I built at OSC was shattered by the deadly car ride in that 1942 Oldsmobile convertible that turned over unexpectantly, much like my life did that fateful day.

My severe injuries ended my future as a basketball and baseball player at OSC. My athletic life, as I knew it, was over. The top was a long way from where I so quickly fell. That innocent Sunday drive on a warm spring evening became a tragic affair, changing my life dramatically from an amazing high to being disabled. My wounds took me through two years of recovery and rehab after five operations, with some consequences still lingering today.

After my retirement from teaching at Canby High School, I rose again to the top at age sixty-five. Single after my recent divorce from Karen and living in my condominium in Scottsdale, I tried to forge a comfortable life without a wife. Karen and I had been married forty years, so single life proved challenging.

I saw my son, Eric, in Arizona and my grandchildren Sofia and Jordan often, as they lived in Arizona, too. I also was in touch with my daughter, Ann, in Oregon. I kept busy on other days, playing golf and cards with Al Kehrli, Mike Grimmett, and Howie Fritcher. Life was good, but about to ascend.

I became acquainted with Patricia Brooks, who had recently moved next door to me at Camelback House. She was pretty, young, and a Democrat. She also shared a lot of my interests and views. My star soared upward as we became close friends. We married four years later and are still happily together.

Sometimes as we go through life, we realize how darn good the past was to us when we look back. We were often in a good place and didn't appreciate it enough at the time. Those moments we now understand as we grow older. It is wonderful when we see the positive side of our reminiscing. It reminds us to enjoy our life in the present. We see what was important as we look back on our lives. Love and good health make it complete and happy.

I wish I hadn't hurried through certain events when we were young. But that's the way it was supposed to take place. Remembering the enjoyable parts of our past, when we are older and can understand their significance, adds to our lives. Hopefully, I will always look back and smile and realize I had a good life.

Mary's Peak

As a first-year student attending Oregon State College in 1953, I encountered a slight difference of opinion with a senior brother at our Sigma Chi Fraternity. One night, I was pulled out of bed and taken off the sleeping porch of the fraternity house. They blindfolded me and drove us to the top of Mary's Peak, west of Corvallis and OSC. The peak was a prominent landmark at 4,097 feet in elevation, the highest point in the Coast Range in Oregon.

The reason three fraternity brothers saw fit to rouse me out of bed in the middle of the night, take me to the top of the peak, and leave me there was for something I supposedly did that broke the rules of the fraternity. I do not know exactly what the rule was, but it did not matter. It was a personality conflict from the beginning.

Our Sigma Chi chapter had an unwritten understanding that when a brother is out of order with the rules of the fraternity and won't change his demeanor, his brothers can take him on a ride in the middle of the night. To enforce the idea that he needs to change his ways, the brother who is going for a ride cannot resist his departure.

As it turned out, this incident happened not because I had done anything against the fraternity or some brother. It was because one of my fraternity brothers did not like me. He was a senior who despised my attitude and the way I walked and talked. In other words, it did not take much for me to irritate him. That night, he talked a couple of other seniors into his plan to straighten me out. There was not any

Intestinal Fortitude

way I was going to change my attitude for him, so the inevitable hazing requirements of our fraternity took place on a chilly night in the spring of 1954.

I know several of my fraternity brothers from the Sigma Chi House found it hard to believe these incidents occurred. They were under the spell of the brotherhood, too, and had a tough time admitting anyone would not be friends with all brothers in the house. Personality clashes came into play all the time.

I do not hold any animosity toward the Sigma Chi fraternity. In fact, I am proud to be a member. I pushed a little too much. I was a little hard to keep up with as a first-year student and stepped on seniors' toes occasionally. I was still operating as hyper-kinetic, impulsive, and explosive, a condition left over from childhood. I was always in motion with an abundance of energy.

When the brothers rolled me out of bed, they did not give me a chance to put on some clothing or grab a jacket and shoes. They blindfolded me so I would not know where I was when we arrived at our destination. When we reached the summit, I was dressed only in pajamas. They did bring along a blanket and left it with me.

Sigma Chi rule #1: No fighting amongst the brothers. I did not resist, even under these circumstances.

Mary's Peak usually had snow on it, and this night was no different. The temperature had to be below thirty degrees. I stood at the crest of the peak as I heard them drive off down the mountain back to Corvallis. With my blanket draped over my shoulders, I looked like an American Sioux Indian standing in the South Dakota prairie. I was beginning to understand Crazy Horse's lament. I must have been a forsaken sight to the animals safely hiding in the foliage.

As the snow started to fall, there was only one way to go: down the mountain. The Kalapuya Indians called Mary's Peak a "place of spiritual power." I must have picked up a little of the Indian's spirit because I told myself, "They can't beat me. I'll win this battle."

I started walking down the mountain in my bare feet, leaving the snowy peak behind. After twenty minutes, I was halfway down to the main highway that runs between Corvallis in the Willamette Valley and Newport on the Oregon Coast of the Pacific Ocean. I caught a lucky break as a huge logging truck, with a full load, pulled out of a forest road to my left.

The screech of the truck's airbrakes sounded like music to my ears as the truck came to a stop next to me on the gravel road. The driver promptly offered help and kindness in the dark. I gladly climbed up into the truck's warm and welcoming cab. He was going past Corvallis to a lumber mill in Albany, so he offered to drop me off at the OSC campus on his way.

The driver figured out quickly I was a college student involved in a hairbrained fraternity initiation. It was easy to tell he was a good guy because he laughed a lot and didn't pass judgment. His memorable name, I never forgot: Xander Schauffe. We talked all the way to Corvallis. He was quite interested in fraternity life since he had not gone to college, especially the part about how some brother left another brother on top of Mary's Peak in the middle of the night. He felt fraternity life would not suit him very well. I saw his point.

As we neared Corvallis, the highway from Mary's Peak skirted the south side of the Oregon State College campus. If he let me out along the highway, I'd still have to hoof it across the entire campus in my pajamas to get to the Sigma Chi house. As I mentioned, this log truck driver was a good guy. By then, I also sensed he had a wild streak himself.

He said, "Hang on. I'll take you to your fraternity."

"It's probably against the law to drive a logging truck full of logs across the OSC campus," I replied.

I guess because it was about five o'clock in the morning and still dark with no cars and people about, he thought it would be okay to do what he did next. He turned the big rig north off Highway 20 and drove past Gill Coliseum, up by Weatherford Hall, the Student Union, and the Quad, to 23rd Street and directly in front of the Sigma Chi fraternity house door.

I thanked him profusely and jumped down out of the cab. As he pulled the big truck away from the curb, he gave three blasts on the truck's air horn that must have awakened my Sigma Chi brothers and half of the houses on fraternity row.

What started out as a dubious attempt to teach me a lesson by a disgruntled senior, turned into quite an adventure for me. I met a memorable log truck driver who delivered me safely from Mary's Peak back to Corvallis and across the OSC campus to the hallowed door of the Sigma Chi house. I could not have found better service unless I'd called a taxi to pick me up from the top of Mary's Peak and the taxi driver had done it for no charge.

    I talked to another first-year member, Wally Zwingli, that morning about my nocturnal ride. He encouraged me to let it go and not confront anyone. The seniors who had pulled me out of bed and left me on Mary's Peak were uncomfortable around me the remainder of the year. They were surprised I returned to the fraternity house so quickly, about an hour behind them. They presumed I would be many hours trying to get back in my blanket and pajamas. The log truck driver became a heroic figure to me. I'll never forget him.

Heart Attack

In February 2001, I walked toward the parking lot at the Camelback House condominiums, where I lived on 68th Street in Scottsdale, Arizona. I didn't know at the time, but I was about to meet up with my new neighbor, Patricia Brooks, who would become my future wife. We had talked once, weeks earlier, at the community mailbox area and had waved at each other a couple of times in passing, but this meeting would be different… our conversation much more comfortable.

I was about to slip into my car when the pretty auburn-haired younger girl backed her red Pontiac Grand Am out of her parking space near me. I say "girl" because she is fifteen years younger than me. I was sixty-five and she was fifty.

She rolled her window down and asked, "Would you like to go on a 'Heart Walk' with me next Saturday?"

I was pleasantly surprised and walked over to her car to tell her I was on my way to work at the Phoenician Resort. I was employed part-time as a shuttle driver for the golf course.

"I won't be able to accept your invitation since I work mornings driving the hotel guests to golf." I thought, How easy it is to talk to her, and how pretty she is too. Her full lips and green eyes caught my imagination, and her straightforward confidence enticed me, too. I decided this girl was incredibly special.

That was the extent of our conversation. She drove away and I went to work. During the winter months, I held an excellent position at the Phoenician Resort to earn extra cash and meet people in a fun way while driving an oversized golf cart around the property to take guests to their rooms, the golf course, the tennis club, or the spa area.

This position enabled me to meet myriad people, including celebrities who visited the five-star "gem" in the desert. The Phoenician was the finest resort in Arizona during the six winters I worked there, attracting the wealthy show-business types, too, and well-known sports figures. The Phoenician was the place to stay at the time, especially in Scottsdale.

Meeting people wasn't the only good thing about the job. More importantly, the tips people gave me when we arrived at their destination on the property were a nice benefit over my minimum wage salary. I averaged seventy-five dollars a day in tips. Twenty years ago, that was good for that type of job. I now had money to cover my golfing habit, my card playing after golf, a little money for good restaurants, and, eventually, a new girlfriend.

Not everyone tipped me, but enough did to make my coworkers in the service area envious of my job. Another favorable feature was the open-air cart I drove in Arizona's beautiful winter weather. I also worked independently with no one looking over my shoulder since the job wasn't in a specific location.

I told them when they interviewed me, "I am an old schoolteacher and coach. I will be on time and do my job." They thought that was worth something, didn't ask any more questions, and hired me on the spot.

After meeting Pat that morning and turning her down for the Heart Walk, I went to work and, astonishingly, suffered a heart attack. As I drove around the resort at nine thirty in the morning, taking care of guests, I started to feel off my usual game. I felt a little tightness on the left side of my body. It worsened as time went on.

After driving the cart up to the main entrance of the resort, I sat down and waited to see if the feeling passed. I began to think heart attack. Upon finding an aspirin in my pocket, I took it. A weak feeling came over me, making it tough to move my body in any fashion. Realizing this wasn't a drill but the real thing, and serious stuff was going on in my body making me lightheaded, I knew making it to the hospital was paramount.

I asked a young bellman named Matt, who was working the front of the hotel welcoming guests, to call me a limousine. I felt an ambulance would take too long to appear and limos were always at the resort, waiting for guests who needed transportation. A Lincoln Continental limo pulled up almost immediately. I made it into the back seat with the help of two or three bellman who, taking note of my heavy breathing, realized I was in big trouble. They knew whatever was happening to me was unquestionably a genuine problem. No practice session—this was the main event.

The hospital was three miles away, so we arrived quickly. The driver helped me out of the car and into an available wheelchair for transportation to the emergency room. An attendant came by immediately.

I whispered to the attending doctor, "I'm under assault by my heart."

He said, "You sure are!" He used a comical sounding voice to keep me calm. He then put me in the critical care unit.

They kept me in the hospital for two days and did a multitude of tests but found no damage to my heart. My cardiologist, Dr. Dooley, let me watch the screen as he found the blockage of a small vein on my heart causing a blood clot. He put a wire in a vein in my groin that led up to my heart and located the blocked vein. He pushed the wire through the blood clot and opened the vein again while I watched on a monitor. I was impressed he could do such a procedure with a wire. It was hard to believe such a small vein blockage could cause me to be so incapacitated. After he removed the clot, I felt better.

Dr. Dooley didn't show much empathy about the seriousness of the blocked vein. He was a funny guy. Although impressed by his actions, I was a little worried with his attempt at humor, as it didn't seem genuine. Dr. Dooley was an eccentric character who made light of my heart attack with a loose bedside manner. He didn't think my episode was too severe. He told me the joke about the golfer who explained to his wife the reason he was late for dinner was his playing partner Charley had suffered a heart attack. To complete his eighteen holes, the golfer had to hit a shot and drag Charley, hit a shot and drag Charley...

Do doctors get that way after seeing a hundred scenarios like mine? Was he trying to calm me down or refocus the situation? When he cracked the joke about heart attacks, I could hardly laugh and rolled my eyes in disbelief.

The Phoenician kept track of my recovery and, after two days, when I checked out, they sent another Lincoln Continental limo to take me to my condominium. It was classy treatment. No wonder they're a five-star resort.

After four days of taking it easy in my condominium, I ventured out and back to the Phoenician Resort to work. Coming home after my first day back, I saw Pat again in the parking lot of the condominiums, also arriving home from work. I hadn't seen her for a week.

"Where have you been?" she asked.

"Oh, I had a heart attack and have been in the hospital."

She initially did not believe me and thought I was trying to be funny about a serious malady to gain her attention.

The coincidence of her inviting me to go on the Heart Walk, then me having an actual heart attack the same day, was hard for us to fathom. I showed her my "heart pills" stuffed in my pocket, and she still had a tough time believing me since the story was so coincidental. With persistence, I finally convinced her I was telling the truth.

A couple of days later, I invited her out to dinner, knowing she would say yes because she cared about what happened to me. She came around and agreed to an evening out.

The dinner was a casual outing. "Let's see what the days bring," I said to her that night.

It was a quick courtship in some ways, with heading to Oregon for the summer, but we had a connection with the heart attack and being neighbors. We both knew our relationship was meant to be by our ease in communicating and how much we enjoyed each other's company. So, we pursued it. Four years later, I asked her to marry me. We wed on October 29th, 2005, in a small chapel in Las Vegas with a dozen of our family members in attendance.

CLOSURE

Patricia and I flew to Portland, Oregon, in August of 2017, excited about my upcoming short two-part book tour with my newly published memoir, *Bounce Back*. On the trip, we would also meet the Rampton family in Corvallis.

I was nervous about the book signings and getting up in front of groups, an audience to speak to, even if they were mostly my friends and family. By rewriting my talk and rehearsing several times, I prepared extensively to talk about myself and my memoir.

We landed in Portland, rented a car, and headed to Tillamook on the Oregon Coast, about a two-hour drive. My presentation planned there in my hometown was scheduled at the Yo Time Yogurt shop downtown on Main Street. It was Fair Week, and a lot of people were in town. I anticipated a good turnout. We offered a yogurt treat choice for all attendees and had sent invitations earlier with coupons. We were prepared.

The *Headlight-Herald*, the local newspaper, helped me promote the event with an article in the sport's page. They honored my past athletic endeavors, which are a big part of the stories in the book. Many helped me announce the event on social media. My success on both the basketball court and the baseball diamond for Tillamook High School had led me to Oregon State University and two scholarships. In my local circles, I was well known for those reasons and the accident. The book tied it all together.

Intestinal Fortitude

We met Abby and Jeff Hoffert, owners of the yogurt shop, and their son Cody the day we arrived in town to introduce ourselves. They are related to Pete Hoffert, who was a friend of mine while growing up in Tillamook in the 1950s. He drove a 1957 Chevy, which was as cool as you could get in the 1950s. Jeff said his dad was still a "cool" guy!

Abby Hoffert let us use a room in the back of her shop for my presentation and book signing. It was just the right size for the thirty people who showed up that day. Patricia and I promised to bring in business for them with our offer of yogurt to the attendees, a small incentive. A large group of friends and townsfolk attended, and Abby sold a lot of yogurt while I signed books.

Prior to this presentation, Ruby Fry Matson invited me to display and sell my book in the Pioneer Booth at the Tillamook County Fair. I signed quite a few books that day with the help of George Widnmer and Gordon Crowston.

George's family owned a dairy farm on the lower Wilson River just above the tidewater where my brothers and I swam as kids. He graduated from high school with my older brother Chuck in the late 1940s. Gordon was from Vernonia but had lived in Tillamook for many years after marrying Lelanie Batke, a friend of mine from school. They were the right people to help me move some books that day since they had known me all their lives.

They, with their friendly banter and good attitude, introduced me to the people who dropped by the booth. They persuaded folks that the book contained interesting stories of Tillamook. The strategy worked... I sold twenty books.

Also, while at the Pioneer Booth, I took a short break from selling to walk over near the carnival rides. Patricia took over for me in the booth while I visualized the small one-room concession stand sitting in its place near the midway. It brought back memories of our family living in it from 1937 to 1939. I reminisced later with my friends about running to the outhouse in the rain. Another memory that came to me was of the music on the midway that played along with the noise of the carnival rides.

My biggest concern on this trip was meeting the Ramptons, Alice's family. They were a part of the book in an incredibly unique way. We had never met before, and I did not know they existed until just months prior. Patricia and I had only recently begun Facebook conversations with Alice Rampton, the sister-in-law to deceased Alice.

When I started writing *Bounce Back,* I had my grandchildren in mind. I wanted to share with them what had happened in my past. I came to realize the auto accident was momentous. It made me want to seek out more information and meet somebody in Alice's family. Writing about the accident was important and meeting the Rampton family would be valuable and critical to confronting my PTSD.

The Ramptons were eager to read the book, which I dedicated to Alice, and hear my thoughts. They had all been small children when Alice died. They would now learn the circumstances of her death, sixty-two years later.

We met Jean Rampton Nelson and her husband, Charles, at the Blue Heron Restaurant north of Tillamook for lunch. Jean is the oldest sister of the Rampton siblings and not currently living in Corvallis. While I attended Oregon State, Jean was at Brigham Young in Utah at the time. She couldn't attend the Corvallis meeting we planned for the following week, so we met earlier so neither of us missed the opportunity for closure.

As I awaited our meeting, I was tense and anxious. She was nervous, too, because of the questions she wanted answered when meeting me for the first time. Jean was a tall woman who commanded respect without seeking it. She led the conversation immediately. Even though she fidgeted, she was calm and collected, a sign to me she had prepared for our meeting.

"I don't hold you responsible in any way for Alice's death," Jean said with a loving smile on her face. Her body language showed she was relaxing by the drop in her shoulders.

"Thank you," I responded and breathed easier as I felt my burdensome past leaving my concealed inner guilt.

"She was sitting next to you, wasn't she, Earl?" she inquired.

"Yes, she was."

I'd carried my survivor's guilt for sixty-two years. For a long time, I imagined the worst about how the Ramptons felt about me, which was partly why I had suffered from PTSD since the accident. Al and Alice visited daily in my thoughts. Why them and not me? A question I pondered for all those years. I needed to make peace with it this week.

"Were the two of you 'kissing and hugging' prior to the car crash?" Jean inquired sheepishly a little later.

With a bit of a grin, I assured her, "None of that took place that day. I hardly knew her."

Jean was noticeably relieved. She told us she had been living with that question since the time of her sister's death. Her sister was a high school girl, and I was a college guy, which made the question all that more important. Jean's being away at school at the time of the accident added to it as she'd learned what happened via a phone call. She'd flown home alone to Oregon to be with her family, all of whom were distraught.

Our meeting with Jean concluded amicably, with us both feeling lighter.

Patricia and I were set to have a meeting over dinner with the remaining siblings of the late Alice Rampton later in the week at Mark and Alice (Henderson) Rampton's home just outside of Corvallis. How ironic he married an Alice.

Mark had been home with two other siblings, all quite young, when the accident happened. The late Alice had been fifteen at the time of her death and was the middle child. Her siblings were now in their upper sixties and seventies.

Because I wrote extensively about the accident and Alice Rampton's death, along with my roommate Al Smith's, in *Bounce Back*, the Ramptons were anxious to read what I had written. I was eager to share copies for all of them at this meeting and to clear the air for all of us. I was also apprehensive for a lot of reasons, especially the forgiveness. I so desperately wanted it for my part in the accident in agreeing to pick up high school girls and take them for a ride. I was anxious, as well, to convey to Alice's siblings how innocent the episode was before it turned to tragedy.

Patricia and I drove to Corvallis from Tillamook for our meeting with the Ramptons. We checked into the Hilton Garden Inn next to the Oregon State University campus. It sat across from the Beavers' football stadium, which loomed overhead. We headed to the Ramptons' house, eager to meet them and learn more about what transpired in their family after the accident. I wanted to share my story too.

We expected a pleasant evening since we knew them a bit through Facebook correspondence and meeting Jean earlier. The entire family was gracious, open, and down-to-earth, and we had a wonderful dinner in the dining room before moving to the living room for dessert. Alice was an excellent chef, and the couple proved to be wonderful dinner hosts, making me feel comfortable in an otherwise awkward situation.

In the comfort of their living room, we discussed the accident that killed their sister. They were meeting the once twenty-one-year-old ballplayer and college student who'd ridden next to Alice in the car when she died. The young man, they found out, who had just met Alice that day by happenstance through his roommate Al and Alice's friend Patty, who also survived.

They told me Patty had stayed in touch briefly in the beginning, was sent away to school in Washington state, and had a difficult life. They did not expand on that, but we knew it was hurtful to them as them claimed to have tried repeatedly to stay in touch. They gave us a cell number to call her later, but she never responded to our messages.

Alice's brothers and sisters, their husbands and wives, and their children all wanted to meet me and know what I knew about the accident. They pressed for all the details and circumstances before, during, and after the collision. This family needed answers and had less information on the subject than I anticipated they would before our meeting.

I felt incredibly nervous sitting before a video camera, a tablet on Alice's lap, a phone recording in Mark's hand, and other family members such as her sister, Chris, who looked to me for resolution. I wished I could have been even more forthcoming to their inquiries about the conversations in the car, the speed of the car, and clearer about my time with Alice. They appeared eager with their intent listening to attempt to understand my frustration too.

It was a prolonged period of six decades since the tragic episode had taken place, but I remembered much of the story, more than they knew, and shared with them things they did not even ask about that night. The emotions of the group were amiable, with some tears welling up, and some thanks to God for the opportunity to find closure, marked by concern for Alice's actions the evening she died. They were all searching for relief. My persistent survivor's guilt and PTSD, in many ways, helped me keep the incident alive all through the years so I could be there for them that night. I told them I had thought about her every day since 1956 and often could see her face. A few smiles assured me they felt a bond with me, a kinship about the accident.

Mark Rampton reiterated what his sister Jean told me. "We don't hold you responsible for Alice's death. My parents did not, nor would not, believe all the rumors of alcohol in the car and speeding that circled around the story."

I then felt I could forgive myself and confront my grief. When I discarded some of the burdens, a weight lifted off my shoulders. It appeased my enigma and PTSD.

During the meeting, they revealed Alice had been babysitting her younger brothers and sisters sitting before me. She'd left them alone, sleeping, that day and stepped into the fateful red 1942 Oldsmobile convertible. She had only agreed to take a ride around the block, not a drive out of town. I don't recall why or when Al decided to take a longer drive and, to this day, I wish we had only gone around the block.

The siblings of Alice sat with me and my wife as adults seeking the true story from a long time ago. They found comfort in the facts and the truth of what really happened. I thanked them for inviting us into their home so I could tell my side of the story about the condition of the car, myself, Al Smith, and the road we traveled that night.

"We barely saw the oncoming cars' headlights as they approached us and forced us off the road," I said to them. "It seemed like just minutes before I realized I was under the car and injured, and Alice was lying near me. I thought she was asleep. I was unable to move to help her."

Our meeting was beneficial to all of us. I came away with a sense of gaining new friends while helping them and myself. The Ramptons were more accepting of their sister's death when they heard the truth their parents never knew. I saw some peace in their faces through their kind smiles. I had been trying to ascertain their reactions to my comments and they provided them.

"Our mother took the rumors extremely hard. She was ill for about six months with her grief and sadness," Mark said. "She heard it from church and from the neighbors."

Rumors had circled during those early days around the town and the campus, but now these siblings could rest. Their underage sister, with adult-aged college boys, eluded any of that behavior.

I owe my wife, Patricia, and Mark Rampton's wife, Alice, a big thank you for organizing the gathering between us and their family. The opportunity to meet their children was comforting too. We learned about their large family and how they eventually dealt with the incident through prayer, church, family support, and their faith. It was hard to say goodbye to them that night, but it came time to go. A lot had happened in those few hours, and I needed to digest it all and begin to move on with the closure I so graciously received.

The next morning, my wife and I entered the Gill Coliseum on the OSU campus for me to take what might be my last look at the place where I played basketball so many years earlier. I asked her to take some pictures, too, and she did. When I looked across the basketball court, I became nostalgic, feeling the flashbacks from a time when I was young, not knowing if I would ever travel back that way again. It felt good to see the campus even though the accident had changed everything in my life.

We left for Portland later that day to meet my daughter, Ann, in Lake Oswego for lunch. After eating a lovely meal, she came with us to check out Mother Foucault's Bookshop, where a book signing was planned for me the next day.

The bookstore, in downtown Portland near the Willamette River on the east side, was perfect for my talk and signing. The brown wood interior and carved wood figureheads made it look like it was out of the Elizabethan period. It had a small wooden stage and lectern with a lot of vintage books wrapped around the stage. That enhanced the feel of an authentic bookstore that had stood the test of time. The scene was warm and homey, and I felt comfortable there.

Craig, the owner of the shop, was a young man in his thirties, who might not have combed his bushy hair for many years. He was an "old hippie" in a time warp, not knowing or caring. He was easily his own man, independent and self-reliant. We liked him.

"Hello, welcome," he said as he showed us around a little before anyone else arrived.

"Thank you for having us," I said as we settled in to arrange my books.

My book talk and signing at Mother Foucault's Bookshop was a success because I now had the Rampton's meeting to add to my repertoire. Among a dozen of my closest relatives and friends, I wove my tales. They listened intently to my talk, laughed with me, offered comments, asked questions, and bought books. Patricia videotaped the event off to my right, so I didn't feel intimidated. I know I did well with the talk because it was a lot of fun. I wanted to do more presentations because I felt like an author that day. We took pictures with those who bought books and disbanded after a couple wonderful hours of feeling proud of my accomplishment.

One of those who attended was my friend Brian Bailey. He said some wonderful things that night about our friendship over the years. We'd known each other since growing up in Tillamook and sharing our college years at OSU in Corvallis.

I can't say enough about how I changed with the event in Corvallis, being so moved by everyone's generosity. I reflected on all of it in conversation with my wife many times after it was history, working my way through the grief and gratitude we experienced together.

We were ready for this success after months of emails, text messages, and phone calls to set up our vacation that year. The follow-up on the book events and the meeting with the Ramptons was nothing less than a miraculous healing for me. My wife is the absolute best at orchestrating this type of thing. I was immensely proud of her, and myself, for a job well done.

We were extremely grateful for the ten days, which ended with our sharing the eclipse of the sun at a local restaurant patio in Lake Oswego. A perfect ending to a trip meant for forgiveness of myself and Alice's family, a feeling of relief to take with me, and no more regrets. We went home to our writing life in Scottsdale, knowing the joy of seeing old friends, meeting new ones, and helping me and the Rampton family move on with our lives.

REQUEST FOR REVIEW

If you enjoyed this book, please consider writing a brief review on the "Earl Llewellyn Goldmann, *Intestinal Fortitude*" Amazon book page. I would appreciate even a couple of honest sentences.

ABOUT THE AUTHOR

Earl Llewellyn Goldmann launched his first memoir *Bounce Back* in 2017 at age eighty-two. Born and raised in Tillamook, on the Oregon Coast, he now resides in Scottsdale, where he moved after retirement.

He taught history and government at Canby and Estacada high schools in Oregon while coaching girl's golf and boy's track, and basketball for more than twenty-five years. Earl also sold textbooks, managed a golf course, and owned a bar/restaurant.

He played basketball and baseball at Oregon State University in the 1950s, only to lose his scholarships after a horrific car wreck. After a lengthy recovery, he later earned two degrees from Portland State University, including a master's degree in education.

Earl and his wife, Patricia L. Brooks, an award-winning author and his partner in their publishing company, have been together twenty years. They not only author books but consult with other writers as well. They enjoy an active lifestyle by walking daily, reading, and enjoying the arts.

egoldmann@cox.net
480-941-0891
www.brooksgoldmannpublishing.com
intestinalfortitudebook.com

www.ingramcontent.com/pod-product-compliance
Lightning Source LLC
Chambersburg PA
CBHW070420010526
44118CB00014B/1833